THE REVOLUTIONARY

PERSONALITY

WRITTEN UNDER THE AUSPICES OF THE
CENTER OF INTERNATIONAL STUDIES,
PRINCETON UNIVERSITY.
A LIST OF OTHER CENTER PUBLICATIONS
APPEARS AT THE BACK OF THE BOOK.

the revolutionary personality

LENIN, TROTSKY

GANDHI

BY E. VICTOR WOLFENSTEIN

PRINCETON, NEW JERSEY
PRINCETON UNIVERSITY PRESS

First Princeton Paperback Printing, 1971

Second Printing, 1973

L.C. Card: 67-11035

ISBN 0-691-02450-2 (paperback edn.)

ISBN 0-691-08611-7 (hardcover edn.)

Printed in the United States of America

by Princeton University Press

TO BOO AND LENNY

PREFACE

This book is an attempt to elaborate some of the psychological characteristics of revolutionists. The empirical bases of the inquiry are the lives of Vladimir Ilyich Lenin, Lev Davidovich Trotsky, and Mohandas Karamchand Gandhi, men who shared a commitment to ending an existing political order and replacing it with a new one. The life of each man is examined in some detail, leading to a personality model of each, on the one hand, and a more general model of a personality type which may be applicable to a wide range of men involved in revolutionary activity, on the other.

It has not been my goal in this effort to achieve the "definitive" psychological portrait of any of the men involved, nor to test the validity of the general hypotheses the study contains. Rather my aim has been to indicate in a preliminary way some of the personality traits which help to explain the political behavior of these three men, and to formulate hypotheses about revolutionary psychology, not to confirm them. Only more detailed analysis of the data available on the lives of the men than there is room to present in a study of this scope could add plausibility to the inferences drawn about their personalities, and only the rigorous operationalizing and testing of the more general concepts could give us more than an intuitive confidence in their validity.

The theoretical basis of the inquiry lies in psychoanalysis, and in the attempts to apply the insights of that field to the world of politics. Hence in a sense the greatest intellectual debt is to Freud, and to those who have most boldly and successfully applied his findings to politics, principally Erik H. Erikson and Harold D. Lasswell.

More personally, I am grateful to my teachers at both Columbia, where I did my undergraduate work, and Princeton, whose additive influence did much to make possible work in "psycho-politics." Especially Nicholas Wahl, Harry Eckstein, Manfred Halpern, and Glenn Paige, all of whom read and criticized most constructively the earlier draft of the manuscript, have my warmest thanks. Bryant Wedge of Princeton, who read the manuscript with great care, was also extremely helpful. And fellow graduate students at Princeton, especially William Daley, and the internal war seminars at the Center of International Studies did much to sharpen the focus of the study and to help me refine somewhat the theoretical constructs which resulted from it.

My deepest appreciation, however, goes to my aunt, Dr. Martha Wolfenstein, from whom I learned most of what I know about psychoanalytic theory and whose insights into the personalities of these three men are ubiquitous in the pages that follow.

I am also appreciative of the long and lively discussions I have had with my colleagues and students at UCLA, especially to the constant probing and receptiveness of the latter.

I would, in addition, like to acknowledge Sarah Campbell's considerate and reliable help in the preparation of the thesis version of the manuscript, and John McHugh's assistance in compiling the index. My research was supported in part by the Center for Research in Social Systems (formerly SORO), The American University, under Department of the Army Contract DA 49-092 ARO–7. I also appreciate the support of the Center of International Studies, Princeton University, and its director, Klaus Knorr. Finally, I am grateful for the sensitive editorial assistance of Roy Grisham of the Princeton University Press.

E. V. W.

August 1966

CONTENTS

Preface   vii

1. introduction   3

Freud and Politics   4
Comparative Psycho-Political Biography   11
Revolution and Leadership   19
Lenin, Trotsky, and Gandhi: An Overview   26

2. childhood and adolescence   33

The Youth of Vladimir Ilyich Ulyanov   33
The Youth of Lev Davidovich Bronstein   49
The Youth of Mohandas Karamchand Gandhi   73
The Propensity to Revolt   88

3. young manhood   103

Ulyanov: Disciple of Marx   103
Bronstein: Words and Deeds   124
Gandhi: The Search for Truth   138
Why Does a Man Rebel?   158

4. adulthood 1   174

Lenin: The Tactics of Revolutionary Leadership   175
Trotsky: Permanent Revolution   191
Gandhi: *Satyagraha* as Revolution   207
The Psychological Bases of Revolutionary Leadership   222

CONTENTS

5. adulthood 2   240

Lenin: The Utilization of Power   240
Trotsky: The Loss of Power   259
Gandhi: The Avoidance of Power   275
The Transition to Power   292

6. summary   302

Bibliography   319
Index   327

THE REVOLUTIONARY

PERSONALITY

I CONCLUDE THEN

THAT FORTUNE VARYING AND MEN

REMAINING FIXED IN THEIR WAYS,

THEY ARE SUCCESSFUL AS LONG AS THESE WAYS

CONFORM TO CIRCUMSTANCES,

BUT WHEN THEY ARE OPPOSED

THEN THEY ARE UNSUCCESSFUL.

NICCOLO MACHIAVELLI

The Prince

CHAPTER ONE

introduction

Politics is a human activity. It is men who run for office, wield power, make decisions, execute policy. And just because men are the actors in the drama of politics, their personalities are important contributors to the character of their political participation. Indeed, students of politics from Plato to the present have tried to explicate the connections between man's nature, as they have understood it, and his politics. In this study I will use one such theory of human nature—the psychoanalytic—in an attempt to add to our understanding of the motivations for revolutionary activity. In order to facilitate an analysis of this type of man, of the "revolutionary personality," I will examine in some detail the lives of Vladimir Ilyich Lenin, Lev Davidovich Trotsky, and Mohandas Karamchand Gandhi, three men who occupy rather different positions along the spectrum of revolutionary involvement. In so doing, I will be guided by the following overarching questions: why does a man become a revolutionist? What personal qualities will help him to be an effective leader of men? And what characteristics enable a man to make the transition from revolutionist to administrator of the state?

Underlying this study is the conviction that psychoanalytic theory gives us, in a sense for the first time, the opportunity to study systematically what before has been either ignored or, as in Plato's case, grasped by intuition alone. Psychoanalysis has taken Plato's insight that "unlawful" desires "bestir themselves in dreams, when the gentler part of the soul slumbers and the control of reason is withdrawn," that in his phantasies man "will not shrink from intercourse with a mother or anyone else, man, god, or brute, or from forbidden food or any deed of blood"[1] and transformed it into a relatively integrated body of knowledge about the relationships between the conscious and unconscious aspects of the mind, and the complicated ways in which these are combined to produce motivated behavior. Yet, with a few conspicuous exceptions, psychoanalytic theory has seldom been applied to politics. And when it has been used it has frequently been for the analysis of parties, nations, and even civilizations, instead of to the material out of which it grew and which it was devised to explain: the motivations of individual human beings. Here an effort is made to apply psychoanalysis to politics in what one would therefore think to be the most natural way, that of studying life histories and generalizing from them. This is, in essence, the method Freud used to develop his notions of personality types, and we may expect that the technique of comparing and generalizing from life histories will do us good service in a psycho-political, as well as a psychopathological, context.[2]

Freud and Politics

Perhaps the best way to orient ourselves to the task of understanding psychoanalytically the motivations of political actors is by briefly examining the ways in which Freud himself applied the theory to politics. It might be said, in fact, that psychoanalytic theory was political from its inception. Its major construct, the Oedipus complex, takes its name from a king who is involved in a classic political dilemma, a conflict between private happiness and the well-being of the state. Man's inner nature is in this way immediately politicized. Moreover, in *The Interpretation of Dreams*, his earliest exposition of the ideas that were to become his hallmark, Freud often used political metaphors to vivify his conception of the mind. For example, in discussing the

[1] Francis Cornford, ed. and trans., *The Republic of Plato* (New York, 1945), pp. 296-97.

[2] The method used in this study is elaborated later in this chapter.

kinds of distortions of thought which occur in dreams, which he attributes to a censoring function in one part of the mind which prevents material originating in another part from manifesting itself undisguised, Freud uses the analogy of the political critic, who must write in allusions and allegories in order to get his criticisms past the watchful eye of governmental censorship.[3] By implication Freud thus posits that political conflict must be comprehensible in the same terms as man's inner conflicts; that dreams and ideologies are both manifestations of human nature, so that a greater understanding of one leads to a better grasp of the other.

Aside from thus creating a nexus between man's psyche and his politics, Freud also examined directly certain kinds of social and political phenomena. The groundbreaking work in this area was *Totem and Taboo*, written in the winter of 1912-13. The argument of the book is based on the observation that there were some striking similarities in the perceptions and actions of primitive peoples, certain kinds of neurotics (especially those of the "compulsive" type), and children. All three groups were found to have, in some form, a tendency toward the worship of totems; the utilization of taboos or taboo-like vows to ward off unwanted impulses, especially those relating to incest and aggression; and the treatment of thoughts and wishes as if they were actions, to indulgence in a self-conceived "omnipotence of thought." Freud explained the relationship between taboo and forbidden impulse by treating it as a manifestation of a fundamental emotional ambivalence in man, which finds its most powerful expression in the Oedipal conflict. This connection is especially plausible when one notes that the most widespread taboos, the inadmissibility of sexual relations with the parent of the opposite sex and the prohibition on murder, coincide with the demands placed on the child during the so-called phallic period,

[3] Sigmund Freud, *The Interpretation of Dreams*, in A. A. Brill, ed. and trans., *The Basic Writings of Sigmund Freud* (New York, 1938), p. 223.

[5]

namely, to renounce the parent of the opposite sex as a sexual object and to stifle hostility towards the parent of the same sex. In this manner Freud brought under one rubric primitive religion, art, ethics, and sexual life. These themes, and the related ideas concerning the origin of civilization in the demise of man's horde existence and the slaying of the primal father, were subsequently elaborated in *The Future of an Illusion, Civilization and Its Discontent,* and *Moses and Monotheism.*[4] Here, however, we are more interested in Freud's analysis of primitive kingship in *Totem and Taboo,* which serves as a necessary corollary to the psycho-political analysis found in his *Group Psychology and the Analysis of the Ego.*

Relying heavily on James Frazer's *The Golden Bough* and related sources, Freud drew the following picture of "the taboo of rulers."[5] The ruler is a man who "must be both guarded and guarded against." He is potentially a force of great beneficence, but he is also deeply mistrusted. He possesses a "mana," a special gift of power from the gods, but this can be used for good or ill. An ordinary man dare not touch a king, for fear that he would die as the result of his action; yet the king's touch is also a healing force. Relations between ruler and ruled are thus fraught with danger, and a special class of intermediaries are developed to mediate between the two.

Although the king is worshiped almost as the gods themselves, he is also so bound by ritual and ceremony that he is practically devoid of freedom—his people make him suffer for the honor they pay him. Yet the ruler is conceived to be so powerful that he can "regulate the course of the world"; but if the rains do not come or the winds blow too

---

[4] Norman O. Brown's *Life Against Death* (New York, 1959); Herbert Marcuse's *Eros and Civilization* (New York, 1962); and Philip Rieff's *Freud: The Mind of the Moralist* (Garden City, N.Y., 1961), are perhaps the most important analyses of the philosophical implications of Freud's work in general, but especially of these late productions.

[5] Freud, *Totem and Taboo,* A. A. Brill, trans. (New York, 1946), pp. 56-69.

hard, the king must bear the consequences for "his" failure.[6]

Taking these observations as a whole, it would appear that we have in exaggerated form some of the normal components of modern, as well as earlier, political life. It is as if many of the mutually conflicting ideas which people might have about politics were being expressed simultaneously. Indeed, this is what Freud believes is happening here. Just as a young child is able to entertain contradictory ideas and ambivalent emotions without being aware of the inconsistency, and just as the unconscious region of the adult's mind is similarly free to believe in opposites, so in primitive politics the manifestations of ambivalence easily coexist, without leading to the total exclusion of one desire or another. The subjects love and hate, fear and trust, honor and punish their kings with equal intensity. Freud goes on to emphasize that these emotional extremes are highly reminiscent of the attitude of the child towards the father. In fact a web of attitudinal similarities is hereby established: son to father, savage to ruler, follower to leader, a religious man to his god, a paranoid to the imago central to his illusions, and, during the transference, the patient to the analyst. And because, in the life of any individual, the intensely ambivalent emotional involvement with the father precedes any of these other possible relationships, it becomes plausible to hypothesize that the later attitudes are modeled on the earlier one. Moreover, with

[6] Freud's data, and his treatment of it, bears an interesting relationship to modern socio-political analysis. For example, William Kornhauser, in his *The Politics of Mass Society* (Glencoe, Ill., 1959), stresses the problem of autonomy and interaction between ruler and ruled. Also the "mana" of the leader or king and his obligation to constantly prove his power to his followers is highly reminiscent of Max Weber's conception of charisma, as in his *The Theory of Social and Economic Organization* (New York, 1964), pp. 358-63. And any student of the American presidency or any other high executive office surely finds the "suffering of office" a familiar phenomenon. All of which suggests that a psychological theory which sheds light on primitive kingship will not be without its value for understanding contemporary politics.

the introduction of the dynamic conception of repression (that is, of the idea that one part of the mind may force from consciousness unwanted desires, which nonetheless remain alive and in search of satisfaction), it becomes credible that an individual may be strongly impelled to feel towards later objects of authority the way he felt towards earlier ones. This idea, the explanation of adult emotional involvements at least partially in terms of an individual's earliest object ties and their perpetuation through the intrapsychic dynamics of the human mind, is fundamental to the present study.[7]

From Freud's analysis of kingship in *Totem and Taboo* it is clear that he conceived that followers or subjects have a strong emotional involvement with their leaders. In *Group Psychology and the Analysis of the Ego*, first published in 1921, he attempted to specify more precisely the nature of this bond.[8] He concluded that the revolutionary mobs which LeBon described in *Psychologie des foules* and such organizations as the Catholic Church and armies share a common psychological basis, namely that groups of this kind involve "a number of individuals who have substituted one and the same object for their ego ideal and have consequently identified themselves with one another in their ego."[9] Although there are a number of theoretical complexities involved in this formulation, essentially Freud argued that the individuals involved abrogate their moral judgment to the leader of the group, obeying without question his directives; and because they share this relationship

[7] A very brief exposition of some of the basic concepts of psychoanalytic theory is included later in this chapter. The following works provide a much more comprehensive overview of the subject: Freud, *A General Introduction to Psychoanalysis* (New York, 1938); *New Introductory Lectures on Psychoanalysis* (New York, 1965); and Otto Fenichel, *The Psychoanalytic Theory of Neurosis* (New York, 1945).

[8] R. E. Money-Kyrle, in *Psychoanalysis and Politics* (London, 1951), and Saul Scheidlinger, in *Psychoanalysis and Group Behavior* (New York, 1952), attempt to develop further the concepts Freud introduced in his *Group Psychology and the Analysis of the Ego* (London, 1948).

[9] *Ibid.*, p. 80.

with the leader, they tend to see something of themselves in the other members—and of the other members in themselves. This twofold process of what we may call identification results in binding the follower tightly to the group, inhibiting thereby libidinal or love relationships with individuals outside the group and the development of independent judgment and intellectual functioning. In addition, this kind of relationship creates the necessity of finding some way of minimizing the ambivalence inherent in man's emotional life. In order for the group to persist, the negative or aggressive component of the ambivalence must be split off from the leader and the other members and directed against some external object. This splitting of ambivalence, the forced separation of love and hate which were once directed towards the same object, we will find to be basic to our understanding of the revolutionist. We will see, moreover, that if an individual is to become a leader of such a group, he must break this tight web of emotional involvement with his peers and superiors.

It will have been noticed that in the discussion thus far no mention has been made of an analysis by Freud of the characteristics of the leader himself, the subject of particular interest here. In fact, Freud did not give any systematic attention to the personality of the man who fills the leadership role. He was interested only in the function of leadership, the effect which leaders have on those who follow them. Accordingly, his brief characterization of the leader as a man of a "masterly nature, absolutely narcissistic, but self-confident and independent" tells us little which is neither true by definition or by common sense.[10] Only the idea of the leader's narcissism, of his lack of emotional involvement with others, and an earlier reference to LeBon's contention that the leader has a fanatical belief in the ideas which he advocates strike one as important components of a description of a leader's personality. We will find, moreover, that Freud overstates the leader's narcissism and that

10 *Ibid.*, p. 93.

[9]

intense belief is one of the things which we would like to have explained. In short, Freud gives us little idea of the adult dynamics of the leader's personality and no conception of his development, of his psychogenesis. It should again be mentioned that Freud had no intention of analyzing the leader as such, and that psychoanalytic theory does provide insight into this kind of man. Yet, despite his claims to the contrary, Freud did treat "great men" with something akin to awe. The very fact that he compares a leader of a group to his terrifying image of the primal father of the horde, that he refers to the latter as "the *Superman* whom Nietzsche only expected from the future," indicates that Freud felt great leaders were in some sense unapproachable.[11]

This is not to say, however, that Freud refrained entirely from analyzing great men. His studies of Leonardo da Vinci, Moses, and others were attempts to get at some of the motivations of men of heroic achievement. And under the influence of Otto Rank, Freud also paid some attention to the idea of heroism as such, the first hero being conceived to be the "man who by himself had slain the [primal] father."[12] The motives for the hero's action seemed clear: the wish to win for himself libidinal freedom and the sexual possession of women.

Yet when analyzing great men Freud operated under a twofold rule. First, one must treat one's subject as a man and not a god. Although the great man appears to us to have almost superhuman "decisiveness of thought," "strength of will," "self-reliance and independence," and "conviction of doing the right thing," to have, in sum, all the majesty and awesomeness of a powerful father to a four year old child, we must not forget that the "father was also once a child."[13] There should be nothing sacred and taboo about the lives of great men, nothing which we should refrain from analyzing.

[11] *Ibid.*   [12] *Ibid.*, p. 113.
[13] Freud, *Moses and Monotheism* (New York, 1939), pp. 140-41.

Freud's second rule is that we must also be aware of our limitations, be ready to admit that there are things which we do not as yet understand. Freud did not feel that psychoanalytic theory could make fully "comprehensible the attainments of the great man."[14] Hence, in this study, while examining what might be termed great men, I specifically refrain from discussing their "greatness." I hope to uncover something about the motivations for revolutionary involvement, and of the prerequisites for leadership, but eschew the broader and more ambiguous topic of greatness.

Comparative Psycho-Political Biography

As we have seen, Freud himself did not really undertake to analyze the personalities of political activists. His politically oriented work, however, does give us some sense of the psychological character of political roles; and, what is more important, his theory and methods are applicable to political, as well as to other, men. Although he did not study the life histories of political actors, he did study life histories, and in the process worked out a general model of personality development and dynamics that has fruitfully guided some subsequent inquiries into the psychological nature of political man.[15] In order to insure a common basis of

[14] Freud, *Leonardo da Vinci* (New York, 1947), p. 108.

[15] There is a fairly large body of literature in which psychoanalytic theory is applied to political actors. See Fawn M. Brodie, *Thaddeus Stevens* (New York, 1959); Gustav Bychowski, *Dictators and Disciples* (New York, 1948); K. R. Eissler, *Goethe: A Psychoanalytic Study*, 2 vols. (Detroit, 1963); Erik H. Erikson, *Young Man Luther* (New York, 1958); Alexander and Juliette George, *Woodrow Wilson and Colonel House* (New York, 1956); Gustav Gilbert, *The Psychology of Dictatorship* (New York, 1950); Alex Gottfried, *Boss Cermak of Chicago* (Seattle, 1962); Leopold Haimson, *The Russian Marxists and the Origins of Bolshevism* (Cambridge, 1955); Edward Hitschmann, *Great Men* (New York, 1956); Harold D. Lasswell, *Politics: Who Gets What, When, How* (New York, 1958), *Power and Personality* (New York, 1960), and *Psychopathology and Politics* (New York, 1960); Nathan Leites, *A Study of Bolshevism* (Glencoe, Ill., 1953); and Arnold Rogow, *James Forrestal* (New York, 1963). Recently, Freud's collaborative study with William C. Bullitt of Woodrow Wilson has also been published.

[11]

understanding, let us pause briefly to indicate the characteristics of the psychoanalytic view of personality.[16]

I will begin by indicating how the term "personality" is
to be used in this study. It is, after all, a particular type of
personality that we are studying, hence it seems best to be
as clear as possible about what is meant by the word—
especially because it is a term with a multitude of connotations. Accordingly "personality" refers to a relatively stable
organization of the ways in which the individual deals with
his internal psychological conflicts, and his involvement in
and conflicts with external reality. The performance of the
functions of conflict management thus results in a personality, one which to be adequate must be both highly integrated and cohesive, and flexible enough to allow the individual to cope with changing internal and external conditions. My interest here is in that kind of personality which
maintains a stable or equilibrious condition and remains
adaptive to the exigencies of its environment by participating in revolutionary activity. We want to know what kind of
life experiences lead a man to have this kind of personality,
and we want to be able to specify in some detail the characteristic psychic qualities of such a man.

The term personality thus implies a cut into the continuing developmental process which is a human life. It is a
cross-sectional view, at some given point or period in time,
of the forces interacting within the individual, and of his
characteristic ways of reacting to the demands of his environment. If we wish to understand this cross-section,

---

[16] It might be noted that there are several branches of contemporary
psychology which are in some sense psychoanalytic. The concepts
outlined below belong to a particular tradition in psychoanalysis,
that exemplified by Freud himself in all of his works, but in particular
in *New Introductory Lectures on Psychoanalysis* and *The Ego and
the Id* (New York, 1960). Some of the others who have carried
forward this work, with its emphasis on the interaction among the
various components of the mind, are: Anna Freud, *The Ego and the
Mechanisms of Defense* (New York, 1946); Erik H. Erikson, *Childhood and Society* (New York, 1963); and Heinz Hartmann, *Ego
Psychology and the Problem of Adaptation* (New York, 1958).

however, it is necessary to examine it in the context of the person's full life history, to indicate its psycho-genesis as well as its current status.[17] Psychoanalytic theory, in its formulation of the stages of psycho-sexual development, gives us a useful implement for carrying on this examination. The oral, anal, phallic or Oedipal, latent, and adolescent phases are concepts which help us to analyze the problems and opportunities which life presents to every individual. And just because all men live through these phases, the concepts provide a natural basis for comparison. In this study I will use Erik Erikson's formulation of the developmental course of the ego to compare systematically the lives of my three subjects. I will seek to locate in each phase the similarities and differences in the men's experiences which help to explain the similarities and differences in their adult personalities and political activity.

The Eriksonian conception of ego development will be elaborated in some detail as the study progresses.[18] Some statement about the nature of psychodynamics, however, will serve to make more easily comprehensible the ensuing analysis. Psychoanalytic theory views the human mind as a system of psychic energy, such energy having predominant either a sexual (libidinal) or aggressive character. The source of this mental or emotional energy is the id, the deeply unconscious area of the mind. At birth, in fact, the mind is all id, an undifferentiated mass of energy seeking discharge (that is, pleasure or satisfaction). In response to the exigencies of impinging reality, however, the mind develops the capacity to delay pleasure-seeking activity in order to insure the organism against unpleasurable or dangerous side effects. In technical terms, the pleasure principle

[17] A clear exposition of the relationship between dynamic (that is, personality) conceptions and genetic ones in psychoanalytic theory can be found in Nathan Leites, "Psycho-Cultural Hypotheses about Political Acts," *World Politics*, Vol. I, No. 1 (Oct. 1948), 102-19.

[18] The basic expositions of Erikson's concepts are his *Childhood and Society*; *Identity and the Life Cycle* (Vol. I, No. 1 of *Psychological Issues*); and Chapter 4 of *Insight and Responsibility* (New York, 1964).

to some extent gives way to the reality principle; that is, man's conscious and preconscious life becomes increasingly dominated by the task of mediating between the demands of the id, of his unconscious, pleasure-seeking impulses, and the external necessities of his situation. The agency that develops in the mind to perform this dual function is termed the ego.

Clearly, the ego is destined to lead a beleaguered existence, for it is far from easy to keep the countervailing claims of id and reality in balance. Moreover, the ego must serve a third master as well. During the phallic phase the individual develops a set of internalized moral standards, which are in a sense a part of the ego, but which also possess the quality of being able to stand apart from the ego and judge its actions and desires. The agent of these moral demands is the superego, or, to use a more common sense and conscious terminology, the conscience.

In order to keep some peace among these contending forces, the ego employs a set of characteristic techniques, the so-called mechanisms of defense.[19] The most basic of these is repression, a process in which the ego uses some of its energy to drive from consciousness, and from motility, impulses unacceptable to the superego or the environment. These repressed impulses do not die, however; they remain alive in the unconscious, seeking some mode of discharge. It is because important impulses are repressed early in life, and do not find ready release thereafter, that they can remain such crucial determinants of later behavior. We shall see in the lives of the men we are studying that much of their political activity can be understood as a way of managing their repressed impulses, of relieving internal conflicts by working them out in a political context. Indeed, one of our major tasks will be to uncover the ways in which these repressed drives are converted into what we recognize as political motives.

There is, of course, much more involved in psycho-

[19] See Fenichel, Chapters 8-9, for his discussion of the motives and mechanisms of defense.

analytic theory than can be included in a brief outline. Moreover, there is far from universal agreement, even among analysts, on how certain terms should be used; nor can it be said that psychoanalysis represents a completely developed and perfect theory of human nature. There are some psychic phenomena which psychoanalysis has investigated too hurriedly, and others which do not seem well explained. But it is not to my purposes to rehash the debates of the "school days" of psychology.[20] Rather it is a premise of this study that one justifies the use of any approach to a subject matter only by producing interesting and useful results, be they hypotheses or proofs. Evaluation on the basis of a priori disposition towards a method can yield no more than a comfortable confirmation of one's pre-existing view. Only by examining the ideas generated are we in a position to estimate fruitfulness.

In this study I will be using psychoanalytic theory as a tool of comparative analysis. In such a manner I hope to arrive at a model of the psychological roots of revolutionary involvement and leadership that will be valid for a fairly wide range of cases.[21] This necessitates a certain sacrifice in depth and in the amount of supporting evidence I will be able to bring forward for the interpretations made. Hopefully this sacrifice will result in a more useful model. By studying three men who differ from each other in as many ways as do Lenin, Trotsky, and Gandhi, and yet who were each dedicated to revolutionary activity, we increase the likelihood that we will be able to identify those causes which lead most directly to the given political consequence.

It should be stressed that the result of this exploration

[20] The following provide useful discussions of the scientific standing of psychoanalysis: Ernest R. Hilgard *et al.*, *Psychoanalysis as Science* (Stanford, 1952); Sidney Hook, ed., *Psychoanalysis, Scientific Method and Philosophy* (New York, 1959); and Paul E. Meehl, *Clinical vs. Statistical Prediction* (Minneapolis, 1954). Robert E. Lane, in Part III of *Political Life* (Glencoe, Ill., 1959) gives a good review and analysis of both statistical and clinical concepts as they have been applied to the study of politics.

[21] The kind of rebel the model is meant to depict will be discussed in the following section.

will not be a tested theory of revolutionary commitment. Rather I am here engaged in the construction of hypotheses, not in their testing. It will take the independent study of other revolutionists to create a strong presumption of validity for the model. Here it can only be claimed that the generalizations which will be made do seem to fit the three cases being studied and that it may be worthwhile to see if they cover other cases as well.

The model of the revolutionary personality resulting from our explorations will not be an exact copy of reality, or even of the lives of the men here being studied. Many factors have to work together to create the actuality of revolutionary participation and leadership. Here I am only concerned with a set of motivational and affective preconditions of this kind of activity, and with a simplified psychodynamic portrait of the revolutionist. In order to augment the understanding of such psychological factors I am forced, for the time being, to hold equal the wealth of other elements which impinge upon the phenomenon. This does not imply that economic, social, and political systemic determinants of revolutionary behavior are deemed unimportant. These kinds of factors have been rather extensively studied, however, while the psychology of the revolutionist has been rather neglected.[22] It is here conceived that personality factors of the kind to be elaborated are necessary conditions for revolutionary behavior. They are clearly not necessary and sufficient conditions. Thus the hypotheses tentatively put forward can only claim to be a partial explanation of the highly complex phenomenon of revolutionary activity.[23]

[22] An introduction to the systematic study of revolution may be obtained from the following: Hannah Arendt, *On Revolution* (New York, 1963); Crane Brinton, *The Anatomy of Revolution* (New York, 1952); Harry Eckstein, ed., *Internal War* (New York, 1964) and "On the Etiology of Internal War," in *History and Theory*, Vol. IV, No. 2, 1965; Lyford P. Edwards, *The Natural History of Revolution* (Chicago, 1927); Karl Mannheim, *Ideology and Utopia* (New York, 1936); and George Sawyer Pettee, *The Process of Revolution* (New York, 1938).

[23] This methodological stance is essentially that taken by Max

In a general sense the methodology I am using here derives from Freudian theory and Weber's investigative canons. More specifically, comparative psychopolitical biography grows out of the work of Harold Lasswell. In *Psychopathology and Politics*, written in 1930, Lasswell, arguing that "political science without biography is a form of taxidermy," undertook to apply the methods and insights of psychoanalysis and related theories to the life histories of politicians. Classifying his cases as men who were agitators, administrators or theorists, he sought to find the personality traits common to the men who played each role, and to all of the men as political activists. As in Lasswell's work, in this study the lives of several political actors are examined in an attempt to find some of the psychological motivations which underlie political commitment.[24]

As already mentioned, in this study I hope to facilitate the use of Lasswell's comparative psychological orientation by analyzing the three men in terms of Erikson's adaptation of the Freudian categories of personality development. One concomitant of using these categories is that we are made aware of how necessary an understanding of childhood is for a comprehension of adult behavior. As Erikson puts it,

> One may scan work after work on history, society, and morality and find little reference to the fact that all people start as children and all peoples begin in their

---

Weber in " 'Objectivity' in Social Science and Social Policy," in his *The Methodology of the Social Sciences*, Edward Shils and Henry Finch, trans. and ed. (New York, 1964).

[24] Gustav Bychowski's *Dictators and Disciples* approximates some of the characteristics of this approach. He does have a general theoretical concern (that is, to delineate the psychological preconditions for the emergence and prevention of dictatorship), and he uses psychoanalytic theory to study the lives of Julius Caesar, Cromwell, Robespierre, Hitler, and Stalin. But, like the early works in comparative politics generally, *Dictators and Disciples* is essentially a set of separately conceived case studies all under one cover, with some general remarks at the beginning and end but no comparative development in between.

nurseries. It is human to have a long childhood; it is civilized to have an even longer childhood. Long childhood makes a technical and mental virtuoso out of man, but it also leaves a lifetime residue of emotional immaturity in him.[25]

This does not imply, nor does Erikson mean it to imply, that all psychological development ends with childhood. Throughout life, as men have to deal with new situations, they continue to develop, to grow—at least in many cases. But in all cases the potential for such continued growth, the limit to adaptability, is to a considerable extent set by earlier, particularly childhood, experience.[26]

The crucial nexus for the transformation of childhood emotions into political motivation is adolescence. During this phase the young person's involvement in the psychological dilemma of drawing together the hitherto unintegrated aspects of his personality is joined to the need to make some decisions about what to make of his life. Hence two processes, those of identity formation and vocational choice, become merged; and the solution to the problems posed by one of them tends to imply resolution of the issues raised by the other as well. Of course, although this phase is often turbulent, the amount of distress and suffering is variable. Again, to take Erikson's view:

> In some young people, in some classes, at some periods in history, this crisis will be minimal; in other people, classes, and periods, the crisis will be clearly marked off as a critical period, a kind of "second birth," apt to be aggravated either by widespread neuroticisms or by pervasive ideological unrest. Some

[25] Erikson, *Childhood and Society*, p. 12.

[26] To some extent political science has been turning attention to developmental considerations in recent years. Following the lead of Talcott Parsons and Edward A. Shils in *Toward a General Theory of Action* (Cambridge, Mass., 1951), men like Gabriel A. Almond and Sidney Verba in *The Civic Culture* (Princeton, 1963); Herbert Hyman in *Political Socialization* (Glencoe, Ill., 1959); and others have been studying political socialization, the process of teaching the young of a country certain political values or norms.

young individuals will succumb to this crisis in all manner of neurotic, psychotic or delinquent behavior; others will resolve it through participation in ideological movements passionately concerned with religion or politics, nature or art. Still others, although suffering and deviating dangerously through what appears to be a prolonged adolescence, eventually come to contribute an original bit to an emerging style of life; the very danger which they have sensed has forced them to mobilize capacities to see and say, to dream and plan, to design and construct, in new ways.[27]

The men we are studying did struggle through a "prolonged adolescence" and did contribute something original to their cultures. And as we shall see, the one who suffered most (Gandhi) also contributed most that was original and inventive to the politics of his—and our—times.

Revolution and Leadership

Having outlined the perspective which will guide the inquiry, we may proceed to a more specific elaboration of the nature of the subject matter itself. Because the word revolution is used in many ways (one standard dictionary, for example, lists the following as synonyms: anarchy, confusion, disintegration, disorder, insubordination, insurrection, lawlessness, mutiny, rebellion, revolt, riot, sedition, and tumult), it seems wise to make as unambiguous as possible the present usage of the word, the range of behavior it will be used to denote. Accordingly, revolution is defined as a form of politics characterized by the extensive use of violent or other illegal means in competition for control of governmental power and authority, such control being desired in order to change (a) the ways in which and by whom control is to be attained and exercised in the future and (b) the fundamental life patterns of the inhabitants of the relevant society.[28]

[27] Erikson, *Young Man Luther*, pp. 14-15.
[28] In "Internal Wars: A Taxonomy" (unpublished memorandum for the Center of International Studies, Princeton University, March

Several of the terms used in this definition warrant elaboration. Politics is taken to be that form of human activity which is predominantly characterized by the quest for and maintenance of control over the most inclusive structure(s) in a society in terms of which individuals make authoritative decisions.[29] Effective decisions of this type, of course, involve both adequate amounts of power allocated to the decision-maker and sufficient authority or legitimacy to satisfy subjects that the decisions are rightful.[30] Finally, fundamental life patterns are those which the members of a society ideally and actually consider to be the most important indices of an individual's status or selfhood. They are, in other words, those beliefs, thoughts, and emotions in terms of which the individual conceives himself to exist, which make him comprehensible to himself and others.

In short, revolution is the politics of rapid and usually violent social change, either because the society is already in the throes of upheaval or because the revolutionary

---

1960) Harry Eckstein provides a taxonomy of the forms of intranational violence. Revolution as defined above would be only one form of internal war, although it does not exactly correspond to any one of the types Eckstein delineates. Chalmers Johnson, in "Revolution and the Social System" (paper presented to the 1963 meeting of the American Political Science Association) also deals with the question of the nature and types of revolution, especially in Part II of the paper. Lyford P. Edwards, in one of the ground breaking studies of revolution, defined the same as "a change brought about not necessarily by force and violence, whereby one system of legality is terminated and another originated." (*The Natural History of Revolution*, p. 2.) This definition, which is quite close to the one used here, also resembles George S. Pettee's conception of the "great revolution" in *The Process of Revolution*.

[29] This formulation is essentially derived from the definition of "political system" which Harry Eckstein presented in his paper "The Concept Political System," at the 1963 meeting of the American Political Science Association; and, like it, it suffers from identifying certain kinds of competitive behavior too closely with the formal structures of government. For present purposes, however, politics and revolution as defined here should serve to adequately denote the activity I will be discussing.

[30] On legitimacy see Weber's discussion in *The Theory of Social and Economic Organization*, pp. 324-28.

actors desire political power in order to make sweeping changes in the very nature of society. The revolutionist is consequently most simply defined as an individual who participates in revolutionary activity.

The propositions that will be formulated in this study are meant to hold, at least in a general way, for all men who participate in revolutions of this sort.[31] This means, however, that some men who are termed revolutionists in ordinary parlance would not be explicable in terms of our model. Men who seek to restore a status quo, who work for gradual political and social change, who participate in palace rebellions, simple coup d'etats, dynastic controversies, and other forms of political activity which do not have the characteristic means or goals of revolution as it has been defined will be of a different psycho-political type or types.

Within the class of individuals who are revolutionists of the character of Lenin, Trotsky, and Gandhi, there are still several important possible sources of variation. First might be mentioned the degree to which any given individual approximates the definition of a revolutionary participant. The less an individual is dedicated to radical social change and a total displacement of the ruling class, the less he will be likely to embody the psychological attributes of the revolutionary personality. The more he is inclined to the use of peaceful or traditionally legitimate political means, the less likely he will be to have a revolutionary psychology. In this regard we may anticipate that Gandhi will deviate from the model in certain respects, for his was a nonviolent (although not a legal) revolution.

Another important distinction that may be drawn among revolutionists is the degree to which they are revolutionists in particular or politicians in general on a vocational or an avocational basis. As Max Weber uses these terms, a person is involved in politics avocationally when political ac-

[31] Undoubtedly somewhat different formulations would be needed to explain the motives of female revolutionists. This interesting task must, however, be left for another time.

tivity is only "occasional."[32] Similarly, then, an avocational revolutionist is one whose reasons for participation are secondary to the central purpose of the activity. He is involved in revolutionary activity as a kind of game, because his friends are dabbling in it. Or he may see in revolutionary activity a way of advancing financially. It may also be that clandestine politics is a dominant mode of extracurricular activity at school, as it was so strikingly for the members of Nasser's generation in Egypt. Or he may work for revolutionary goals only because to do so is opportune politically. In all of these cases the person will abandon revolutionary activity as soon as the secondary motivations that occasioned the activity cease to be operative. And clearly such people will be psychologically very distinct from the individual for whom revolution is a lifelong enterprise.

The revolutionist by vocation is primarily devoted to the goals of the organization of which he is a member or the ideology which he espouses. Revolution is a long-term involvement and other vocational or avocational interests are decidedly secondary to the purposes of the revolutionary cause. In many cases, in fact, all secondary interests die out and the individual becomes entirely devoted to the cause itself. The three men we are studying were all of this type, men who identified themselves as revolutionists—and who conceived of revolutionary activity as a perfectly suitable occupation. We are not interested here in men who luxuriate in a passive and disengaged nihilism. We are interested rather in the man who feels that he has a job to do, just as the businessman has a job to do, but in this case it is the work of revolution, of bringing about a new order of things. Accordingly, the model is meant to depict the emotions only of those who are revolutionists by vocation.

By using the term vocation to describe revolutionary movements we are led to an important realization: revolu-

[32] Hans Gerth and C. Wright Mills, ed. and trans., *From Max Weber* (New York, 1958), p. 83 [From Weber's "Politics as a Vocation"].

tion is not a simple form of social deviancy. For a man to choose a revolutionary vocation there must be an established revolutionary tradition, a recognized and accessible outlet for his revolutionary energies. Otherwise the role of criminal, outcast or deviant will have to substitute for the more creative and politically significant role of rebel. This in turn reminds us that the questions this study raises do not have a simple, individual motivational answer. As mentioned earlier, a consummated revolutionary involvement, as well as successful leadership, takes the interaction of a complicated variety of social, economic, cultural, and political factors. In this study only motivational variables of a particular kind are being elaborated. Again, this in no way implies a desire to minimize the importance of other aspects of the problem.

Another source of variation within the general type of the revolutionary personality is what might be termed the "psychological role propensity" of the individual. As Lasswell argues, certain types of personal experience lead to an inclination to perform certain political functions, so that one can discern an administrative, an agitational, and a theorizing type of political personality. Or to use a different role typology, it seems likely that those who enjoy being bureaucrats, and are effective in that context, will be psychologically distinct from those who base their authority on charismatic grounds. For example, of the three men, Lenin was the most effective administrator, Trotsky was the most impressive agitator, and Gandhi surpassed the other two men in charismatic appeal. Personality differences, it will be seen, help to account for the variations. But a shared revolutionary personality exists as well.

One final, and important, source of variation is the degree to which a given revolutionist is a leader or a follower. All of the men we are studying, and whom the model is meant to describe, are individuals who attained high, if not the highest, leadership roles. The psychology of the ordinary member of a revolutionary movement, of the true believer, to use Eric Hoffer's term, will differ in some impor-

tant ways from that of the leader.[33] To the extent such individuals vary in fundamental ways, in their basic perceptions of the nature of the revolutionary experience, other
constructs must be used to make them intelligible. This
question, however, is peripheral to the major purposes of
this study.[34]

The revolutionary leader, then, the primary object of
our concern, is a man who exercises power and authority
with respect to some body of followers in terms of a revolutionary ideology. Just as a man may be more or less a
revolutionist, so, too, he may be more or less a leader. We
would judge him to embody leadership to a higher degree
when he need obey no superior leader, controls a wide
range of the activity of the people who follow him, controls
more rather than fewer people, and can exact obedience
with a relatively small expenditure of his vital resources,
emotional, political, and other.[35] By these criteria Lenin
and Gandhi attained a higher level of leadership than did
Trotsky. Part of my efforts will be directed towards an explanation of this difference in achievement.

It should be stressed that this is not a study of leadership
as such, but of the leader. Having defined what the leader
does, I am now interested in what psychological qualities
enable him to do it. The important questions of the leadership context, of the interaction between the leader and his
followers, will not directly concern us. We will not be asking, for example, why Gandhi appealed to the Indian people. Rather we will assume that his actions and words had
something to do with his effectiveness, and shall ask what it

[33] Eric Hoffer, *The True Believer* (New York, 1951).
[34] Hannah Arendt's *The Origins of Totalitarianism* (New York,
1958) and Sigmund Neumann's *Permanent Revolution* (New York,
1942) contain important examinations of the structure and gradations
of revolutionary leadership.
[35] A good review of the literature on leadership from a biographical
point of view is provided by Lewis Edinger in "Political Science and
Political Biography," *The Journal of Politics*, Vol. XXVI, Nos. 2 and
3 (May and August 1964). A good general review of leadership
studies is Bernard M. Bass, *Leadership, Psychology and Organizational Behavior* (New York, 1963).

was that led and enabled him to perform those actions. Moreover, we are not even going to be investigating all aspects of the leader himself, or of his development. A host of sociological and other factors will have to be left to one side so that we may bring sharply into focus the underlying motivations of the men we are studying.

It is obvious that in politics leadership and greatness are closely allied. By most standards Lenin and Gandhi, if not Trotsky, would certainly qualify as great men in politics. And indeed, part of the justification for studying these men is that they were in some sense heroes, that their impact on the course of events was enormous.[36] But a set of questions related to their impact on the politics of their times must, like the questions related to the interaction of leaders and followers, receive only peripheral attention in this study. In order to focus adequately on the issues of the motivation and psychological requisites for revolutionary participation and leadership, I must forego the opportunity to address myself to a broader range of concerns. Hopefully, however, our understanding of these more general issues will be augmented in the long run by more specifically focused studies of the present variety.

It has already been mentioned that one of the reasons Lenin, Trotsky, and Gandhi were chosen as the protagonists in this study is that their impact on the world in which they—and we—live was very great. More importantly, they were selected because they represent important variants of revolutionary participation. Lenin was primarily the leader and chief ideologist for a revolutionary organization, as well as a man who adjusted maximally to wielding power once the party came to power. Trotsky was a brilliant orator, administrator, and theorist, who nonetheless failed to understand the nature of political organizational

---

[36] Sidney Hook, in *The Hero in History* (New York, 1943), p. 153, judges a historical actor to be a "hero" when he is an individual "to whom we can justifiably attribute preponderant influence in determining an issue or event whose consequences would have been profoundly different if he had not acted as he did."

activity and who was unable to realize the highest level of leadership. Gandhi, unlike the other two men, deplored violence and built a revolution on the basis of his own charisma and suffering. Here, clearly, are men who are different enough from each other to shed light on the varieties of revolutionary involvement. Yet, at the same time, they were all revolutionists, in our sense of the term, and hence ought to share important personality attributes. We shall see to what extent we are able to understand both the similarities and the differences in the chapters ahead.

Lenin, Trotsky, and Gandhi: An Overview

Our theory and method dictates that we begin with an analysis of the available material on the childhood experiences of the three men. In order to give the reader some idea of where this analysis is leading, however, a brief sketch of some of the central characteristics which marked the political behavior of each man seems appropriate. The burden of the following chapters will be to try to explain, in psychoanalytic terms, why the men had these attributes.

The mature Lenin did not seem to have the doubts and indecisiveness, nor the predilection for irregular habits and a bohemian existence, which were the hallmarks of the Russian revolutionary emigrés in Western Europe in the first years of this century. He was so matter-of-fact and direct in his purpose, so narrow in his range of interests, that the intellectuals who were his contemporaries, and indeed many of his subsequent biographers, have found it difficult to understand him.[37] How could a man who appeared so ordinary, of such pedestrian interests and tastes, command the loyalties of so many men who had a far greater scope of intellectual concerns than he did? Those who did understand him as Trotsky did to some extent, realized that the tight focus of his interest and his ability to command the obedience of other men were two sides of the same coin.[38]

[37] Louis Fischer discusses his difficulties in working with Lenin in *The Life of Lenin* (New York, 1964), p. 679.
[38] Leon Trotsky, *Lenin* (New York, 1962), *passim*.

The one subject in which Lenin was vitally interested was the impending revolutionary overthrow of the Tsar in Russia.[39] With an intensity of concentration that was a constant source of wonder to his contemporaries, he turned his enormous analytical and organizational powers to one question: what could men do to help bring about the revolution in Russia? He ruled out no means if they could help him achieve this end and assumed that his opponent would similarly use any means at his disposal to crush revolutionary socialism. His view of the coming revolution was clearly apocalyptic: out of the bloody destruction of the existing order would be born a new society, devoid of conflict and that inequality which is the father of conflict. The issue would be met between the forces of good, the vanguard of the working class leading forth an army of militant proletarians, and the forces of evil, the tsarist autocracy with the allied, large capitalist interests of Russia and the world; the loser in the fateful conflict would die.

With the final battle not far off, Lenin found himself living in what appeared to be a dangerous world: he was keenly sensitive to the possibilities of betrayal, out of malicious intent or human inadequacy, even from those who were closest to him.[40] Mistrustfully, to guard against the weakness of will or the treachery of the material with which he had to work, Lenin built up a tightly hierarchical organization, which he governed with the aid of impersonal rules of conduct which were to leave the members of the party no choice but to do the right thing: as long as they obeyed the dictates of the leader there would be harmony among comrades and the assurance of ultimate success. Should a member disagree with the leader, and persist in his disagreement after the Old Man, as Lenin was called, had done everything possible to persuade him of the inadequacy and dangerousness of his views, then he would be cut out

[39] Cf. Fischer, pp. 56-92; Bertram D. Wolfe, *Three Who Made a Revolution* (New York, 1964), Chapters 8, 9, 12-15; Stefan T. Possony, *Lenin: The Compulsive Revolutionary* (Chicago, 1964).

[40] Leites, *A Study of Bolshevism, passim.*

of the organization as if he were an infectious cancer. And when, as in 1903, Lenin was unable to maintain strict control over the minds and policies of his cohorts, he was willing to split with any and all of the other leaders of Russian social democracy in order to insure his freedom to follow those policies which he felt—which he knew—to be the only ones, at the given historical moment, which led to successful revolution.

However, Lenin never remained in the wilderness, isolated from followers, for very long; his analyses of the turn of events, the unbearable sarcasm of his polemical thrusts and his readiness to reinstate any man who would acknowledge his mistakes and follow the correct, hard, and unbending line, usually proved to be irresistable to those similarly concerned with the course of Russian socialism. Moreover, Lenin had the conviction, which he conveyed to others just because he felt it so deeply and could act upon it with the sure and natural movements of a man apparently born to wield authority, that he, and at times he alone, correctly read Marx, that the question of his leadership was not one of personal volition or ambition but of the necessity for all men to recognize the truth, the Marxist truth which it was given to him to understand.[41] And because he viewed his authority in these peculiarly impersonalized terms he seldom gave others the impression of personal ambition. He seemed, as it were, cut from the whole cloth of revolution, a perfectly integrated embodiment of revolutionary truth and motivation.

Trotsky, by contrast, had a terrible personal visibility about him.[42] Where Lenin the man seemed to disappear into Lenin the leader, Trotsky always overwhelmed others with Trotsky. He was a brilliant orator and writer, the master of a direct, witty, and caustic style. He delighted in dis-

---

[41] Max Eastman comments that a verbal victory for Lenin always appeared to be simply an enunciated truth, in *Leon Trotsky: The Portrait of a Youth* (New York, 1925), p. 166.

[42] This quality is reflected well in A. V. Lunacharsky's sketch of Trotsky, which is reprinted in Max Eastman, *Since Lenin Died* (London, 1925), pp. 131-35.

membering his opponent's arguments and when he had done so, as he almost invariably did, he expected his erstwhile foe to recognize the correctness of his position and the brilliance of his exposition—and then to applaud the effort. He did not have Lenin's way of making his position appear to be the inevitable outcome of the correct analysis of the current situation, but rather gave one the impression of forcing his own highly individualized formulations upon a recalcitrant reality. As a result Trotsky left one with the feeling that it was not just the revolution that was important, but his own role in it as well. Actually, Trotsky had very mixed feelings about the kind of position or positions he wanted to fill once the revolutionary movement came to power,[43] but he nonetheless appeared extremely ambitious and bent on self-aggrandizement.

Trotsky's very visibility and oratorical brilliance, his great gift for taking the center of the stage of events and not relinquishing it, suited him perfectly for playing the role which made him the second ranking leader of the Revolution. In 1905, again in 1917, at Brest-Litovsk and during the Civil War Trotsky was the voice of the proletariat, the tribune of the people. But during the quiet periods, the lulls before and after the revolutionary storms, when heroics— and heroic speech—were out of tune with the times, Trotsky's clear calls to revolutionary action and sacrifice sounded grandiose instead of grand, theatrical instead of dramatic.[44]

Trotsky differed from Lenin in other ways as well. Lenin concentrated all of his energy, all of his time, on the revolution. Trotsky, although always speaking from a revolutionary Marxist position, was also a commentator on life in general, on morals, literature and art, drama and music; his interests were more diffuse than Lenin's and in this respect he was much more the prototype of the Europeanized Russian intellectual. He was, however, more of an activist,

---

[43] Leon Trotsky, *My Life* (New York, 1930), p. 339.
[44] Isaac Deutscher, *The Prophet Unarmed* (London, 1959), pp. 23-27.

much more attuned to the possibilities and drama of the revolutionary process itself than, say, the Mensheviks, the "right" wing of the Russian Social Democratic Party. He did not have the Menshevik repugnance for shedding blood, and during the heroic days of 1917 and the ensuing Civil War, he did not suffer from their paralysis of will. But, like them, he was a polyglot, a mixture of ideas and emotions which did not hang together as did the rock-like and solid unity that was Lenin. Trotsky was a convinced activist and the originator of what is perhaps the most voluntaristic form of Marxist theory; and yet at times he was extremely passive in the face of political crisis. A man who was devoted to his friends and capable of great loyalty, he found it impossible to work in tandem with others. The greatest speaker and writer of the Russian Revolution, a man keenly sensitive to the dramatic possibilities of both forms of communication, he was quite deaf and blind to the personal antipathies he aroused among his peers.[45] Next to Lenin, the acknowledged leader of the Revolution and a man reputed to be bent on primacy, he was nonetheless unable to take those actions which might have brought him and the ideas he so prized to the top in the struggle for power over Lenin's position when the latter, through illness, was increasingly forced to turn the reins of power over to others.[46]

Both Lenin and Trotsky—although the latter was not without his hesitations and doubts—were men of violent means. Trotsky was less mistrustful than Lenin, easier therefore to betray, but he shared Lenin's vision of a world divided into two warring armies, the strongest and best armed of which would win when the battle was drawn. Gandhi, the third of our subjects, also viewed the world as divided between opposing forces, between those of *maya* (illusion) and reality, spiritual truth, and material falsehood.[47] In India in the first half of the present century the British represented the gross materialistic and aggressive

[45] Eastman, *Since Lenin Died*, pp. 40-50.
[46] Deutscher, *passim*.
[47] Louis Fischer, *The Life of Mahatma Gandhi* (New York, 1962), pp. 37-44.

falsity of the West, and, before Gandhi, it was unclear how the spiritual truth of the East was to manifest itself. It was Gandhi's great achievement that he provided the way—*satyagraha*, truth-force, mass civil disobedience based on the desire to convert one's enemy through love so that he willingly acknowledges one's dignity and rights. Gandhi brought the principle of *ahimsa*, nonviolence, into politics. He led a revolution against British colonial authority in which the meekness of the oppressed (and their numbers) became a tool in gaining relief from their oppression.

Gandhi shared with Trotsky a focus on man's dignity as well as his courage, but in Gandhi's hands these values took on quite different forms than they had with Trotsky. Where Trotsky seemed intent on gaining recognition of his personal status, his personal superiority, Gandhi put himself forward as the most humble of men, the lowliest servant of his fellows—albeit one that God had especially blessed and through whom God spoke to this world.[48] Unlike Trotsky (and Lenin) Gandhi defined courage in terms of the ability to suffer pain and face death rather than to inflict pain and guard against death.[49] He shared with Trotsky a generally optimistic view of the world; like him he had a pervasive faith in the ultimate success of his cause. But he resembled (and outdid) Lenin in his asceticism and self-denial. His simplicity of dress, his sexual restraint, his rigorous vegetarianism were legend well within his own lifetime. He was, in brief, the closest thing to a saint that modern politics has seen.

In the next two chapters we shall examine the childhood, adolescence and young manhood of these men, seeking from these periods a knowledge of the origins of their adult personalities and an answer to the question of why a man

[48] Gandhi sums himself up well in the introduction to his *An Autobiography: The Story of My Experiments with Truth* (Boston, 1957), pp. xi-xv.

[49] Susanne Hoeber Rudolph, "The New Courage: An Essay on Gandhi's Psychology," *World Politics*, XVI (October 1963). See also her later contribution, "Self-Control and Political Potency: Gandhi's Asceticism," *The American Scholar*, XXXV (Winter 1965-66).

becomes a revolutionist. Then in the fourth chapter we shall examine the first phase of their mature lives, the period in which they did or did not establish a basis for leadership. Here we will be concerned with both the actions which insured (or deprived) them of ascendancy and with the ideologies they used to justify their actions. In Chapter 5 we will turn to the period of the revolutionary struggle for power and after, looking for answers to the questions of why men do or do not respond well to the conditions of revolutionary turmoil, why some men acclimate themselves to being in power when others do not and of how the revolutionary leader approaches the question of succession. In the last chapter the findings of the study will be briefly restated.

CHAPTER TWO

childhood and adolescence

As Erikson says, we seldom pay much attention to child-hood.[1] Moreover, even if we did, there would be no guarantee that we would know very much about the early lives of leaders—we do not know in advance, for example, that a bright Jewish Ukrainian schoolboy named Lev Davidovich Bronstein is going to turn out to be the famous Leon Trotsky. For two of our men (Gandhi and Trotsky), however, we do have autobiographies, which, whatever their ambiguities and hidden traps, are at least a personal record of the men's lives, including their childhoods. Thus Lenin becomes the greatest problem, for he seldom discussed his early life, never wrote about it at any length, and was not given to indulging in public introspection. Our picture of Lenin's youth must be reconstructed from all too unreliable reminiscences of family and friends. Nonetheless, there are some important things which we may surmise about and from his early life.

The Youth of Vladimir Ilyich Ulyanov

Vladimir Ilyich Ulyanov was born on April 22, 1870 in the village of Simbirsk on the Volga River. His father, Ilya Nikolayevich Ulyanov, was a school teacher and administrator, who through diligent work and unswerving loyalty to the prevailing regime advanced to the rank of "Actual Councillor of State" by the time of his death in January 1886.[2] His mother was Maria Alexandrovna Ulyanov (neé

[1] Erikson, *Childhood and Society*, p. 12.
[2] Actual Councillor of State was an hereditary rank of nobility,

[33]

Blank), apparently of German ancestry, a relatively well if informally educated person for a provincial backwater like Simbirsk.[3] Both of Lenin's parents, in fact, were atypical both for Simbirsk and Russia as a whole. His father was a highly methodical, extremely conscientious person who devoted long hours to both his job and related benevolent work, especially free tutoring. That such qualities were both esteemed and relatively rare is shown by the status that he achieved as a result of his work. Anna, the eldest sister, described her father as follows:

[Ilya Nikolayevich] was conscientious and patient in his explanations, treated his pupils pranks with indulgence and used to prepare poor pupils for examinations free of charge. He was a born teacher and was fond of his work. . . . As a form of recreation from his work he preferred talking to people interested in this work. He also liked to rest in the family circle, looking after the upbringing of his children, and he was very fond of chess. . . .[4]

Anna thus paints a picture of the ideal father—as if everything connected with Lenin had to be perfect. But while we may question the tone of her remarks, the factual content seems plausible; thus we may envision Lenin's father as a devoted and talented teacher, a man whose personality synchronized well with his occupation. It also seems likely that he was a loving father, who devoted substantial time to gently teaching his children how to behave. He taught his children to play chess, and played other games with them as well.

Ulyanov's official duties, however, kept him away from

---

fourth out of fourteen among the "Table of Ranks." See Fischer, *Life of Lenin*, p. 6; Wolfe, *Three Who Made a Revolution*, p. 46.

[3] Louis Fischer is the most thorough of Lenin's biographers in tracing back the national and racial characteristics of Lenin's parents and ancestors.

[4] *Reminiscences of Lenin by His Relatives* (Moscow, 1956), pp. 14-15.

home "for weeks, occasionally months at a time, traveling by train, carriage, and sleigh to the remote reaches of his educational realm."[5] The general agreement that exists on his love of teaching and the time he devoted to it also supports the impression of a father often absent from home and family, and perhaps somewhat too much of a pedagogue when present—but a loving teacher, ungiven to harshness. We shall see presently that Lenin identified strongly with his father. Many of his father's leading characteristics, such as his pedagogical manner, his patience, and his devotion to his work, were to be Lenin's as well; but Lenin blended these attributes with others, and applied them to tasks his father would have been unlikely to condone.

Just as Anna gives us what is probably a touched-up portrait of her father, so she sketches her mother in rosy hues:

> [Vladimir Ilyich's mother] was of a steadfast and firm disposition, but at the same time cheerful and friendly. A woman of great capacity, she studied foreign languages and music and read a great deal. . . . She never raised her voice, hardly ever punished her children and yet secured their love and obedience. Her favourite relaxation was music, of which she was passionately fond, and which she played with great feeling. And the children liked to fall asleep and, later in life, to work to the sound of her playing the piano.[6]

Again, while the emotional texture of the picture is perhaps inaccurate, it is probably safe to assume that Lenin's mother was relatively well educated, devoted to the well being and advancement of her children, and of a steady character and firm disposition. She taught her children to read and play the piano, helped them compose a weekly handwritten family magazine and often led the family in singing.[7] The reports of her reactions to the death of her

[5] Fischer, *Life of Lenin*, p. 6.
[6] *Reminiscences of Lenin*, pp. 16-17.
[7] Fischer, *Life of Lenin*, p. 6.

eldest son (Alexander, who was usually called Sasha), as well as her fortitude and control in meeting the adversities caused by the political involvements of all of her children, tend to substantiate the picture of a woman of great emotional control and self-discipline.[8]

Anna also gives us her impression of the relationship between her mother and father:

> Nor were there ever between her and her husband —they always lived in harmony—any arguments or disagreements concerning the upbringing of their children which are always a bad thing for the children. They usually discussed any doubts they had in private, and the children always found a "united front" facing them. . . . The childhood of Vladimir Ilyich and his brothers and sisters was happy and cloudless.[9]

And so we complete the picture of the ideal family. Loving and temperate parents, devoted to each other and to their children, and the children in turn devoted to each other and their parents. How much of this picture is fact, and how much fiction, is hard to discern. But unless Anna is completely falsifying the situation, it at least is likely that the family was not bothered by unusual stress or disruption.

The family, it might be noted, was rather large. In addition to Vladimir, Anna (born in 1864) and Sasha (born in 1866), there were three other children who lived to maturity: Olga (born in 1871), Dmitri (1874), and Maria (1878).[10] On the whole this considerable brood of chil-

---

[8] In his *Lenin: The Compulsive Revolutionary*, Possony evokes an image of marital strife, motherly moodiness, and depression and paternal weakness (p. 5). The evidential basis which underlies his analysis, however, is unclear.

[9] *Reminiscences of Lenin*, pp. 16-17.

[10] Fischer reports a boy named Nikolai, who was born and died in 1873 (*Life of Lenin*, p. 6), and Possony reports a girl, also named Olga, who was born and died in 1868 (p. 6). Wolfe notes neither. For purposes of understanding Lenin it is not important to know of siblings that died before his birth—unless such a death had a pronounced effect either on his parents or older siblings. But the death of a younger son would fit well with the interpretation which will be

dren seems to have gotten along without anything more
than the usual amount of familial squabbles and annoy-
ances. Those closest in age tended to pair off, so that Anna
and Sasha, Volodya (Vladimir) and Olga, Dmitri and
Maria were the most frequent companions. Sasha supposedly strongly resembled his mother in both appearance
and personality, while Lenin took after his father. Wolfe
sums up the impressions recorded of the boys in the following way:

> Yet, in physique as in temperament, they were as
> different as two brothers could possibly be. Alexan-
> der's face was long and brooding; his skin milky white;
> his hair, thick, turbulent, frizzy, deeply rooted, stood
> up in all directions from a line far down on the fore-
> head. His eyes, set deep on a strange angle in a nobby,
> overhanging brow, seemed to turn their gaze inward.
> It was the strongly chisled face of a dreamer, a saint,
> a devotee, an ascetic. But Vladimir's head was shaped
> like an egg, and the thin fringe of reddish hair began
> to recede from the forehead when he was twenty, leav-
> ing him bald, like his father, in young manhood. His
> complexion was a blend of grayishness and full-blood-
> edness; his eyes, tiny, twinkling, Mongoloid. His whole
> aspect, except in moments of intense thought or anger,
> was jovial, humorous, mischievous, self-confident, ag-
> gressive. . . . [He] was noisy and boisterous, a player
> of practical jokes, an inveterate tease, quick at re-
> partee, sharp of tongue. He loved to exhibit the grow-
> ing powers of his mind by raillery at the expense of
> his littler brothers and sisters, young cousins and play-
> mates. The one bad mark in his high school record
> came from playing pranks on a French teacher whose
> pomposity he disliked. Various people testify to the

---

presented of Lenin's reaction to Sasha's death. It is not, however,
necessary that such a younger brother died for the interpretation to
stand, and accordingly we will treat Lenin's family as if there were
six children.

fits of ill-temper to which young Vladimir was subject on occasion, while his mockery and intellectual superiority created a certain wall between him and the other lads his age. ("Vladimir Ilyich enjoyed the love of his schoolmates," writes the pious Anna, "although he had no very close friends.")[11]

Vladimir thus appears to have been a somewhat shy boy who was not in very close contact with people outside of the family.[12] Within the familial context he was loud and strident, given somewhat to boasting and bullying, but on the whole well liked and likeable. Sasha by contrast was more reserved and introspective. He also seems to have been somewhat melancholic, which Vladimir was not.

With one exception, the picture we get of Lenin's childhood, of his preadolescent years, is one of normal and healthy development. A hint of loneliness and compensatory over-assertiveness (often manifested in sarcasm and other thinly disguised aggressive forms) are indeed to be found, leading one to suspect that Vladimir was outwardly more aggressive than Sasha; but it is certainly not a picture of lack of adjustment to his immediate environment or of loss of contact with reality. His easy success in school work, the esteem in which he was held by teachers, from whom, with the exception Wolfe noted, he never received anything but very high grades, the memories the other children have of playing games with him—all attest to Lenin's having been a bright, assertive, and not unusual lad.

The extended absences of his father, coupled with paternal attentiveness when his father was present, however, put a limit on the picture I have drawn of Vladimir's relatively happy childhood. Although it was and is far from

[11] Wolfe, p. 55. Anna's description of Lenin as a child can be found in *Reminiscences of Lenin*, pp. 18-22. Fischer, *Life of Lenin*, pp. 7-8, provides a good if all too brief summary of Lenin's first fourteen years.

[12] All in all, Possony's picture of Lenin as a child seems overdrawn in its bleakness. Cf. Possony, pp. 5-8.

uncommon for a child to grow up with minimal contact with his father, this fact does not make such lack of contact any less important for any given individual. The prolonged absence of one of the most important loved ones during childhood tends to create feelings of insecurity and mistrust, as well as a possibly pervasive feeling of being neglected.[13] It must have had a strange effect on young Lenin's mind when a loving and attentive person was there one day and gone the next—and often gone for weeks running. The loving, temperate attention of his mother undoubtedly provided a stiff leavening of stability and control; but the pattern of alternating great attention and prolonged absence (and hence inattention) which characterized Lenin's relationship with his father probably produced strongly ambivalent feelings with regard to a person toward whom, in any case, emotions are prone to be unusually mixed. These feelings were probably further intensified by the kind of disciplinary measures Ilya Ulyanov apparently used, a rule of firm moral suasion, rather than physical coercion, which left little room for anti-paternal rebellion with a clear conscience.[14] The high moral rectitude of the father undoubtedly resulted in an unusually demanding superego for the son, so that young Lenin probably was unable to think or express the feelings of resentment which seem sure to have followed his father's absences and disciplining without experiencing guilt as a consequence. (The striking similarities already noted between Lenin's adult personality and that of his father point to a deep emotional involvement with his father, which would have resulted in the very ready internalization of his father's moral standards.) This ambivalence might have diminished after adolescence as a normal by-product of growing up and coming to accept one's parents as human beings with frailties and virtues

[13] Fenichel, *Psychoanalytic Theory of Neurosis*, p. 44.
[14] Freud discusses the effects of restrained disciplining on superego formation in *Civilization and Its Discontents* (New York, 1961), pp. 70-80, especially p. 77.

like all other human beings, had not, in Lenin's case, the normal course of development, with reference to both his father and elder brother, been cut brutally short.

Before turning to the critical events of Lenin's adolescence, it might be noted that there is one fact in Lenin's childhood which might tend to substantiate the impression that family circumstances set the occasion for a degree of mistrust and insecurity, of lack of confidence in the reliability of others. This is that Lenin did not learn to walk until he was almost three years old.[15] It is possible, of course, that strictly physiological factors prevented him from walking earlier, and hence any hypotheses about the reasons for the delay are very speculative. But assuming it was not strictly physiological in origin, such as some neuromuscular difficulty, it is worthwhile to venture a psychological explanation.

Perhaps then, young Lenin's progress towards walking was slowed down after his sister Olga was born (Olga was eighteen to twenty months younger than Vladimir). It is common enough that young children attempt to copy the behavior of newly born children in order to get the attention newborns receive. That Vladimir finally started to walk when Olga did suggests this possibility. Such a regression or fixation, however, would not have been either very likely or as persistent if the child felt secure and well loved; his developing self-esteem, based on loving parental care, would suffice to prevent such a severe reaction to the birth of a sibling.[16] Therefore, if we temporarily rule out physical causes, it seems likely that by the time Olga was born, Lenin had already developed a basically mistrustful nature, either as the result of the unreliability of those who supplied affection, warmth, and food, or for some other reason. Young Lenin may have delayed walking because he was uncertain about how his environment would react, about

[15] Wolfe, p. 54.

[16] On regression and fixation during early childhood see *Fenichel*, pp. 65-66; also Anna Freud, *Normality and Pathology in Childhood* (New York, 1965), pp. 54-107, *passim*.

whether or not he could safely venture this new activity. This mistrust and felt lack of attention would have then been accentuated by Olga's birth. It is of interest in this regard that Erikson, among others, hypothesizes that basic attitudes of trust and mistrust originate in the experiences of the first year of life.[17]

If the above explanation of Lenin's late walking is correct, then important characteristics of Lenin's adult behavior, above all his mistrustfulness and the aggressiveness which grows out of mistrust (there are, needless to say, other sources of aggression as well), had deep roots indeed in his life experiences. A predisposition would exist towards viewing the world in kill-or-be-killed terms; an underlying receptivity to the danger signals in his environment would have been established. This mistrust, assuming it existed, was not so great as to impair Lenin's grasp of reality. But it did result in a certain perception of reality which, in the context of revolutionary politics, had important consequences.

Whatever the causes of Lenin's late walking, the fact itself indicates a highly cautious attitude—which is possibly the result of underlying mistrust but which also might derive from the amount of time Lenin must have spent watching rather than doing during his first three years. Where other children were learning by trying, young Lenin learned by watching, waiting, and then trying. This lack of impulsiveness was one of Lenin's characteristics throughout his life. Any new action or policy which Lenin put forward was always preceded by a long period of silent and absorptive gestation. As we shall see later, this way of learning and acting is strikingly different from the ways of both Gandhi and Trotsky. Both of the latter learned publicly, Lenin privately; Trotsky and Gandhi often acted impulsively, Lenin almost never.

Turning to Lenin's early adolescence, we find that it was marked by an increase in assertiveness, boisterousness, and

[17] Erikson, *Childhood and Society*, pp. 247-51. Cf. also the work of Melanie Klein and her followers.

sarcasm. It was when he was about fifteen that he was involved in ridiculing his French teacher, the incident which resulted in the one low grade referred to earlier.[18] The earlier hero-worship for his brother changed to a mild contempt for Sasha's passive ways (the latter was engaged in a long-term study of worms) and friction between them increased.[19] Earlier young Lenin tried to be "the same as Sasha" in everything he did, but now he struck out on paths of his own.[20] Thus it seems that Lenin was going through a rather typical period of adolescent rebellion, rejecting earlier models for his behavior, starting to feel that he was as much of a man as his father and older brother, and hence able to stand his ground against them. All this, it should be stressed, was being played in a low key. There were no dramatic crescendoes of antifamilial rebellion. Lenin's feelings of aggressiveness were probably very strong, but he had imbibed enough of the family tradition of emotional control, as a consequence of the affection in which he held other members of the family so that, for example, when his father reprimanded him for his abuse of his French teacher, Lenin submitted to parental authority and promised that no further incidents would take place.

Then unexpectedly, in January 1886, Lenin's father died. Lenin did not react to his demise with prolonged mourning or a cessation of other activities. Within a year of his father's death, however, he did give up whatever religious beliefs he had previously held.[21] He became increasingly hard to manage, insulted his mother at least once (although supposedly jokingly), and was generally obstreperous, so that eventually quarreling broke out between him and Sasha, now, as eldest son, head of the family.[22]

Sasha did not give up his usual activities either—he con-

[18] A. I. Ulyanova-Yelizorova, in *Reminiscences of Lenin* (Anna), p. 25.

[19] Fischer, *Life of Lenin*, p. 11.

[20] *Reminiscences of Lenin*, p. 18. The words in quotation marks Anna recorded as Lenin's own.

[21] Fischer, *Life of Lenin*, p. 9.   [22] *Ibid.*, p. 12.

tinued his work in biology at the University of St. Petersburg, returning home only for vacations, and not even interrupting his studies to attend his father's funeral. Yet despite the superficial appearance of control, Sasha was deeply disturbed. He told his sister Anna that at one point during the year after his father's death he had contemplated suicide.[23] Instead of killing himself, however, he directed his energies into revolutionary activity, first, importantly enough, participating in a memorial demonstration at a cemetery near the university in honor of dead revolutionists, and eventually participating in a pitiful and inadequate plot to kill Tsar Alexander III.[24] The plot was easily discovered by the Tsar's agents and Sasha was arrested. During the course of his trial and after it was over, several opportunities were given him to deny responsibility or ask for pardon. All were rejected; he even went so far as to take upon himself responsibility which was not his—except where he felt he would be claiming false glory for himself.[25] In May 1887 he was executed.[26]

Sasha's revolutionary activity appears to have suicidal overtones. His feelings of guilt, resulting from his father's death, may have impelled him to seek his own death—his patricidal urges must have been very strong indeed for him to have sought to bring about his own destruction through the killing of "father" Tsar. Sasha said he wanted to die for his country.[27] More basically, I would guess he wanted to die as atonement for his sins, to pay for his aggressive impulses towards his father. Here we have, in fact, in very disturbed form, the classic question of how a boy becomes

[23] *Ibid.*, p. 14.

[24] Several good accounts of this can be found in biographies of Lenin. See the first chapter of Fischer's *Life of Lenin*; Wolfe, Chapter 3; and Possony, pp. 9-11.

[25] Adam Ulam claims that before his death Sasha did give in to his mother's pleas and ask for pardon. See his *The Bolsheviks* (New York, 1965), p. 94.

[26] See especially Wolfe's discussion of the trial and its aftermath as cited above.

[27] Wolfe, p. 64.

〚 43 〛

a man. Clearly he does so by becoming *like* his father, but in its earliest form this goal is expressed as actually becoming the father, replacing the father in his relationship with the mother. But the burden of such thoughts is guilt and fear, guilt stemming from the strictures of the superego, fear that the father will perceive the clandestine desires and revenge himself. Hence Sasha would seem to be a person who could not manage this complex relationship, in whose mind the replacement of the father remained all too literal a desire. When his father died, Sasha was thus overcome by guilt at what his thoughts had led to (at least, what his superego told him they led to) and sought for a path of alleviation. That he took part in cemetery ceremonies rather than some other form of demonstration is just one sign of his concern with death and of his desire to atone to his father for missing his funeral; that he sought to kill the Tsar is an indication of the depth of his aggressive impulses; that he refused all offers of escape from his situation, of avoidance of execution, is a token of the unbearability of his guilt, of his desire to even all scores by allowing his own destruction.[28]

No one in his family knew of Sasha's activities until he was arrested. No one, in fact, was terribly sensitive to the politics of the day, least of all young Lenin, who mainly concerned himself with his school work, games, and the novels of Turgeniev.[29] Yet when Sasha was arrested, Lenin

[28] Sasha's ideological commitment in this matter is unclear. He apparently, as did so many of his generation, held some blend of populist and Marxist ideas; it would seem the former more strongly than the latter. However, others holding similar beliefs, even the others involved in the plot, did not view the situation in such self-sacrificial terms.

[29] Lenin's youngest sister, Maria Ulyanova, reports that when Lenin heard the news of his brother's execution he said "No, we won't take that path. That isn't the path to take." (*Reminiscences of Lenin*, p. 95.) Wolfe—rightly, I believe—calls the veracity of this report, as well as several other legends about Lenin, into question (pp. 75-77). In the present case, the only ones available to hear Lenin's tactical dictum were thirteen year old Dmitri and nine year old Maria, who supposedly remembers it. Given Lenin's political uninvolvement, and the nature of the audience, the remark seems unlikely.

became the acting head of the family, and it was he who brought the news to his mother.[30] From then until Sasha's execution it was the mother who carried the burdens of pleading with Sasha to accept one of the outs open to him, of being with him at the execution itself. Lenin continued his schooling and graduated later that spring with highest honors from his high school. Again, to a substantial extent, Lenin's behavior appeared to be unaffected by familial death. His attitude towards his mother did soften, however, and within a brief span of years he became a revolutionist.

How, then, does one explain Lenin's immediate overt reaction, or rather, lack of overt reaction, to the deaths of these two important people in his life? One might well expect that a young man who lost, in short order, two people he loved very much would react to the loss with substantial manifestations of grief, that he would at least manifest the usual signs of mourning, such as depression, lack of interest in other people and in his usual activities, and so on.[31] Or Lenin might have been overwhelmed by the experience, as Sasha was by his father's death. But Lenin did not react in either of these ways. We have no record of a substantial period of mourning, nor did Lenin sink under the weight of the events as Sasha did.

Still it seems unlikely that Lenin would be unaffected by this double bereavement. I believe that he was indeed very deeply affected, but that he was unable and, in part, unwilling to respond to the events at the time they occurred. Rather it took Lenin a period of years to work out an acceptable solution to the emotional and other problems which the deaths presented, a period which ended with Lenin's affirmation of revolutionary Marxism.[32]

One of the reasons why Lenin did not appear to be re-

[30] *Ibid.*, p. 65.

[31] Freud describes the symptoms of mourning and speculates on the psychological work which mourning performs, in "Mourning and Melancholia," in his *Collected Papers*, Joan Riviere, trans. (New York, 1959), IV, 153-54.

[32] The transformation of this problem into Lenin's revolutionary identity is discussed in Chapter 3.

acting to this experience is that he probably repressed the feelings aroused by the crucial events. Even before the deaths of his father and brother, Lenin had manifested a substantial capacity for emotional self-discipline. Self-control was, after all, an esteemed Ulyanov family trait, and Lenin would have been expected not to give way to his emotions. As a result Lenin probably found it necessary to suppress his grief, and thereby to increase the feelings of guilt which he had as a result of the aggressive feelings he harbored towards father and brother. (Sasha, too, it might be remembered, had felt it necessary to keep his distress to himself.) Without the possibility of expressing his grief, and thereby expiating his guilt, Lenin would have been left little choice but to use his powers of self-discipline to repress his aggressive feelings, to drive from consciousness all trace of his dislike for his father and brother. It should be emphasized that such an action would not have been necessary had not Lenin loved his father and Sasha quite deeply. It was this combination of love and hate, this ambivalence, that created for Lenin the central problem of his life.

It was not, however, just the family tradition of self-control that prevented Lenin from mourning and thereby severing his intense emotional bonds with the deceased. It is also possible that Lenin, about sixteen when his father died and not quite seventeen at the time of Sasha's death, was not yet emotionally old enough to mourn. For mourning, the painful process by which we learn to accept a person's death by testing our desire that the person not be dead against the reality of his nonexistence,[33] does not seem to be possible before the individual has first experienced the quasi-mourning which is the process of late adolescent liberation from parental control:

> The predominant tendency . . . [in children who lose a parent during childhood or early adolescence] is that emotional response is inhibited, and on a level slightly

[33] Freud, "Mourning and Melancholia," *Collected Papers*, IV, 153-54.

below the surface the reality of the loss is denied. While the child acknowledges verbally that the parent is dead, he continues to daydream that the parent will return. We observe here a splitting of the ego—what is accepted on one level is denied on another. Feelings of grief are more or less interfered with; there is a great intolerance for protracted distress. Inhibition of affect and denial of the reality of the loss mutually reinforce each other. If one does not react to the event, it is as if it has not occurred. What is most strikingly absent in children and adolescents is . . . the "work of mourning."[34]

In other words, Lenin's lack of overt reaction may be an indication not only of the degree to which he repressed his emotions, but of the denial of the reality of the loss as well. And this denial can be viewed in a twofold light. On the one hand, Lenin was denying the loss of loved objects, of people who provided him with warmth, stability, and security. He was battling against the feeling of being deserted by benevolent authorities. It is in this regard that we can understand Lenin's loss of religious faith after his father's death: his inability to believe in God is a reflection of his increasing inability to believe that his father is alive, of his feeling that paternal or Godly love has deserted him, and therefore is no more.

On the other hand, Lenin's unconscious denial of his father's and brother's deaths was an attempt to assuage his feelings of guilt about their deaths. If his father and Sasha are not really dead, then his aggressive wishes could not have killed them. But Lenin's feelings of guilt were not so great, nor was his contact with reality so poor, that he could allow himself to slip into a truly delusional world. Consciously he knew full well that his father and Sasha were dead. Thus his sense of reality, and his rational control

[34] Martha Wolfenstein, "Death of a Parent and Death of a President: Children's Reactions to Two Kinds of Loss," in Martha Wolfenstein and Gilbert Kliman, eds., *Children and The Death of a President* (Garden City, New York, 1965), p. 64.

over his emotions, were at war with intense internal conflicts over these events. Lenin was in need of a way of bringing these emotions under conscious control, and of a way of dealing with them that would reduce the strain of his psychic conflicts.

More concretely, after his father's death, Lenin might be viewed as having a need to express his aggressive feelings towards paternal authority, but without having a way of justifying such feelings nor an object towards which such aggression might be turned. As a result, these aggressive feelings would not be directed outward, but inward, resulting in strong feelings of guilt which denial of the reality of the death would not be adequate to prevent. For a while the full force of this internal conflict could be warded off by treating Sasha as a substitute for paternal authority, by displacing ambivalent emotions away from the deceased father to the living older brother, who after the father's death was head of the family. This relationship between Lenin and Sasha would be extremely tense, however, for in it would be not only Lenin's ambivalent feelings towards his father, but also his already ambivalent attitudes towards Sasha as a brotherly rival for parental esteem. Hence, when Sasha died, there would result the repressed emotional distress discussed above.

We must put off until the next chapter the attempt to analyze the way in which Sasha's death served as the catalyst by which Lenin's internal conflicts were transformed into revolutionary involvement. Louis Fischer, however, does give us an impression of the connection between his brother's death and Lenin's later political activity:

[Sasha] became a hero to Vladimir Ulyanov (Lenin) whose shock and fury were enhanced by the worst of all feelings: regret, regret not to have been close to the hero brother, not to have appreciated him, to have underestimated him. When as a university student, Lenin was first arrested, a colleague in a cell asked him what he thought he would do after his release. "What is there for me to think?" Lenin replied. "My path has been blazed by my older brother."[35]

In a sense, Lenin was to spend his life working out the relationship between his emotions, his feelings of love and hate, and the rights and powers of authority. Unlike most men, who outgrow intense concern over questions of authority as they gradually liberate themselves from the dictates of parental control, the deaths of his father and brother forced Lenin to struggle with such questions again and again. And, as I try to demonstrate in the following pages, Trotsky and Gandhi also came to have revolutionary identities as a result of essentially interminable conflicts with parental authority.

The interpretation of Lenin's development presented in this section has been highly speculative. Because there is a real paucity of reliable and indicative information on his early life, I have been forced to reconstruct and infer even more than is usual for work of this kind. The situation with regard to Trotsky, to whom we now turn, is considerably better. For here we have the rich fund of information that is *My Life*, his autobiography.

The Youth of Lev Davidovich Bronstein

In his masterful biography of Trotsky, Isaac Deutscher devotes about thirty pages to Trotsky's first eighteen years, which is a lot, by normal biographical standards. Yet Trotsky himself, in his autobiography covering his life until about 1929, devotes about 115 pages, almost one-fifth of the work, to this same period, and this despite the fact that he had many reasons for wanting to ignore his childhood. If quantity is any indication of the importance a writer attaches to a subject, then Trotsky, more or less consciously, considered his childhood to be of rather great significance for understanding him and his actions—and not only his actions but the general principles for which he fought as well. As he wrote to Max Eastman sometime in the early

---

[35] Fischer, *Life of Lenin*, p. 17.

1920s when Eastman was seeking permission to write a biography of him:

> Many people find their way to the *general* through the *personal*. In that sense biographies have their right.[36]

Although the events of his childhood which Trotsky expressly thought were crucial for understanding his relationship to the "general," to the course of human history, will not be our central focus here, he nonetheless has provided us with a rich source of information which I will try to utilize in order to aid us in understanding both the "personal" and the "general."

Lev Davidovich Bronstein was born on November 7, 1879 on his father's farm in Yanovka, a small agricultural community in the southern Ukraine, not far from Odessa. His father, David Leontievich Bronstein, had just moved to Yanovka from a small Jewish agricultural community where Trotsky's grandfather had settled in the 1850s.[37] David Bronstein's father was one of a small number of Jews who broke away from the stifling atmosphere of the urban ghettoes to try to build a better life on the Russian steppes; under the strict regulation to which Jews were subject in tsarist Russia such a move provided practically the only means of escape. But even this was narrowed with passing time, David Bronstein himself becoming a partial victim of the *ukase* of 1881 which forbade Jews to buy land, although it did not take away land already owned.[38]

David Bronstein was a hard working and determined agricultural entrepreneur, uncultivated and crude but intelligent and dignified. He was known for his shrewd appraisal of the qualities of other men no less than for the vigorous management of his expanding estate. He had a strong, steely voice and an equally strong will.[39] He was immensely respected, if not loved, both by those who worked for him and his less industrious, and eventually less

---

[36] Eastman, *Leon Trotsky*, p. vii.
[37] Deutscher, *The Prophet Armed*, p. 6.   [38] *Ibid.*, p. 8.
[39] *Ibid.*, p. 7. Also Eastman, *Leon Trotsky*, p. 5.

wealthy, neighbors. Trotsky himself describes his father in the following manner:

> My father was undoubtedly superior to my mother, both in intellect and character. He was deeper, more reserved, and more tactful. He had an unusually good eye both for things and people. My father and mother bought very little, especially during our early years; they both knew how to save every penny. My father never made a mistake in what he bought. . . . He judged people by their manners, their faces and their habits, and he always judged them correctly. . . .

* * *

> When we children were young, my father was quieter and gentler with us than my mother. My mother would often lose her temper with us, sometimes without reason, and would vent her fatigue or her chagrin over some domestic failure. We always found it more remunerative to ask our father for favors than our mother.[40]

Trotsky's mother was virtually as hard driving and devoted to the growing estate as his father. She was by birth an urbanite, and at first had trouble adjusting to the regimen of the farm. With time, however, she became a steady source of support to her husband. Trotsky's mother was emotional and rather conventional, to the extent that conventionality was possible for a Jewish woman of essentially urban values leading a peasant's life. She tried to keep the Sabbath as long as others were watching and strained both her energy and abilities to maintain some minimal level of literacy.[41] Eastman reports that her neighbors remembered that

> She was an "insistent" character, and a "great manager," and that the Bronsteins' estate was as efficiently run, and their household as spic and span and punctual

[40] Trotsky, *My Life*, pp. 18-19.   [41] *Ibid.*, pp. 17-19.

to its dates, as the famous military train of the Commander-in-Chief of the Red Armies. They remember that she was a handsome woman, with "a face full of goodness," and that neither she nor her husband was "the kind to sit down in front of any kind of work."[42]

Trotsky devotes a fairly large number of pages in *My Life* to describing his parents in one way or another, but the following sketch says most of what must be said:

Once in a while in the evening we played old maid, from which a great deal of noise and laughter resulted, and sometimes a little quarrelling. We thought it particularly amusing to cheat my father, who played carelessly and laughed when he lost. My mother, on the other hand, played better, and would grow excited and watch my oldest brother sharply to see that he was not cheating her.[43]

The most striking thing about Trotsky's sketches of his parents is the lack of idealization, the absence of any conspicuous attempt to build up an image of superhuman benevolence such as Anna Ulyanov presents with reference to Lenin's parents. The good is here mixed with the bad: Trotsky's father was hard working but given to carelessness and inexactitude; he abused his peasants but no more than other landowners; he could be gentle and jolly but became harsher as time went by; he was devoted to his wife but allowed her to toil unceasingly; he was uncultivated but a shrewd judge of character; and so on. Trotsky's mother, on the other hand, was efficient and orderly, persevering and hard working, but also rather hypocritical, less emotionally controlled, more given to taking out her weariness on her children than was her husband. Such a picture seems to be realistic appraisal, a substantial coming to grips with parental authority. By this I do not mean that Trotsky is depicting here some kind of final and objective truth about his parents' characteristics. As we shall see, there are un-

---

[42] Eastman, *Leon Trotsky*, p. 8.　　[43] Trotsky, *My Life*, p. 15.

doubtedly distortions involved in the portraits; but the distortions are not so great as to make Trotsky's parents unrecognizable as human beings.[44]

Early in this chapter it was noted that Lenin shared many characteristics with one or the other of his parents. Hopefully I will be able to demonstrate in the following chapters that these characteristics and their manner of acquisition are important for understanding Lenin's political actions. Similarly, Trotsky accepted and rejected certain of his parents' attributes which are highly relevant to his subsequent behavior. Aside from physical characteristics over which he had little control (his general appearance and powerful voice were very similar to his father's), Trotsky emulated above all his parents' industriousness, managing to combine his father's initiative and imagination with his mother's orderliness. Later his experience in school accentuated these tendencies, but the basis was set first in the familial context. His penchant for personal cleanliness is accordingly attributable to both his mother's influence and later experience; his fierce pride and unbending will, however, developed essentially out of his identification with his father. But to describe such characteristics (industriousness, imagination, orderliness, cleanliness, independence) is neither to explain them nor bring out their implications. To do both of these things I must indicate how and why such qualities were acquired. For this task Trotsky himself provides the best guidelines.

Looking back from approaching middle age, Trotsky viewed his childhood in the following terms:

> My childhood was not one of hunger and cold. My family had already achieved a competence at the time of my birth. But it was the stern competence of a people still rising from poverty and having no desire to stop half-way. Every muscle was strained, every

[44] Trotsky's ability to view his parents as mixtures of strengths and weaknesses contrasts sharply not only with Lenin's sister's idealization of her parents, but also with the picture Gandhi draws of his mother—although not his father.

thought set on work and savings. Such a domestic routine left but a modest place for the children. We knew no need, but neither did we know the generosities of life—its caresses. My childhood does not appear to me like a sunny meadow, as it does to the small minority [the rich]; neither does it appear like a dark cave of hunger, violence and misery, as it does to the majority [the poor]. Mine was the grayish childhood of a lower-middle-class family, spent in a village in an obscure corner where nature is wide, and manners, views and interests are pinched and narrow.[45]

In reading this passage one is immediately struck by the way Trotsky links his own life to general social forces. His childhood is gray because it is *lower middle class*, because his parents are working long hours to escape poverty. On the one hand this leap from the concrete (the small amount of time the parents spent with the children) to the abstract (their lack of attention is explicable only in terms of their class situation) is good—and important—sociological analysis; on the other hand it is bad introspective psychology. As the following passage helps make clear, the lack of parental attention and affection in Trotsky's early life was profoundly important to him. He had to find ways to explain why it was that his parents did not love him more; at the same time he was unable to consider the possibility that the fault lay either in him or in them—although he does come close to blaming them:

Of the eight children born of this marriage, four survived [an older brother and sister, Trotsky, and a younger sister]. I was the fifth in order of birth. Four died in infancy, of diphtheria and of scarlet fever, *deaths almost as unnoticed as was the life of those who survived.* The land, the cattle, the poultry, the mill, took all my parents' time; *there was none left for us.* The seasons succeeded one another and waves of farm work swept over domestic affection. *There was no*

[45] Trotsky, *My Life*, p. 1.

display of tenderness in our family, especially during my early years, but there was a strong comradeship of labor between my father and my mother.[46] (Emphasis added.)

Young children do not think in terms of general social causes. If their parents are not affectionate, they think of this as some failure of their own or some failure of the parents. In this passage Trotsky practically screams out his grievance: *I was ignored and unloved, even the cattle got more attention than I did and what love was displayed was between my parents—I was excluded!* This is the cry of a lonely child, trying hard not to blame his parents, but hating them for their lack of solicitude just the same. Looking back on it from the age of fifty, Trotsky could not admit to himself that he was simply a lonely boy crying for parental attention; he had to see it in some more general terms, in terms less personal and less painful. Yet the signs of his feeling of deprivation are plentiful throughout the descriptions of childhood—passages on long hours spent waiting for parents to return to the house from the day's labor; of amusing himself, all the time unnoticed, in the machine shop or elsewhere on the farm; of calling the servants to keep him company when the empty house became too omnipresent in its stillness. The grayness in Trotsky's young life was the color of loneliness, of feeling unloved.

The picture Trotsky paints is gray, however, not black. It is not a picture of continual deprivation or parental meanness. As cited earlier, the family was usually together in the evenings, often playing cards, telling stories or entertaining guests. The children were given music lessons and taught to read, and childish mischief seems to have been largely tolerated and understood.[47] Trotsky, in fact, seems to have been the favorite child; Eastman states, for example, that "he is so sweet-tempered and has such a merry disposition that his parents cannot get along without

[46] *Ibid.*, p. 17.   [47] *Ibid.*, pp. 14-15.

him."[48] At a very early age he was helping his father with the accounts for the farm and being proudly displayed to neighbors and relatives when he started writing poems and essays, also very precociously. He easily surpassed the achievements of his older brother, who seems to have had neither his intelligence nor his charm, and apparently was much loved and fondled by his sisters.[49] Moreover, many of the servants seem to have treated him quite indulgently, especially Ivan Vasilyevich Gryeben, who ran the machine shop and whom young Trotsky much admired. When all this is taken into account, one wonders that Trotsky characterized his childhood even as gray. That he did so points to the enormous importance of parental love and attention for the child. All the advantages of his familial situation served only to mitigate the effects of the lack of, especially, motherly presence. His mother's absence, moreover, exacerbated Trotsky's relations with his father. It is hard enough for a child to accept the father's relationship with his mother in circumstances where the mother is at home with the children; where the mother is not home explicitly because of her bond with the father (where all tenderness is between mother and father, as Trotsky noted), then the tension between father and son becomes almost overwhelming.

If, additionally, the father is generally kind and indulgent, as Trotsky's father appears to have been, the relationship is infused with ambivalence, with love and respect for the father on the one hand, resulting in the internalization of the father's moral standards, and hate for him on the other—which, when combined, result in pervasive feelings of guilt and anxiety.[50] Thus out of somewhat different situations Lenin and Trotsky emerged with similar, although *not* identical, problems. Lenin had to deal with love and hatred for his father growing out of a pattern of alternating

[48] Eastman, *Leon Trotsky*, p. 2.
[49] Deutscher, *The Prophet Armed*, p. 8.
[50] On the formation of the superego see Freud, *The Ego and the Id*, pp. 18-29.

indulgence and deprivation of fatherly love. His father's death, coming when it did, became crucial for his subsequent development. For Trotsky the ambivalence stemmed from the degree to which he felt an otherwise predominantly benevolent father deprived him of his mother's love. (Needless to say, Lenin's relationship with his mother was important—he and his father did not live in isolation. In his case, however, there was less reason for feeling the father deprived him of mother's love, and hence less strain in that regard.)

Trotsky's conflicts were, in a sense, more complex than Lenin's; they were not sharply focused on one set of traumatic events, the successful management of which would imply mastery of the problems. Rather, the conflicts were diffuse and wide-ranging, rooted so early in his life that he was almost unable to come to grips with them. As a result, his life was marked by indecision and hesitation at certain crucial moments, as well as waverings with regard to some basic ideological concerns. Lenin's, by way of contrast, was not.

Eastman captures, somewhat inadvertently, the ambivalence of Trotsky's feelings for his father in the following impressions:

> Trotsky is proud of his father, proud of the fact that he died working and understanding. He loves to talk about him.

* * *

> Trotsky was devotedly attached to his mother in those early days. His relation with his father—according to the testimony of one who lived often in their house—was "none too cordial." That must have been the fundamental fact of his emotional life . . .[51]

Trotsky did indeed love to talk about his father—the early chapters of *My Life* are full of generally, although not exaggeratedly, favorable remarks about David Bronstein. When Trotsky discusses his *relationship* with his father,

[51] Eastman, *Leon Trotsky*, pp. 7 and 10.

however, elements of strain are manifested.—when he was eighteen he finally broke openly with his father, or "ran away" from him, as the latter put it.

The grayness of these early years was mitigated by the company of peasants and servants, among whom Trotsky spent much of his time and with whom he partially identified in their conflicts with his father. Yet he was not a peasant or a servant, hence at times he would find himself the object of their scorn.[52] He was uncomfortable being both his father's son and the workingmen's companion—the claims and obligations of these roles were conflicting, increasing thereby the strain he already felt. An incident which occurred the summer after his second year in school in Odessa, when he was about ten, made a deep impression on Trotsky and symbolizes the basic nature of his relationship with his father. Trotsky was dressed up in his best school uniform and felt "simply magnificent." Desiring to show the world how splendid he looked, he went out with his father on a tour of inspection of the fields. At one point in the trip his father stopped to test the quality of the wheat being harvested:

> [In cutting the wheat with his scythe,] Father made simple, homely movements, as if he were not actually working but only getting ready to begin, and his steps were light and tentative as if he were looking for a place to get a better swing. His scythe was also moving simply, without any swagger about it, and even—or so it seemed—not quite firmly. And yet it was cutting very low and very evenly, with each swift shave laying the ears in a straight belt running along on his left. Arkhip [one of the peasants] looked on with one eye, clearly approving Father's skill. . . .

* * *

> After Father had left for another field, I also made an attempt to wield the scythe. "Strike the hay on your

[52] Trotsky, *My Life*, p. 24. Trotsky's subsequent espousal of the cause of the lower classes, his comfort and ease in speaking before them, is related to this early identification.

heel, boy, on your heel; keep your toes free, don't press." But in my excitement I couldn't quite see where that heel of mine actually was, and on the third swing of the scythe my toes dug right into the earth. "That will soon finish the scythe, if you go on like this," said Arkhip. *"You'd better learn from your father."* A woman binder . . . gave me a sneering look. I stepped out of the ranks with decided haste, still in my badge-adorned cap, from under which the sweat was coming down in streams. "Go and eat cakes with your mother," came mockingly from behind. . . .

* * *

As I returned home from the field I saw a barefooted woman at our door-step. . . . She had walked seven versts to our house to get one rouble that was owed her. . . . It made my heart tighten to look at that figure—the embodiment of poverty and submission.[53] (Emphasis added.)

A large number of themes are interwoven here. Trotsky obviously admires his father and his father's skill at his work. The admiration of others for this skill increases his father's stature in his eyes. How much he wants to be like his father, to share in his skills and admiration (and to share in the possession of his mother). So bravely he steps into his father's shoes—only to fail miserably, to earn taunts instead of praise. He is told to "learn from his father": he is not yet a man, not yet his father's equal. Urban values, especially intellectual prowess as symbolized by his school uniform, have no currency in the country. Trotsky must thus either learn from his father or find some other kind of work, some other basis of achievement, in which to surpass him, in which he might find his manliness.

Then, while retreating to the house, he sees a helpless woman who is waiting for his father. She, too, is inferior to the latter and, seeing something of himself in her and per-

---

[53] *Ibid.*, pp. 80-81.

haps something of his mother, Trotsky feels immediately sympathetic. With time those feelings of sympathy and iden- tification are to intensify—and to change somewhat in the process. For Trotsky will come to realize that he is stronger than these weak, passive people; perhaps he is not as strong or as skilled as his father, but he is superior to the peasant, the worker, the servant. On their behalf he can set himself up as a man in opposition to his father, when speaking for them he can feel secure and proud.

Before passing on to Trotsky's school experiences, al- luded to above, certain other aspects of his preschool life must be discussed. First, as Trotsky remembers it, he was constantly living with humiliation and failure—he wets his pants and is scolded, he tries to imitate his older brother and fails, tries to ride a horse and falls off, he injures him- self while trying to help his father, he asks for information and is brushed off or ignored, the peasant boys make fun of him and abuse him, the older servants laugh at him. The incidents stream on in endless profusion. Of course, his life could not have been all failure—we know from Eastman and others that it was not. But his memories of his actions as always having ill consequences and of other people as treating him with contempt indicate that failure and humili- ation were important to him, that these were aspects of his life he would have to overcome. Significantly, by the time he reached the upper grades in school, he had made con- siderable progress as a result of his academic ability. From that time, consequently, good ideas and intellectual prowess were to be the root aspects of his conception of worthwhile achievement; he would use both as weapons with which to humiliate his foes.

The second point is that Trotsky started writing quite early, easily and, as it were, clandestinely:

> Scarcely had I mastered the art of writing when it se- duced me. Once, while alone in the dining room, I be- gan to put down in printed script such special words as I had heard in the shop and in the kitchen and

which I had never heard from my family. I realized that I was doing something which I should not be doing, but the words lured me just because they were forbidden. I had decided to hide the little paper in an empty match-box and then to bury it behind the barn. I was far from completing the list when my elder sister entered the room and became interested. I seized the paper. My mother came in after my sister. They demanded that I show them the writing. Burning with shame, I threw the paper behind the divan. . . .[54]

Somewhat later Trotsky wrote letters for servants which got him into trouble; he was also forced to read verses he wrote, which embarrassed him, at least at first. Thus writing, from a very early time, seems to have been invested by Trotsky with ideas of danger and self-assertion, something to be done in privacy. Eventually he began to take pride in what he wrote, to think of himself primarily as a writer; throughout his life, however, it was to be linked with illegal activity.

Third, Trotsky often found that adults betrayed his faith in them, did not live up to their promises.[55] Later, in school and throughout his life, especially after 1924, betrayal and the unreliability of others' promises were to be elements of Trotsky's life. Whether he read betrayal back into his childhood after subsequent experience or was somehow very susceptible to it from an early age is hard to tell. At a minimum, however, it seems that he expected people to keep their promises and to honor confidences; he was basically trusting—both with respect to peers and elders (or later with respect to comrades and authorities)—and hence easily deceived. He did not have Lenin's wall of mistrust to keep him safe from betrayal. This difference between the men, it might be noted, would have been unlikely to result from their adult experience; both men lived in the same hotbed of intrigue and counterintrigue throughout their postadolescent lives. Thus the difference must originate in childhood, probably in the first few years of life.[56] Trotsky,

[54] *Ibid.*, pp. 39-40.   [55] *Ibid.*, p. 4.
[56] Erikson, *Childhood and Society*, pp. 247-51.

whatever his complaints against it, must have found the world warm and rewarding in his earliest years. In fact, his sensitivity to its "gray" elements probably resulted from the contrast between his first years and the ones that followed. At first the absence of his mother may have been less important, for his nanny and older sister doted on him. With developing consciousness, however, Trotsky's demands on his environment increased; and with that increase in consciousness an increased capacity for disappointment and frustration arose. Lenin, on the other hand, had relatively little confidence in his environment from the start (at least so it would seem if my speculations on his late walking are correct); accordingly, there was less the people who formed that environment could do to shock or dismay him.

Trotsky's trust of his surroundings is apparent even, or perhaps especially, in his careful recording of his youthful humiliations and failures, many of which were marked by the spontaneous and immediate imitation of the actions of others. He was constantly trying things and then, sometimes, not having them work. While Lenin from an early age was watching and absorbing, Trotsky was imitating and displaying. Lenin was wary of the response he might get from his environment, Trotsky relished and looked forward to it, was always trying to provoke the response. This expectation that other people will respond favorably to one's efforts, which can result in attempts to stimulate the environment to provide such responses, is a precondition for some kinds of self-display[57]—and in the present case underlies Trotsky's love of the dramatic discussed below. For Trotsky, desiring applause, was an extremely colorful figure; Lenin, distrusting applause even when he got it, was gray and prosaic in comparison. Lenin's lack of display, however, was a very great asset, for it was a sign of Lenin's self-sufficiency and self-confidence.

Trotsky's formal schooling started when he was sent to

[57] Fenichel, *Psychoanalytic Theory of Neurosis*, p. 72.

Gromulka to learn Hebrew and Yiddish at the age of seven. He felt very out of place in this inbred Jewish environment and his parents soon allowed him to return to Yanovka. While he was there, however, he learned the rudiments of writing and reading and started to mix more Russian into his native mixture of Russian and Ukrainian. The following summer his cousin Spentzer came to visit the family, and brought with him a radical change in Trotsky's life. Spentzer was a well educated and quite cultured liberal from Odessa who had been forced to drop his university education as a result of some political misdemeanor.[58] He was offended by the harshness and cruelty of rural life, and Trotsky, who quickly came to idolize him (throughout his life Trotsky was quick to form attachments to older and respected men—Lenin, Axelrod, Martov and Parvus were all loved and respected guides at one time or another), picked up something of his reaction.[59] When Spentzer got married later that year, Trotsky's parents decided to send him to Odessa for schooling, where he could get a good education and live in the congenial environment the Spentzers would provide.

After a year of preparatory work, Trotsky entered St. Paul's *realschule* (in 1889). He was a quick learner and became first boy in his class within a period of months; he also became an ostentatious student, searching out bits and pieces of information which could be used to embarrass his teachers. At the same time, however, a genuine passion for writing and reading was developing, and before he was ten he was attempting to put out a small magazine.[60] Both at school and at the Spentzer's home this boy who had felt so ignored drew an increasing amount of attention—most of it highly favorable. At first, he had felt a little ill at ease in the Odessan environment; he quickly discovered that the manners and language of Yanovka were inadequate for the city. Because he was already so fastidiously clean and

[58] Deutscher, *The Prophet Armed*, p. 120.
[59] Trotsky, *My Life*, pp. 41-42.
[60] *Ibid.*, p. 66.

wanted so much to fit in, however, he quickly picked up the accouterments of urban living.

Visits to Yanovka, in fact, became an increasingly mixed pleasure, each time he went the rural atmosphere and his father's way of life seemed more coarse, alien, and unalluring. Gryeben's machine shop was rapidly losing out to the Spentzer library, printing press, and literary atmosphere. On the farm Trotsky was just the owner's son, a child to be unfavorably compared to the father; and at Yanovka Trotsky had to live under paternal discipline. In Odessa he was treated as something of a prodigy, his intelligence and rapid learning became the means of securing love, applause, and respect. Thus in the city he did not have to face the conflicts that predominated in the home environment. But this separation from the home environment when his conflicts with his father were still unresolved, when he had not overcome his feelings of being unwanted as well, meant that he would, on the one hand, intensify his blame of his father for taking him away from his mother, and, on the other, retain undiminished his childhood love and respect for the elder Bronstein.

In some ways, Trotsky's extensive separation from his father during his boyhood and adolescence is similar to Lenin's relationship with his father. In each case the son had but limited contact with the father, contact which terminated abruptly during adolescence. Lenin, however, until his father's death, remained at home while his father was away, so that after each separation the father returned to the family and was reabsorbed into it. Trotsky, by contrast, was the one who journeyed away from home, so that every time he returned to Yanovka he found himself more estranged from his father's way of life, less competent at the skills esteemed on the farm. The consequence of this difference is that Lenin tended to identify increasingly with his absent father, each contact with the elder Ulyanov providing fresh material for such an identification, while in Trotsky this tendency towards identification was offset by the developing disparity between his world and his father's.

The death of Lenin's father to some extent, however, created a situation more nearly parallel to Trotsky's separation from his father. For Lenin now had to deal with not the familiar father of chess games and croquet, but an earlier, more primitive, image of the father as an almost suprahuman power and moral authority. The father's death, I inferred, aroused the feelings of guilt which would evoke this earlier image of the father. Trotsky also had to deal with a magnified conception of his father, one which combined his early impressions of paternal authority and the later image of his father as the master of life at Yanovka. Because both young men were separated from their fathers before these conceptions could be replaced with more realistic ones, because the normal process of outgrowing paternal authority was cut short, each had to continue to come to terms with an idea of great and powerful authority deeply and solidly imbedded in his unconscious, an image of authority no longer easily amenable to modification by contact with the reality of the son's developing manhood and the progressive aging of the father.

Lenin had, in this regard, by far the more difficult task, for his father was gone for good, and an intense complex of emotions had resulted from his death, from this one, sharply traumatic, incident. The possibilities for psychic failure were very great here, but so too were the opportunities for striking success. In Trotsky's case the situation was neither as intensely difficult nor as sharply focused. As a result, Trotsky retained a more ambivalent attitude towards authority. This intense and persistent ambivalence, as noted earlier, will help us to understand many aspects of his adult political behavior.

Two aspects of Trotsky's school experience might be mentioned to fill in the picture of his early adolescence. The first was referred to above—Trotsky liked to learn not so much for its own sake but for what it could bring him in terms of his relations with others. On the one hand, learning enabled him to outrank his fellows, to receive a disproportionate amount of respect from his elders; on the other, the bits and pieces of esoterica he picked up enabled him to humiliate his teachers (who were not, on the whole, a very bright lot). Knowledge enabled him to turn the tables on the people in his environment. From a little boy humbled by peasants he became a young lad who humbled his elders. Moreover, he could finally start to feel superior to his father, whose learning was commonsensical and practical, not literary or scientific. This form of achievement had an important side effect; that is, it had highly theatrical and highly aggressive elements. Trotsky used his intelligence to draw attention away from others and towards himself; he did not want merely good marks, he wanted the best. More than anything else, he wanted them to impress his father—and was quite disappointed when his father was not unduly impressed.[61] And because Trotsky wanted attention, from his father and others, he tried to present himself and what he knew in the most striking possible way. In later life this taste for the dramatic was to be one of his greatest advantages at one point and greatest disadvantages at another.[62]

Trotsky's budding intellectualism[63] was aimed not only at building up his own self-esteem, but at lowering the self-esteem of others. He wanted his teachers to feel that they were less intelligent than he was. Later in life, as well, Trotsky would not rest content merely with getting his ideas accepted; he would attempt to make his rivals look stupid in the process.

The second point which should be noted about Trotsky's school days is that on the whole he was an extraordinarily dutiful and obedient student. Several minor scrapes do little to mar the serene picture of the diligent young scholar.

[61] Trotsky, *My Life*, p. 78.

[62] It is of interest that during his Odessa period Trotsky picked up a love for the theatre that he never lost.

[63] Eastman, *Leon Trotsky*, p. 17.

Trotsky, like Lenin, developed into a revolutionist only after his school days had essentially ended.

There is, however, one incident from his school experience which Trotsky later recalled as a portent of his later revolutionary life. In the second grade he and his classmates had a Swiss teacher of French named Burnande who had an intense dislike for Germans, which he took out on the German students in the class. One of these was a boy named Vakker, whom Burnande was treating particularly unfairly. Trotsky and some of his classmates decided to protest this injustice by giving Burnande a "concert, to howl at him through closed mouths so that he could not tell who was doing the howling." As a result of this prank, several of the boys were kept after school—but Trotsky, the star pupil, was not suspected. Trotsky says he

> did nothing to obtain exemption. Neither did I accuse myself. I left school rather with a feeling of regret, as staying with the other boys would have promised a jolly time.[64]

The "feeling of regret" might have been tinged with feelings of guilt, a feeling that he should have been blamed too. But the moral code of the schoolboy probably did not include turning oneself in; more likely it was to be expected that everyone would hotly deny responsibility. As often happens, however, some people, to keep punishment away from themselves, blamed others. And the main one blamed, probably rightly, was the star pupil Bronstein. Once his teachers got over their shock at Trotsky's having been involved, they turned on him with real fury: Burnande strode up to him and shouted, "The star student of the second grade is a moral outcaste."[65] Trotsky was then expelled from the school (but with the right of re-entry after a year) after going through days of torment waiting to see what his fate would be. He most dreaded returning home and confronting his father—who, as it turned out, found the inci-

[64] Trotsky, *My Life*, p. 67.   [65] *Ibid.*, p. 68.

dent rather amusing: "pained as he was, he obviously relished the idea that his offspring, despite his title of the star
student, had daring enough to whistle at high officials."[66]
Asserting oneself in this relatively manly way was something Trotsky's father could understand and appreciate.
Thus to an extent Trotsky was given paternal assent in his
protest against authority—later, however, when Trotsky
showed signs of making a career out of such things, his
father was properly dismayed and outraged.

Trotsky, after narrating this incident, concludes by
saying:

> Such, one might say, was the first political test I
> underwent. These were the groups that resulted from
> that episode: the tale-bearers and the envious at one
> pole, the frank, courageous boys at the other, and the
> neutral, vacillating mass in the middle. These three
> groups never quite disappeared even during the years
> that followed. I met them again and again in my life,
> in the most varied circumstances.[67]

Of course, as the very language makes clear, Trotsky was
reading back into this incident something of the experience
of later years. Still the structure of the event is so similar
to later occurrences in his life that it seems indicative of
the existence of psychological predispositions which were
operative here as well as later. First, Trotsky did not expect to get caught. He did not view authority as really malevolent, only distasteful. Thus he was shocked and overcome, not in the least stoical, when authority reacted as
one had every right to expect it would in the Russia of that
time. Later, too, although the naïveté would disappear,
Trotsky would never treat authority with the respect and
caution that Lenin would. He never viewed things in kill-
or-be-killed terms. Moreover, he expected others to remain
loyal to him, to serve his interests (and the interests of the
cause) above their own. Hence he was easily betrayed—

[66] *Ibid.*, p. 71.   [67] *Ibid.*, p. 72.

and viewed as betrayal what others might have viewed in terms of human failure and been less stern and condemning.

Next, the action that led to the punishment was undertaken on behalf of another. Trotsky was led to rebel only in an area where he had no personal grievance. Similarly, in later life he would be fighting for the privileges of a class to which he did not belong. Psychologically, as I will attempt to argue later, fighting for others rather than oneself contributes in certain ways to an individual's self-esteem, while at the same time screening out some of the underlying motivations of the conflict so that the individual need not face up to them. Therefore, while the incident described was probably remembered by Trotsky in part because of what happened to him later, it nonetheless indicates that in nascent form many of his "political" characteristics were already operative at age eleven.

Trotsky was readmitted to St. Paul's after a year's absence and quickly resumed his place as top student. He later missed a year due to what his doctors described as a "chronic catarrh" of the stomach, which Trotsky himself attributes to "nervous shocks." He was to have attacks of this disorder throughout his life. During the year's absence, he was helped by a tutor and graduated on schedule in 1896. Actually he still had a year to complete, for St. Paul's only went up through the sixth grade. As a result, Trotsky was sent to a school in Nikolayev to complete his primary schooling. During that year Trotsky broke with his past mode of life and emerged an incipient revolutionist. During that year he also broke rather sharply with his father.

When he arrived in Nikolayev, Trotsky was far from being in a revolutionary state of mind. He himself admits that he was "poorly equipped politically even for a seventeen-year-old boy of that period."[68] In fact, according to Eastman, he was "very bourgeois . . . and almost a bit of a swell."[69] But he was not complacent; in fact, he was rather

[68] *My Life*, p. 96.   [69] Eastman, *Leon Trotsky*, p. 31.

disturbed in a multitude of ways. He did not know what work to pursue, what profession to enter. And "he thought that his will was sickly. He seemed to be perpetually going around in a desperate circle, considering the pros and cons of every little movement and doing nothing. He did not see how he could ever play the part of a man with this moral impediment!"[70] (It is worth noting that his father was characterized by a very strong "will"—one not in the least "sickly.")

Because he was both a budding intellectual and troubled by this sickness of will, he began looking for a system of justification, for a set of answers to the questions bothering him. At another time, in another place, such strivings might have been worked out in religious terms; in the Russia of the late nineteenth century they were worked out in terms of whether or not, and for whom, to rebel. This crisis was aggravated for Trotsky by the move to Nikolayev; he no longer had his cousin Spentzer's warm home to return to, nor the comradeship of the same students he had been with for several years. As a result, he reports,

> I neglected my studies. . . . [In reference to the main political ideas of the period] There was an odor of putrefaction emanating from populism. Marxism repelled by its so-called "narrowness." Burning with impatience I tried to grasp the ideas instinctively, but they were not so easy to master. I found no one about me to offer sure guidance. Every new conversation, moreover, forced me to come to the bitter, painful and desperate conclusion that I was ignorant.

* * *

> I swallowed books, fearful that my entire life would not be long enough to prepare me for action. My reading was nervous, impatient and unsystematic. . . . My striving for a system became tense, sometimes savage.

[70] *Ibid.*, p. 32.

At the same time, I was repelled by Marxism partially because it seemed a completed system.[71]

It was a while before Trotsky would admit to others that he was not satisfied as a peaceful citizen; when he changed, he changed suddenly, swinging radically leftward so that he soon became the leader of those who were bent on social protest.[72] But, as he notes, he rejected Marxism because it was "completed." In the last two sentences quoted, the ambivalence that marked him throughout life, and especially during this period, comes out unmistakably. At the same time, he was looking for a final and absolute authority for whom he could be the willing servant, one which would answer all questions and make all choices for him—and which would promise fulfillment and rest. On the other hand, he wanted to assert his independence, to create for himself an adult role which would entail no submission, to continuously act and put forward his claims to manhood. It was especially hard for him to accept Marxism because the most ardent young Marxist in the town was a girl somewhat older than himself, whom everyone involved in student protest activities viewed half as a sweetheart and half as a mother.[73] Trotsky's system of thought could not be taken from a person who echoed so many of the conflicts which led to his mental distress in the first place—and who was a love object in her own right (Trotsky was to marry her shortly). Thus Trotsky, searching for an ideological identity, became a populist, a Narodnik.

Many of the conflicts that had marked Trotsky's early years combined as, to quote Eastman, "his revolt against his father and his revolt against the social system now became united."[74] Trotsky had left the dwellings his father had arranged for him and was living with a gardener named

---

[71] *My Life*, pp. 98-99.

[72] Deutscher, *The Prophet Armed*, pp. 22-23, provides an excellent description of this process of radical transformation.

[73] Eastman, *Leon Trotsky*, p. 48.

[74] *Ibid.*, p. 38.

Shvigovsky and several young radicals just outside of town. His father came to reclaim him, stormed into the house and addressed the first boy he saw, in that loud Bronstein voice: "Hello! You ran away from your father too?" Then came a fierce quarrel between Trotsky, who asserted his right to independence, and the elder Bronstein, who tried to persuade and threaten his son into studying civil engineering— so that he could come back and aid him with the expansion of the farm. Trotsky refused to follow his father's course and thereupon was thrown on his own financial resources. Although the quarrel was partially patched up later, and Trotsky did bend so far as to study mathematics at the university in Odessa for a time, essentially he had successfully asserted his independence. The strain, however, was great —and Trotsky felt gloomy and depressed.[75]

The elder Bronstein understood people well and there is something basically correct about his accusation that his son was running away from him. Trotsky could neither submit to his father nor fight him on his father's ground. He could not return to the farm and try to assert his manhood without creating a situation in which guilt and fear would be overpowering. Yet his hatred for his father was too great to allow him docilely to follow paternal direction. He had to find some way to play out his grievances against his father without actually confronting him; and to do so he needed something, some system, to justify his action. At this point he had not yet found it, but the search, with all its torment and strain, was well underway.

In summary, Trotsky at seventeen was already committed to certain modes of action which would characterize him from then on. He would be a wielder of words, for writing had been his major tool of self-assertion and self-esteem throughout his childhood and adolescence. He would be an industrious user of words, highly orderly and systematic. His early identification with parental characteristics, some his mother's, some his father's, was intensified as these

[75] *Ibid.*, p. 56.

same things proved to be respected in the urban and intellectual context he found himself in during his school days. Moreover, words would be a way of drawing attention to himself; he would use them dramatically—and, with experience, occasionally with really startling impact and effectiveness. He was to use his words on behalf of others, but he was not yet sure for whom; he wanted to be a prophet for a cause, but he did not yet know what cause. He was still torn between being his father's favorite son and hating his father. This fundamental tension, a feeling that he must fight against authority to assert his manhood, coupled with gnawing doubt that justice lies on the side of authority and that only submission would lead to righteousness and safety, was the mainspring of Trotsky's life. His strengths and weaknesses grew out of it.

With Trotsky the conflicts and tensions seem close to the surface. Ambivalence is manifested in many different ways. In Lenin the conflict is less apparent, more tightly controlled, and more focused. Gandhi, to whom we now turn, exposes his conflicts even more fully than Trotsky, but the nature of his solution to those conflicts was to have the finality and control of Lenin's. And Gandhi, like Lenin, seems to have been marked more by a specific and distinct sequence of events, also hinging on his father's death, than by problems which were more diffuse and difficult to grasp.

The Youth of Mohandas Karamchand Gandhi

In *My Life* Trotsky is seldom introspective; he makes little attempt to analyze the nature of his internal conflicts. Because he presents such full descriptions of events, other members of his family and other people with whom he came in contact, however, the problems posed by his lack of self-examination are surmountable; his underlying conflicts are apparent in the way he describes others, the kinds of virtues and vices, as well as emotions, he attributes to them. Gandhi, by contrast, in *An Autobiography: The Story of My Experiments With Truth*, attempts to lay bare every aspect of his mental turmoil. As a result, the amount of useful self-analysis we have in his case is really quite phenomenal. On the other hand, Gandhi was so concerned with himself that only very hazy images emerge of the other people in his life. But from his autobiography and other sources we can get some idea of what the family of his childhood was like.

Mohandas Gandhi was born on October 2, 1869 in Porbandar, one of the Kathiawad principalities. Gandhi's father was Diwan, or Prime Minister, of Porbandar, later of nearby Rajkot, and later still of Wankaner. The Gandhis were of the Modh Bania subdivision of the Vaishya, or merchant, caste, third below the Brahmans and the Kshatriyas, just above the Sudras, the caste of the workers, and far above the "untouchables," who were outside and below the caste system. The Modh Banias,

> like other merchant castes, held to a nonviolent ethic suited to commerce, and to ascetic standards which often supplied the moral equivalent of a Protestant ethic for Indian merchant castes. Kathiawad was strongly influenced by the Vaishnavites, with additional influences from Jainism—the most nonviolent of Indian sects.[76]

Gandhi states that his father Karamchand (or Kaba)

> was a lover of his clan, truthful, brave and generous, but short-tempered. To a certain extent he might have been given to carnal pleasures. For he married for the fourth time when he was over forty. But he was incorruptible and had earned a name for strict impartiality in his family as well as outside. . . .

* * *

> He had little education, save that of experience. . . .
> Of religious training he had very little, but he had that

[76] Rudolph, "The New Courage," p. 105. See Heinrich Zimmer, *Philosophies of India, Joseph Campbell,* ed. (New York, 1956), for a clear exposition of the fundamentals of Indian Buddhist, Hindu, and Jain beliefs.

kind of religious culture which frequent visits to temples and listening to religious discourses make available to many Hindus.[77]

Although it is simplified and rather flat, as all Gandhi's observations of others are apt to be, and lacks the subtlety of Trotsky's depictions, Gandhi's picture of his father does not appear to be idealized. In particular, Gandhi attributes two negative attributes to his father: a hot temper and a certain lustfulness. Both of these are characteristics of a passionate nature, and passion was something Gandhi tried to avoid, except where the pursuit of Truth was involved. These two things, then, were aspects of paternal behavior which Gandhi condemned and sought to escape. The former bespeaks Gandhi's resentment at being subject to his father's emotions, the latter reflects Gandhi's horror of sex which grew to a great extent out of his relationship with his father. Both are important themes to which we will return.

Gandhi's picture of his mother, Putlibai, unlike that of his father, is of unrelieved holiness and purity:

> The outstanding impression my mother has left upon my memory is one of saintliness. She was deeply religious. She would not think of taking her meals without her daily prayers. Going to . . . the Vaishnava temple was one of her daily duties. As far as my memory can go back, I do not remember her having ever missed the *Chaturmas* [a vow of fasting and semi-fasting during the four months of the rains]. She would take the hardest vows and keep them without flinching. Illness was no excuse for relaxing them. . . .
> To keep two or three consecutive fasts was nothing to her. Living on one meal a day during *Chaturmas* was a habit with her. Not content with that she fasted every alternate day during one *Chaturmas*.[78]

[77] Gandhi, *Autobiography*, pp. 3-4. Rudolph, in "Self-Control and Political Potency," notes that Gandhi's father was actually married three times, not four.
[78] Gandhi, *Autobiography*, pp. 4-5.

Not only was she a saint, but she was "cheerful," had "strong commonsense" and the "ladies of the court thought highly of her intelligence." Gandhi later stated that "Whatever purity you see in me is derived from my mother, not my father."[79] Thus Gandhi's mother appears as the perfect embodiment of the Modh Bania caste, an immediate and living model of correct Vaishnava behavior for her children. That Gandhi identified with her and eventually tried hard to live up to his memories of the model she provided is agreed upon by most commentators.[80] Yet the very intensity of identification, as well as the idealized terms in which Gandhi depicts her, leads one to suspect that strong countervailing emotions were at work which had to be controlled by casting out all qualifications on his mother's perfection and benevolence.[81] We have two indications that this might be so. First, his mother had little time to spend with him,[82] which would tend to create in Gandhi the same craving for attention and resentment at not getting it that we found in Trotsky. Second, Putlibai's self-suffering had an important aggressive aspect: if she was for some reason dissatisfied with the behavior of another member of the family she would impose some penalty on herself so that, out of love for her, they would cease the activity.[83] Such practices both highlight the ambivalence between child and parent (the child must always give up desired activities to win parental esteem—the classic example being toilet training) and accentuate it, for the child does not merely feel ashamed of not living up to parental expectations but guilty at inflicting suffering as well.[84] We do not know how

[79] Quoted in B. R. Nanda, *Mahatma Gandhi* (Boston, 1958), p. 20.

[80] Cf., for example, Nanda, pp. 19-20.

[81] Adorno *et al.*, in *The Authoritarian Personality* (New York, 1951), pp. 340-46.

[82] Prabhudas Gandhi, *My Childhood With Gandhiji* (Ahmedabad, 1957), p. 25.

[83] Rudolph, "The New Courage," p. 105.

[84] Freud, *Civilization and Its Discontents*, p. 77; also Heinz Hartmann, Ernst Kris, and Rudolph M. Loewenstein, "Notes on the Theory of Aggression," *The Psychoanalytic Study of the Child*, Vol. III/IV, 1949, p. 31.

often Putlibai used this technique in controlling Mohandas, but to the extent that she did he would grow up feeling that his actions and drives were potentially dangerous, that any, even covertly, aggressive action on his part was likely to result in injury to another. Given such a situation there would also be a great temptation to lie whenever maternal wishes were transgressed.

Putlibai's self-suffering had another aspect: it was a tool not only for controlling the children but for making her wishes felt by her husband, who dominated the family as the principal authority but who was to some extent controllable by his wife in this manner. Thus Gandhi had an early model of how to deal with authority, one which he applied quite young when his parents would not indulge his wish to have a Moslem friend over for dinner.[85]

Gandhi's childhood does not appear to have been a happy one. Although he was the youngest child,[86] and supposedly the favorite,[87] he was timid, unathletic, afraid of hobgoblins by night and possible humiliation by his peers by day.[88] Several factors appear to have contributed to this state of affairs. In particular, Mohandas clearly lived in fear of his father, whose temper he commented upon. He hurried back from school to take care of him when he was sick, he quaked at the thought of punishment before confessing an adolescent theft to his father.[89] The fear of burglars and hobgoblins that plagued him, especially after he was married, are also indicative of a fear of vengeful and righteous father. Gandhi's first way of dealing with these feelings, aside from great obedience and service to his father, was to repeat Rama's (that is, God's) name whenever he was

[85] Rudolph, "The New Courage," p. 105.

[86] Gandhi's father had two daughters by previous marriages and four children by Putlibai, three boys and a girl: Lakshmidas (born in 1860); Raliatbehn (born in 1863); Karsandas (born in 1866); and Mohandas.

[87] P. Gandhi, p. 25.

[88] Rudolph, "The New Courage," sums up these impressions, drawn from Gandhi's *Autobiography*, on p. 106.

[89] P. Gandhi, p. 31.

afraid.[90] His nurse Rambha proposed this remedy to him when he was very young and, although he did not use this device during the period of his adolescent fears, with time he returned to it whenever he felt in need of support. Thus Rama (or God or Truth) became a male authority that Gandhi set up in opposition to his father and, later, other authorities, when he felt endangered.

In adolescence, however, Gandhi was rebelling against the tradition of which Rama was a part, hence other means of dealing with these fears had to be found. Gandhi, somewhat indirectly, describes how he faced up to this problem:

> [When I was fifteen] . . . I stole a bit of gold out of my meat-eating brother's armlet. . . .

> * * *

> But this became more than I could bear. I resolved never to steal again. I also made up my mind to confess it to my father. But I did not dare to speak. Not that I was afraid of my father beating me. No. I do not recall his ever having beaten any of us. I was afraid of the pain that I should cause him. But I felt that the risk should be taken; that there could not be a cleansing without a clean confession.

> I decided at last to write out the confession, to submit it to my father, and ask his forgiveness. I wrote it on a slip of paper and handed it to him myself. In this note not only did I confess my guilt, but I asked adequate punishment for it, and closed with a request to him not to punish himself for my offense. I also pledged myself never to steal in future.

> I was trembling as I handed the confession to my father. He was then suffering from a fistula and was confined to bed. His bed was a plain wooden plank. I handed him the note and sat opposite the plank.

> He read it though and pearl-drops trickled down his cheeks, wetting the paper. For a moment he closed

[90] M. K. Gandhi, p. 32.

his eyes in thought and then tore up the note. . . . I also cried. I could see my father's agony. . . .

Those pearl-drops of love cleansed my heart and washed my sin away. Only he who has experienced such love can know what it is. . . .

* * *

This sort of sublime forgiveness was not natural to my father. I had thought that he would be angry, say hard things, and strike his forehead. But he was so wonderfully peaceful, and I believe this was due to my clean confession. . . . I know that my confession made my father feel absolutely safe about me, and increased his affection for me beyond measure.[91]

Gandhi's solution to the problem of fearing his father, here based on his guilt over stealing and concealing the theft, was not to confront his father on some occasion when he perhaps had been unjustly accused of something or when he felt blameless, trying to establish thereby his independence and defying his father to harm him (as Trotsky did in dealing with his father). Rather, Gandhi selected an occasion when he was guilty, when punishment would be deserved. He decided he would have to suffer, and that others would have to suffer, for his sins. Either he would be redeemed or damned, but in either case ambiguity must be relieved.

He did choose a situation which to some extent augered well for him. His father was bedridden and hence the chances of physical punishment, which Gandhi claims not to have feared but which a sister remembers as a definite apprehension,[92] were at least reduced. Even so, he did not quite face up to things; he wrote a note rather than speaking. (It is interesting that for years afterwards Gandhi would be unable to speak easily, at least in public; until he arrived in South Africa he would rely on notes, which others read for him, when he had something to say to any formal audience. And in later years, on his weekly day of

[91] M. K. Gandhi, pp. 27-28.
[92] Cited in P. Gandhi, pp. 30-31.

silence and when he was tired, he would again prepare notes for others to read for him.) All in all, however, he had put himself in a critical situation. He had confessed a "sin" and promised to reform—would his father behave as he was wont to behave and punish himself and berate Mohandas, in which case Gandhi's already low opinion of himself would have been lowered still more, or would he be forgiving, and thereby indicate that the "sin" was not beyond redemption, that he had faith in his son's promise, that he loved him and would not harm him (or himself) despite the boy's guilt? These were the alternatives for Gandhi as a result of his confession; it thus must be considered a bold action, by which Gandhi had much to gain—and much to lose. Gandhi's father proved forgiving, and Gandhi learned from the experience that telling the truth had very great rewards, that facing up to one's guilt could bring relief from that guilt while concealing it would bring only inner torment, too much to bear. Gandhi also learned that the suffering he feared, both his own and his father's, was not so overwhelming after all; he had built up more fear in anticipation of his confession than the results of the confession warranted. Thus Gandhi set up the necessary conditions for overcoming fear and anxiety.

One of the reasons, then, for Gandhi's relatively unhappy childhood was fear of his father, with its related aspect of strong feelings of guilt. Another was his feeling of inadequacy with respect to both his father and his peers. All boys, to some extent, feel inadequate and unworthy when they compare themselves to their fathers.[93] In Gandhi's case, with his father a man of considerable stature outside the family and its truly dominant figure within, these feelings would naturally be accentuated. One way of dealing with this feeling of inferiority would be through imitation of the father among one's peers; although one cannot at once be a man one can at least be a boy—aggressive, athletic, daring, and so on. But this means of expression was

[93] Fenichel, *Psychoanalytic Theory of Neurosis*, p. 77.

also cut off for Gandhi. He was a shy boy and unathletic as well. He was afraid to talk to his fellow students at school for fear that someone would "poke fun" at him.[94] Again, as with his fear of his father, the young Gandhi tried to come to grips with this problem.

Gandhi's first response to his felt lack of manliness, which is in evidence from a very early age but which grew after his marriage in early adolescence, was to try to develop more masculine characteristics. This attempt to be a man—first expressed in meat-eating, smoking, a visit to a house of prostitution, and, somewhat later, in a general imitation of the British model of manhood—continued, although with diminishing force as time passed, until Gandhi at thirty-six renounced sexuality altogether and thereby gave up the quest.

Gandhi's early model in his attempt to become a man, aside from his father, was Sheikh Mehtab, an older Moslem boy who was strong of body, a good athlete, able to bear punishment, and by no means afraid of ghosts or serpents.[95] Sheikh propagated the idea that meat-eating was necessary for bodily strength, that if Gandhi remained a vegetarian (as all Hindus are supposed to be) he would stay weak and unmanly. To some extent the boys seem to have connected this idea with expelling the British, who were reputed to get their strength from meat, but how reliable Gandhi's memory is in this respect is a bit hard to determine. In any case, for many Indians, and for Gandhi as he grew older, the British model of masculinity, with its martial ideals and emphasis on physical courage, was a discomforting one.[96] In fact, it was as alien to the major stream of traditional Hindu ideals to act out one's manhood in British terms as it was difficult for Gandhi to think of himself as a man at all. This "fit" was to be one of the essential aspects of Gandhi's success in Indian revolutionary politics, just as

[94] M. K. Gandhi, p. 6.   [95] *Ibid.*, p. 20.
[96] Rudolph, "The New Courage," *passim*, handles this point extremely well.

Lenin's ready assumption of a paternal role was to aid him greatly in his revolutionary struggle.

At first Gandhi resisted Sheikh's arguments about meat-eating—despite the fact he knew that one of his older brothers was eating meat. Gandhi knew that if he ate meat he would have to lie to his parents, both to avoid hurting them and bringing punishment of some kind onto himself. Eventually, however, the claims of manhood overcame the call of filial duty and Gandhi partook of meat. That night he felt as if "a live goat were bleating inside" him, but he tried meat-eating several more times before the strain of lying to his parents caused him to stop.[97] Sheikh also enticed Gandhi into a brothel, but Gandhi lost his nerve and was shown "the door, with abuses and insults." This incident made Gandhi feel as if his "manhood had been injured, and he wished to sink into the ground for shame."[98] Sheikh also encouraged Gandhi to be assertive and domineering with his wife, but Gandhi's child bride turned out to have a mind of her own, so that Gandhi was forced to retreat from the battle for manhood on all fronts.

Even when Gandhi gave up some of the more overt attempts at being masculine, he did not give up his companionship with Sheikh. He perpetuated what he admitted to be a demoralizing relationship on the grounds that Sheikh could be reformed—by Gandhi. In a similar manner he had rationalized his meat-eating in terms of the need for Indian strength against the British raj. Thus in his teens Gandhi was already engaged upon a long-term attempt to bend all his efforts to highly moralistic goals, an attempt which, in origin, was oriented towards the justification of action undertaken for other reasons.

The first two aspects of Gandhi's childhood, a fear of his father and an inability to live up to masculine ideals, are clearly related to each other. Gandhi's fear of his father was not a simple dread of punishment; it was a complex amalgam of internalized self-reproach, anxiety at the thought of

[97] M. K. Gandhi, p. 22.   [98] *Ibid.*, p. 24.

the loss of paternal affection, and the idea that aggressive actions on his part would have harmful effects on his father (a common aspect of the struggle to attain a masculine role which would be much accentuated when the discovery of rebellious acts, such as stealing and meat-eating, leads to parental self-punishment). Gandhi was, in other words, extremely guilt-ridden, afraid that he was doing things he should not and for which he ought to be punished. At the same time it was necessary for him to act in a manner which exacerbated guilt if he were to attain manhood. He was torn between, as most boys are to a lesser degree, a desire to submit to his father (and his own superego, the internal manifestation of his father's moral standards) and a desire to replace him in his mother's eyes. The aim to be like the father implies overturning the father, which in turn leads to anxiety and guilt.[99]

Gandhi's plight was accentuated by his strong identification with his mother, and his early marriage. The identification with his mother meant that in addition to the ambivalences of his relationship with his father growing out of his strivings toward masculinity, Gandhi also had to resolve an opposition between the goals of masculinity and femininity themselves. This identification provided the third source of strain in Gandhi's childhood, for each time he asserted his masculinity and independence, via smoking and the rest, he was betraying that part of himself which was involved with his mother. In his eagerness to be masculine, to be even more of a man than his father, Gandhi went beyond the degree of manliness his mother respected, so that in a multitude of ways his goals were clashing and contradictory. Gandhi wanted to be a man to win his mother's respect and to be like his admired father; he wanted to de-

[99] See Fenichel, Chapters 5 and 6; see also Freud's summary statement on the Oedipal period in *New Introductory Lectures on Psychoanalysis*, pp. 63-64, and the earlier exposition of this root psychoanalytic concept in "Three Contributions to the Theory of Sex," in A. A. Brill, ed., *The Basic Writings of Sigmund Freud* (New York, 1938), pp. 553-629, especially pp. 617-18 on the re-emergence of Oedipal problems during adolescence.

velop the saintliness of his mother because he loved her and his father presumably loved that quality in her. And for Gandhi these were total ideals—he could not be satisfied with being like his father in some respects and his mother in others. During the period of his adolescence, especially after his marriage, Gandhi tried the solution of complete masculinity. The results, in his own eyes, were disastrous. From then on he moved increasingly towards the model of his mother, of which the "Mahatma" of Indian history was his approximation.

Before turning to his marriage and its consequences, one other aspect of Gandhi's childhood should be mentioned; that is, his lack of masculinity was associated in his mind with shame, with embarrassment, as in the incident at the brothel. Gandhi, like Trotsky, went through his childhood constantly plagued by humiliation. This lack of respect, which Gandhi related to his lack of prowess in several regards, was to be one of his concerns for years, until his own self-respect became sufficient to allow him to bear proudly a great deal of contempt. He was, in fact, virtually transformed from a boy sensitive to the slightest hint of contempt to a man quite immune to the barbs of his enemies.

Although traces of internal conflict appear even in the first pages of his autobiography, Gandhi's problems became almost overwhelming during adolescence. Before that he had been a mediocre and shy schoolboy, but with adolescence and his marriage began the whole set of events that we have been discussing; if he was not exactly happy before adolescence, he was even less so during it. Gandhi was married when he was thirteen, at the same time as an older brother and cousin. Although child marriage was the rule among Hindu families, he was a bit young even by Hindu standards.[100] His marriage took place when it did because it was convenient and economical for his parents to get his

[100] The injury which eventually led to the death of Gandhi's father was incurred in conjunction with Gandhi's marriage, thus creating another association in his mind between sexual activity and bodily injury. See Rudolph, "Self-Control and Political Potency," p. 86.

and his brother's marriages out of the way at the same time. As Gandhi put it, "there was no thought of our welfare, much less our wishes."[101] Thus Gandhi tries to place full blame on his parents for the unhappy experiences which lay ahead.

Gandhi was nervous on his wedding night, despite careful coaching by his brother's wife, but "the impressions of the former birth were potent enough to make all coaching superfluous."[102] Having overcome the first obstacle, he quickly set about to make himself master of his marriage, as his father was the master of his, but Kasturbai, his wife, was uncooperative. She met his demands, sexual and other, with a sort of passive resistance, leading Gandhi to comment somewhat wryly at a much later date that he "learnt the lesson of non-violence from my wife when I tried to bend her to my will."[103] The strains of this marriage were to some extent limited, to some extent amplified, by two facts. First, Kasturbai spent much of her time during the first years of their marriage with her family, thus removing the immediate source of difficulty but also increasing Gandhi's youthful jealousy and anxiety. Second, Gandhi continued to live in his father's home, as was customary, and was restricted in his contact with his wife. This both provided a degree of stability that two children living by themselves would not have had and made him feel that his pleasures were subject to parental regulation.[104]

It was during this period of his life that Gandhi was most involved with Sheikh Mehtab, suffering from fear of ghosts even while in bed with his wife, experimenting with meat-eating and smoking. Then in his sixteenth year everything came to a head. His father had been ill for some time with a fistula on his leg. Gandhi and his mother had been his father's primary nurses, the former hurrying home from school each day to take care of him. At the same time Gandhi's wife was well-advanced in pregnancy. Then one night, when Gandhi was massaging his father's legs, his

[101] M. K. Gandhi, p. 84.   [102] *Ibid.*, p. 11.
[103] Quoted in Nanda, p. 21.   [104] M. K. Gandhi, p. 84.

uncle came to relieve him. Gandhi reports in his auto-biography:

> I was glad and went straight to the bed-room. My wife, poor thing, was fast asleep. But how could she sleep when I was there? I woke her up. In five or six minutes, however, the servant knocked at the door. I started with alarm. 'Get up,' he said, 'Father is very ill.' I knew of course that he was very ill, and so I guessed what 'very ill' meant at that moment. I sprang out of bed.
> 'What is the matter? Do tell me!'
> 'Father is no more.'
> So all was over! I had but to wring my hands. I felt deeply ashamed and miserable. I ran to my father's room. I saw that, if animal passion had not blinded me, I should have been spared the torture of separation from my father during his last moments. But now it was my uncle who had this privilege. . . .

* * *

> This shame of my carnal desire even at the critical hour of my father's death . . . is a blot I have never been able to efface or forget, and I have always thought that, although my devotion to my parents knew no bounds and I would have given up anything for it, yet it was weighed and found unpardonably wanting because my mind was at the same moment in the grip of lust. . . . I may mention that the poor mite that was born to my wife scarcely breathed for more than three or four days. Nothing else could be expected. . . .[105]

Gandhi mentions one of the two emotions which are important for understanding this, what would be for anyone, shocking experience. He felt ashamed of himself, humiliated by his weakness, by someone other than himself having the honor of being with his father at the last moment.

[105] *Ibid.*, pp. 30-31.

He had not lived up to a standard of behavior that was crucial to him; he was trying so hard to be the obedient son and now he was found wanting.

But there is another aspect to this incident, for which the key is the death of his child. It is clear that Gandhi felt his actions, having intercourse with his wife so late in her pregnancy, caused the death of the baby.[106] Sexual activity had led to death—and, one would surmise, in Gandhi's mind it had led to the death of his father as well. One aspect of the Oedipal fantasy is that the son desires the elimination of the father and in adolescence feels that his developing sexual potency will be the instrument of that desire. Thus sexual activity has built into it aggressiveness towards the father, so that, if the father is at all loved, during the Oedipal phase itself and again during adolescence the sexual activity appropriate to each stage is accompanied by feelings of guilt, varying in intensity depending on any one of a number of things.[107] When, as in Gandhi's case, the death of the father almost seems to follow from sexual activity, guilt is extraordinarily heightened. In a sense, Gandhi was to spend the rest of his life seeking to ease the burden of that guilt— by sexual abstinence and by the nursing of others. At the same time that he was trying, as it were, to make it up to his father, however, Gandhi refused simply to submit, to give in and admit his guilt. Instead, for reasons which I will try to indicate in the next chapter, he continued to assert his independence, his right to manhood and the prerogatives of men, but in a strange and disguised form. Passive resistance (or nonviolent action), that peculiar contradiction in terms, was the indirect expression of almost overwhelming guilt—and vigorous self-assertion.

As in the case of Lenin, this traumatic event of adolescence did not prove immediately debilitating. Gandhi was able to finish high school and matriculate at the University

---

[106] In his autobiography Gandhi notes that, with his wife in the advanced stages of pregnancy, "religion, medical science and common sense alike forbade sexual intercourse." p. 29.

[107] Fenichel, p. 94.

at Ahmedabad. But he found the work at the university difficult and unsatisfying and so, like Trotsky, looked for a way of escape. This was provided by a family friend who suggested that young men bent on advancement would be wise to go to England for their education. Gandhi leaped at the idea, taking several arduous journeys in the effort to convince members of the caste that he could go to England without being corrupted. His mother, too, was worried in this regard and gave him her permission to go only after he vowed to abstain from wine, women, and meat.[108] (In a way it was probably fortunate for Gandhi that he was forced to take this vow, for it eliminated a number of difficult choices that might have confronted him otherwise.) Even when he got his mother's permission, however, the battle was not won, for he still had to deal with a general meeting of the Modh Bania in Bombay. Here, despite his normal incoherence when addressing large groups, Gandhi stood up for his right to go to England strongly and persistently—even after he was declared an outcast by the group. That he should have been able to do so, and then to have gone on to London despite the ban, indicates the intensity of his desire to escape from India or, more accurately, his need to escape from himself, from the tortured writhings of his own mind. As we shall see, he took his problems with him and returned to India with his burdens very little, if at all, lightened.

The Propensity to Revolt

It seems appropriate to draw together the material thus far presented in order to form some kind of picture of what our three revolutionists were like as their adolescence drew to a close, to attempt a preliminary comparison of their similarities and differences. For this purpose let us examine our protagonists in terms of the psychoanalytic scheme of personality development.[109]

[108] M. K. Gandhi, p. 39.

[109] The explanatory hypotheses used here were originally developed by Freud, notably in "Three Contributions to the Theory of Sex," and

One of the problems our materials present us with is that while we have a substantial amount of information about the early lives of the three men, it is difficult to determine exactly when the various incidents which have been recorded took place. On the whole, we can tell if something happened before or after the child started school, but usually not whether it happened at age three or five. Given the nature of psychoanalytic theory, the lack of this kind of information is to be regretted; and, as a result, we must use the concepts involved in the psychoanalytic model of the stages of development somewhat more loosely than is desirable, especially for the first three (oral, anal, and genital) stages. Instead of talking about Lenin's behavior during the anal period, for example, I will have to discuss the degree to which Lenin appears to have mastered the conflicts of that stage. It should be noted, however, that by the time we get to the latency period the amount of relatively solid information available on all three men is quite substantial; for once young people get to school they are observed by and have contact with many more people, and develop a much surer sense of sequence. Their lives are no longer as private or as timeless as they were in earlier childhood.

Although it is not absolutely crucial that the developmental sequence of childhood be substantially known, it is vital that we know a good deal about what the individual was like, and with what problems he had to deal, during adolescence. As Erikson puts it, adolescence is the time when

> each youth must forge for himself some central perspective and direction, some working unity, out of the effective remnants of his childhood and the hopes of his anticipated adulthood.[110]

---

our picture of the pregenital period in particular was further developed by Karl Abraham in a series of studies which are reprinted in his *Selected Papers*, Ernest Jones, ed. (London, 1942), pp. 370-501. Fenichel provides a more systematic and complete review of them. The direct model for the present discussion is that used by Erikson, as in *Childhood and Society*, pp. 247-74, as well as in several of his other works.

[110] Erikson, *Young Man Luther*, p. 14.

Thus we must come to grips with an individual's pre-adolescence, for the strengths and weaknesses of that earlier period are the raw material out of which an "identity," as Erikson puts it, must be built during adolescence. And it is in terms of this configuration of psychic and social forces, this identity, that the actions of an individual become comprehensible.

According to Erikson, the developmental concerns of the first five years of life can be discussed in terms of three major "crises" with which the individual must deal. The first of these, the crisis of the oral stage, centers on the development of attitudes of trust.[111] During this period the child learns to respond to a rather undifferentiated environment, the most clearly perceived element of which, under usual conditions, is his mother. He will develop a basically trustful or mistrustful view of his world depending on the degree to which, and the ways in which, the people in his environment, especially his mother, manage to gratify his needs for physical comfort and love. The more they succeed in gratifying his needs, the more trustful he will be; the less they succeed in gratifying him, the less trustful he will be. He will never be, however, either perfectly trusting or perfectly mistrustful. There is inevitably enough frustration in an infant's first months to create a degree of wariness and there must be some minimal level of gratification if he is to survive. But a wide range of variation is possible, from a person who, on the whole, expects favorable and comforting responses from those around him to one who generally expects his environment to be a source of pain rather than pleasure. Needless to say, this underlying orientation can be considerably modified on the basis of later experience, especially if the child's environment changes radically during his early years. If, on the other hand there is a high degree of continuity in his environment and his experience with it, the original orientation is likely to be considerably augmented.

[111] Erikson, *Childhood and Society*, pp. 247-51.

With respect to our three cases, Lenin appears to have had a basically mistrustful, Trotsky and Gandhi a basically trustful, nature. Lenin's late walking and his reticence in making friends outside the family are the only facts we have from his childhood to support this contention; but such as they are they do tend to support the view that Lenin was basically mistrustful. Trotsky, on the other hand, seems to have been highly optimistic; his autobiography is full of the disappointments which are only possible as a result of high expectations. Moreover, his earliest memories are of a confident grasping at the objects in his environment. Gandhi would appear to resemble Trotsky in this respect: his receptivity to the ideas of his friend Sheikh Mehtab and his ready assimilation of his nanny's formula (repeating the name Rama) for warding off evil spirits seem indicative of an essentially trustful outlook.

Although much experience comes between the first year of life and full adulthood, there should be indications in that first year of what the adult will be like and, therefore, of what his political behavior will be like. In the present case, all else being equal, one would expect Lenin to be mistrustful of his environment; he should tend to place little faith in promises, be highly suspicious of the intentions of those around him, relatively less sanguine about the encouraging aspects of any given phenomenon, and hence not easily let down, betrayed or disappointed. His adult behavior should be characterized by attempts to make his environment less risky, both by keeping the initiative himself and by creating structures which would leave him less exposed. Thus we would seem to have here one root of his later creation of an organization subject to his directives alone.

Trotsky and Gandhi, on the other hand, should expect rewards from their environment; they should tend to have faith in and respect promises of other people, assume that the intentions of others with respect to themselves are essentially benevolent, be optimistic about the outcome of any given event, and so on. If this line of argument is correct, and if the facts have been correctly interpreted, then when we turn to the examination of the adult behavior of these men we should find differences and similarities as above.

It thus appears that revolutionists might have a rather variable degree of trustfulness. Should this be so, then neither great trustfulness nor great mistrustfulness can be the distinguishing psychological mark of the revolutionist. Nonetheless, variations with respect to trust may be very important keys to understanding the behavior of any given revolutionist.

The crisis of the second phase of development, the anal phase, Erikson terms the crisis of autonomy versus shame and doubt.[112] During this phase the people in the child's environment expect him to develop a degree of self-control, especially with regard to excretory functions. The greater the degree to which the child succeeds in developing this control, the greater will be his sense of accomplishment, self-respect and autonomy (and the more easily will he develop other kinds of self-control.) To the extent that the child does not succeed, he will be frustrated, ashamed of his failure (as a result of the reactions of others to his failure, such reactions almost always involving some intent to humiliate), and doubtful about his capacities and the worth of his achievement.

Of the three men, Lenin apparently mastered this crisis most successfully. Almost nowhere in the descriptions of his youth or his adult life do we find that Lenin felt deeply ashamed or was bothered by indecisiveness. At many points, however, we find that he was self-controlled and self-possessed, from his earliest school days to his last Central Committee meetings. Trotsky, by contrast, reports many instances of humiliation stemming from lack of self-control—from a pants-wetting incident at some very young age or from his lack of control of his father's scythe in the incident noted earlier. The embarrassments he suffered as a

[112] Erikson, *Childhood and Society*, pp. 251-54.

result of not being able to control what he wrote, as in the incident where his sister caught him carefully writing out his recently acquired vocabulary of "special" words, is another case in point. By the time he got into the upper grades at school, however, he was well on the way to managing this problem—by turning the tables and humiliating others. This particular form of mastery, however, meant that Trotsky would remain susceptible to humiliation; he would use his tongue and pen to ward off what would be felt as attempts to embarrass him. Thus where Lenin would fight singlemindedly for his ideas and cause without any thought of his personal dignity or need for the flattery or attention of others, Trotsky would be fighting constant rearguard actions to protect his easily upset sense of self-respect. Lenin's pride, anchored early in success, would be relatively invulnerable and inconspicuous personally; Trotsky's, imperiled early, would be prickly and all too obvious. And Trotsky would, at various times, display that indecision and uncertainty so noticeably absent in Lenin—as at the end of his school days.

Gandhi, even more than Trotsky, was plagued by the unresolved problems of this crisis. Feelings of shame pervade the early pages of his autobiography, even rise to overlap with his feelings of guilt as a result of his father's death. Gandhi was fighting a veritable war against shame, shame at being a bad athlete, a mediocre student, a liar. He lived in fear of the taunts of his schoolmates and the abuse of prostitutes. Unlike Trotsky, for Gandhi the experiences of school and adolescence provided no relief. Gandhi carried this issue, the question of where to find a firm basis of self-respect, alive and problematical into adult life.

Furthermore, Gandhi, much more than Trotsky, was bothered by lack of self-control and decisiveness throughout his childhood and adolescence. He was constantly making vows to himself in an effort to control what he felt to be his wayward passions and inclinations. It should be emphasized that he was making determined efforts to deal with what he felt to be his weaknesses, but the first real sign we have that Gandhi is not going to give up under the strain of his felt incapacity is when he resolves to go to England and acts perseveringly to bring that resolution to fruition.

As with the question of trust, we find Lenin on one end of the continuum and Trotsky and Gandhi somewhere near the other end. And, as with the attribute of trustfulness, the differences here are more striking than the similarities. Thus we are again dealing with characteristics of, presumably, great explanatory value which are not held in common by the three revolutionists. Unifying psychological themes do appear, however, as we turn to the next phase.

Erikson views the next phase, the Oedipal or genital, as that period in which the child must initially come to grips with the problem of guilt, which grows out of his ambivalent relationship with his parents.[113] For boys, love for and fear of the father results in the internalization of his moral standards as the superego, thereby setting up a conflict between the child's love for his mother, which demands the removal of the father, and his feelings of affection and love for his father, as internally represented by the superego. The child is thus at war within himself—if he fails either in sublimating the conflict (through giving up his mother as a sexual love object and identifying with his father in his assumption of a male role) or in externalizing it, initiative will be stymied. He will use up large amounts of his mental energy in a fruitless and debilitating internal conflict. Here, as with all mental conflicts, the extremes of perfect guilt and perfect guiltlessness are seldom found; but a considerable variation with respect to guilt is possible.

All three of the men seem to have undergone unusually tense strivings during this phase, although Lenin somewhat less than the other two. Lenin's clear emulation of his father and older brother during the latency period indicates that he was well on the way to mastering this problem or that the crisis was less intense than in the other two cases, but the depth of his reaction to the deaths of his father and

[113] Erikson, *Childhood and Society*, pp. 255-58.

brother during his adolescence indicates that a rich basis existed in the earlier stage for the conflicts of the later. In Trotsky's case the conflict was clearly great. His descriptions of the life at Yanovka, which emphasize his feeling of maternal neglect, include many examples of his conflicts with and admiration for his father, as well as the observation cited earlier that such affection as there was in the Bronstein home existed between mother and father. Moreover, during the latency period Trotsky did not imitate his father as Lenin did his. Indeed, he sublimated the conflict, using his superior learning as a basis for asserting his manhood vis-à-vis his father, although he failed to meet the elder Bronstein on his own ground. Lenin, however, could challenge his father on the elder Ulyanov's ground: he could excel in school, as his father had done and as his position as teacher and administrator emphasized, and even beat his father at chess. Trotsky perhaps had the same potential, for he does report early card playing at which his father lost and, had he not gone off to Odessa, he might have challenged his father's superiority as a worker of the land. He was not, however, given that opportunity. He left Yanovka at a relatively early age, so that the predominant image of his father that he carried away was probably one of overwhelming strength and competence. Once he started school he was in Yanovka only in the summer, a time when his father's skills and superiority, and monopolization of his mother, would appear most complete. Thus, as mentioned earlier, Trotsky carried away with him a much magnified picture of his father's superiority, one untempered by the moderating effects of continuous contact with the father into and through adolescence.

Gandhi, too, suffered from strong feelings of guilt, both as a consequence of his experience during the genital phase and as a result of his father's death when he was sixteen. Gandhi's idealization of his mother and partial condemnation of his father for lustfulness—in a sense for ever marrying his mother in the first place—is one indicator of the nature of the conflict. His submission to his father, and his numerous attempts at achieving manliness, both during his early school days when he reproached himself for his timidity and after his marriage when his sexual desires and his longing to be a dutiful son were at war with each other, complete the picture of great internal tension. Moreover, Gandhi's failure to find a satisfying and rewarding basis for achievement during his latency period indicates that he found no ready ground for the sublimation of his hostile feelings toward his father.[114] In his case, as in Lenin's, the events of adolescence were especially crucial for shaping the subsequent nature of the man.

The crisis of the latency period Erikson terms that of industry versus inferiority.[115] It is the period when the individual expands greatly the scope of his world. He must now deal more intensively with many people outside his family—age mates, teachers, and so on. He must find some basis of achievement which will allow him to identify with his father (and perhaps older brothers as well) and relieve his feelings of hostility. Because this period is devoted to a short-run solution of the problems of the preceding phase, we were able to deal with it above in our discussion of the genital phase. Here I need only stress that Gandhi seems to have been least successful during this stage, and Lenin most. All were dutiful schoolboys. Trotsky and Lenin relished their work, or at least their grades; Gandhi did not. Trotsky, on the other hand, was the most impulsive and public learner of the three while Lenin was the steadiest and least ostentatious.

Adolescence, the final stage to be considered in this chapter, is the time when all the strands of childhood must somehow be pulled together into a coherent personality. It is the period when, in the course of normal development, the parents are given up as the central objects of emotional

[114] Although Gandhi was not a bad student, his subsequent devaluation of his own education and the system of education of which it was a part reveals how little satisfaction he was able to find in his school work.

[115] Erikson, *Childhood and Society*, pp. 258-61.

drives and replaced first by a series of less emotionally laden objects and eventually by the individual's new family, wife or husband, and children. During this period, in preparation for the emotional separation that is to take place, the individual internalizes even more of his parents' characteristics, and in the process develops a more realistic image of his parents than hitherto existed. He comes to view them as fallible creatures, neither all good nor all evil. At the same time he has to come to grips with his now greatly expanded universe. He has to learn how others will respond to him and how he should respond to them. He must also make a decision as to his occupation, a decision Erikson stresses is a crucial indicator of the individual's view of himself and his society.[116] In most cases, especially before the advent of modern industrial society, children roughly followed the occupational lines of their fathers, so that their psychological development was highly continuous, a gradual process of increasing assimilation of the way of life of the parents. The striking thing about all three of our cases is that adolescence, the period of the "crisis of identity," was exceptionally stormy, its outcome uncertain, and its consequences great.

Until his father's death, Lenin's adolescence was not unusual. He continued to do well in school, matching the achievements of both father and older brother. When his father died, I inferred, Lenin was beset by great feelings of guilt, as a result of the adolescent reactivation of the Oedipal struggle. Lenin was in the midst of working out his aggressive feelings towards his father when suddenly his father died. Sasha and Lenin seem to have taken this event to signify the fulfillment of their Oedipal desire: the brothers were responsible for the death of the father. Lenin's feelings of aggression, and hence his guilt, were increased when Sasha became head of the family, thus embodying at once paternal and fraternal rivalry for the attention of his mother. And then Sasha was executed.

[116] *Ibid.*, pp. 261-63.

Lenin was now confronted with a double burden of guilt, but also with a way out from under that burden: Sasha's patricidal attempt on the life of the Tsar evoked a very real embodiment of evil authority, namely the forces of tsarism responsible for his brother's death, on which Lenin could focus. After all, it was not he, Lenin, who killed his brother but this malevolent authority. To be sure, Lenin had rejected his early identification with Sasha; but now he could make up for his aggressive feelings with regard to his brother, and his lack of attention to his brother's noble qualities (which is more or less another way of saying the same thing), by taking up his brother's cause—by rebelling against evil authority! He could thus fight against this surrogate paternal authority with a clear conscience—for the Tsar was a bad father against whom the sons were entitled to rebel—without giving up those vital elements of his personality, those crucial feelings of rectitude as well as the specific talents, which he had internalized from his father. At the same time his father could now be felt to be a wholly benevolent authority. Thus his feelings of guilt resulting from his father's death were much alleviated, for his brother had borne the punishment for the patricidal act or intent. Psychologically speaking, the death of his father was not enough to make Lenin a revolutionist, nor was the death of his brother; but the two in combination created a mighty impulse towards revolution. So far, however, there was only an impulse; how it was changed from an inclination into a specific form of revolutionary action is the subject of the next chapter.

In Lenin, then, the relatively smooth course of his emotional development was abruptly interrupted by dramatic events affecting the adolescent resolution of Oedipal guilt. In Trotsky guilt was again at issue, but there was no one set of events on which Trotsky could focus his desire for alleviation from strain. In Lenin, and Gandhi as well, solution to the problems growing out of a limited set of events tended to entail solution to most of the basic psychological problems with which they had to deal. Trotsky, on the other hand, somehow had to deal with a pervasive feeling of guilt which he could not pin down to one simple set of experiences. Lenin's life splits neatly around his father's and brother's deaths—and still preserves a high degree of continuity with his early experiences and the strengths he derived from them. Trotsky's life is a study in discontinuities—between city and country, farmer father and intellectual son, dutiful schoolboy and lifelong revolutionist. Although no man can escape the consequences of his earliest years, for Trotsky they provided relatively little material for a meaningful adult life. Not until he went to school in Odessa did he start to develop talents relevant to the world in which he was to live, while Lenin's personality developed evenly, stage upon stage.

Nonetheless, the problem with which Lenin and Trotsky had to deal was similar in many respects. For both, the issue was, at root, how to deal with paternal authority and the strong feelings of guilt that attached to the relationship of father and son. Trotsky's solution was to avoid the conflict to the extent that he could without submitting. He quickly attached himself to a new way of life which gave him some basis for feeling superior to his father. Using his education as a lever, Trotsky was able to confront his father over his choice of vocation. The tables were now turned—Trotsky had something his father wanted, namely certain skills that would make the farm prosper. But to become an engineer, as his father desired, would be to give in—and eventually would mean confronting his father on his home ground at Yanovka, where the burdens of guilt and humiliation would both be too much to bear. Trotsky, as did Lenin, needed an out. He came upon one in a rather haphazard way. In the midst of his doubts and uncertainties about the future, with the comfortably closed world of school no longer totally available or really satisfying, Trotsky came upon populism. The Narodnik tradition with which he came in contact promised human dignity and liberation from the Tsar, glory and excitement.[117] It constituted a justification for rebellion without guilt, attention without humiliation, and the chance to act for others, not oneself. Trotsky rejected Marxism, for its ideas appealed less than did populism to that side of Trotsky's personality which demanded personal glory. Trotsky was, however, not happy, not guilt-free, in his new mode of bohemian living. There was no crisp break with his father, no clear problem yielding a straightforward solution. There was little satisfaction in just running away.

Trotsky and Lenin, as adolescence ended, were each on the verge of revolutionary activity, although it would take Lenin a little longer than Trotsky to become fully involved. Gandhi, although working tensely with similar problems, was far more uncertain, in a much deeper quandary, than either of the Russians. His adolescence, unlike Lenin's, had been rather frustrating and marked with failure before his father's death. That event, and the death of his son, proved almost overwhelming. His father's death, alone and under less strange circumstances, probably would have been enough to precipitate a major crisis. But coming as it did, when he was in the middle of that act which most directly symbolized his challenge to his father's position, it drove Gandhi away from his wife and away from India, possessed with very great feelings of his own potential for harm, looking for a way of living, and a justification for living, which would somehow combine submission and aggression, femininity, and courage.

Each man, then, carried with him into his adult life unfinished business with his parental generation. Each carried a burden of guilt he had been unable to relieve in the context of the family or, in Gandhi's case, in the context of his family extended to include his wife. Each had to come to grips with a primitive image of paternal authority. There were, as I have mentioned, significant differences as well,

[117] Deutscher, *The Prophet Armed*, pp. 26-27.

with respect to mistrustfulness and shame in particular. But this important nucleus of similarity can be seen to exist.

These common characteristics of the three men I propose to view as necessary conditions for revolutionary involvement.[118] They are clearly not, however, necessary and sufficient conditions for such an outcome, for many men experience early trauma which leave similar problems to be worked out. It seems likely to me that all people who have this psychic configuration as adolescence draws to a close will have a propensity or tendency to become involved in political protest in general and revolutionary activity in particular, but such latent inclinations must be combined with appropriate precipitants and preconditions for revolutionary activity if involvement in revolutionary politics is actually to occur.[119] On the one hand, something must happen to trigger the individual's tendency to revolt. This is what might be termed a precipitant or catalyst, and as we shall see in the next chapter the most salient common characteristic of the precipitant in the cases we are studying is that established political authority acts with unexpected aggressiveness towards the potential revolutionist.

On the other hand, there are the long run, more general aspects of societies and individuals, such as the motivational variables we have been studying, without which catalytic sparks would strike without effect. Of these, we have explored only the motivational aspects of individual participants as preconditions for revolutionary activity. There are a host of other factors which make possible or impossible, successful or futile, such involvement.[120] The

---

[118] It may, in fact, be that these are not necessary conditions for revolutionary involvement, even for the type of revolutionist here being studied. They are proposed only hypothetically. The hypotheses involved must of course be tested against a significant sample of revolutionists before we can treat these ideas as anything more than suggestions.

[119] This terminology is taken from Eckstein, "On the Etiology of Internal War," in *History and Theory*, Vol. IV, No. 2, 1965.

[120] See Eckstein's discussion, *ibid.*, pp. 143-44.

existence of a revolutionary intellectual climate, of certain kinds of economic stress and change, of rapid social change combined with political stagnation—these factors and many more like them are doubtless involved when large numbers of individuals are actually recruited into revolutionary enterprises. By focusing only on some of the individual psychological considerations, I am not in any way denying the importance of these other variables. I do believe that the psychological variables are often given insufficient attention on the part of others who study revolutionary involvement. Hence it seems worthwhile to make explicit what others leave implicit.

young manhood

In this chapter we will trace the development of the three revolutionists from their adolescence through early manhood, from men groping for a way of organizing their lives to men firmly oriented toward the course of action that was to mark their careers. This is the period when all three men worked out a way of dealing with their "crises of identity," one varying in length from a mere half dozen or so years in Trotsky's case to almost twenty years in Gandhi's. Lenin, whom we consider first, took about a dozen years. Needless to say, this period of self-definition and adjustment to reality grew out of the men's earlier conflicts and did not end abruptly at any particular age. Each of the men changed in important ways after the period here under consideration, although in varying degrees, but none broke sharply with the world view or approach to political activity developed at this time.

Ulyanov: Disciple of Marx

Lenin did not react to Sasha's death by immediately taking up the revolutionary banner. Although he was deeply disturbed by his brother's death—and appalled by the behavior of the local "liberals" who deserted the Ulyanovs now that they were tainted with treason[1]—he enrolled in the University of Kazan in the fall of 1887. He entered the faculty of law and political science, for reasons not known.[2]

[1] N. K. Krupskaya, Lenin's wife, notes that the liberal's "widespread cowardice made a very profound impression upon him at that time." See *Memories of Lenin* (New York, 1930), I, 4.

[2] See Wolfe, *Three Who Made a Revolution*, p. 71.

In any case, his tenure at the university was very short—he was expelled in December. The students of the university had assembled to present a petition of grievances to the provincial inspector, and Ulyanov, for reasons which are again unknown, was among them, standing in the front row.[3] As the group disbanded, registration cards were checked and Vladimir's bore the name which his brother had made known. That night he was arrested and subsequently ordered to leave the city of Kazan.

He was ordered to go to Kukushkino, in the province of Kazan, where his elder sister Anna had already been exiled as a result of her innocent contact with Sasha during the period of his revolutionary activity. There he remained until the autumn of 1888. Lenin was undoubtedly bored at Kukushkino, and highly uncertain about his future.[4] He and his mother made repeated efforts to get him readmitted to the university, but to no avail. Neither he nor his mother had any intention of letting him remain idle, but tsarist authority was making it difficult for him to take up the life of a peaceful citizen.

On the whole, Lenin passed the time productively, unlike many men in similar situations who, when removed from the stimulus of active life, allow themselves to sink into despondency and inactivity. He read avidly but somewhat unsystematically, digging out what he could from dated liberal periodicals he found in the area and the books he was allowed to borrow from the University of Kazan. By this time he was certainly trying to piece together his brother's orientations towards political action, but his orderly mind could find no coherent argument in the materials with which he was able to come in contact.[5] During the months in Kukushkino, or perhaps even somewhat

---

[3] Although we do not know specifically why Lenin was involved in this protest, it probably was connected with his brother's death. His position in the front row, however, does not seem to have been connected with his leadership of the activity; apparently he was little more than an observer. *Ibid.*, p. 78.

[4] *Ibid.*, p. 81.   [5] Ulam, *The Bolsheviks*, p. 99.

earlier, he did read Chernyshevsky's *What Is To Be Done?*
This had been one of his brother's favorite books and in it
he found an appraisal of the social situation in terms of
Hegelian dialectics and a call to tough, vigorous action.[6]
The revolutionary message of *What Is To Be Done?* became part of Lenin's orientation to politics; it was firmly
implanted before he turned to Marxism and was never
really displaced by Marxism. Its emphasis on coming to
grips with facts, however, undoubtedly helped to make him
receptive to Marxism, while its voluntaristic leanings and
approval of violence as a political tool gave him an activist
perspective that was not quite Marxist.[7] But it did not provide him with a system of thought adequate for guiding
action. It provided a leaning, a direction, not a tool of analysis or basis of justification.

Psychologically *What Is To Be Done?* was part of
Lenin's image of his brother. As he later told a friend:

> After my brother's execution, . . . knowing that Cher-
> nyshevsky's novel had been one of his favorite works,
> I started to read it in earnest and spent on it, not days,
> but weeks on end. Only then did I understand its
> depth. It is the kind of book that influences you for
> your whole life.[8]

Thus in his effort to understand *What Is To Be Done?*
Lenin was seeking an understanding of what had guided
and motivated Sasha in his sudden and violent action. His
abiding admiration for the book is hence one sign of his
identification with Sasha, of his attempt to play a revolutionary role "like Sasha." As we saw earlier, he was in-

[6] Haimson, *The Russian Marxists and the Origins of Bolshevism*,
pp. 97-103. In particular, Lenin must have been attracted to the character Rakhmetov, who is an apt representation of what was to become
the famous Bolshevik hardness. Cf. N. G. Chernyshevsky, *What Is To
Be Done?*, trans. Benjamin R. Tucker (New York, 1909), especially
pp. 207-22.

[7] Lenin's relationship to Marxists and Narodniks (Chernyshevsky
being one of the most important Narodnik theorists) will be considered in more detail when we come to his writings of the 1890s.

[8] Cited in Haimson, p. 98.

clined to caution from a very young age, and the disastrous consequences of his brother's sudden action (whether it was impulsive or not in fact, it would have appeared so to Lenin, who only learned about it after it was brought to light by the authorities) made him more apprehensive than ever about the probable consequences of precipitous action. Thus Sasha's way was too dangerous; until some other course of action could be found, Lenin would remain torn between the desire to relieve his guilt through identification with his dead brother and a fear that such identification would result in danger, if not death, to himself.

To relieve the tension and reduce boredom Lenin lost himself in chess, physical activity, and helping other members of the family with their studies.[9] Later, when back in Kazan, he even took up smoking, but at his mother's request gave it up. He maintained his self-discipline, but the strain was obviously great.

In the autumn of 1888 Lenin was allowed to return to Kazan but not to enter the University. He spent the winter reading and playing chess and, according to his sister Anna, reading the first volume of Marx's *Capital*.[10] In the spring of 1889 his mother, despairing of getting her son back into a university, bought a farm in Alakaevka in the Samara *Gubernya*. There Lenin was to try his hand at running an estate but, as he told Krupskaya, his "relations with the muzhiks got to be abnormal."[11] Luckily his mother finally secured permission for him to take the law examination at the University of St. Petersburg in the summer of 1890, so that he was relieved of the burden of landowning after a short tenure. Lenin took his examinations in the spring and fall of 1891 as an external student (that is, he was not admitted to a university but was allowed to study on his own for the degree), passing with the highest possible grade—and this despite having to compress a four-year course into

[9] His mother had brought the rest of the family to Kukushkino shortly after Lenin was ordered to reside there.
[10] *Reminiscences of Lenin*, p. 30.
[11] Quoted in Wolfe, p. 85.

one year. In January 1892 he was licensed to practice law and enrolled with an old chess foe, A. N. Khardin, as a junior attorney in the town of Samara, not far from the ill-fated farm. Here he was to remain until the end of 1893, so that Samara was his home for four years in all.

Lenin spent a year and a half of the Samara period as a junior attorney, during which time he participated as the defense attorney in ten clear-cut cases of petty theft, wife-beating, and the like. Not unexpectedly he secured no acquittals.[12] There was one case, however, which he undertook on his own initiative and which he did win. Lenin and a relative were taking a trip, during which a river had to be crossed.[13] The ferrying privileges across the river were held by a man named Arefeev, who by might rather than right allowed no other boats to ferry passengers across but his own. When Lenin and his companion arrived at the river, they discovered that there would be some wait for the ferry, so Lenin persuaded one of the local boatmen to take them over. Arefeev, as was his custom, had the boat turned back and made them wait for his ferry. Lenin was incensed and brought charges against Arefeev and, despite all kinds of tricks by the latter and inconveniences resulting from his influence with the local authorities, won the case.[14]

Here, then, for the first time in his own experience, Lenin came in contact with an authoritative figure who was in the wrong, against whom, by practically any standards, one could fight with a clear conscience. The incident took place in the summer of 1892 and was pursued well into the winter. By this time Lenin was already getting impatient to leave Samara, to try out his Marxist wings. The fight against Arefeev was a temporary substitute for the larger battle he was longing to enter. Several years later, when he was exiled in Siberia, he would use legal defense, although in

[12] *Ibid.*, p. 86.
[13] Dmitry Ulyanov in *Reminiscences of Lenin*, says that Lenin's brother-in-law accompanied him (p. 122); Wolfe claims that it was a sister (p. 87).
[14] *Reminiscences of Lenin*, pp. 122-29.

this case on other people's behalf, as a means of using up some of the energy he longed to devote to revolutionary activity.

Living in Samara were many members of *Narodnaya Volya*, the revolutionary organization of which Sasha and his friends had considered themselves a part. The police had placed them here to rusticate and grow old after their prison terms had expired. From them Lenin tried to learn of his brother's cause, but he found them vague and imprecise.[15] He did learn from them a number of technical skills, like the chemical basis of invisible inks and the ways of getting false passports. Aside from the bias towards terror and voluntarism developed earlier, however, he found little in what these old revolutionists said that was useful. He was looking for two things which Narodism could not supply: first, a justification of rebellion that would be total, that would define all relationships of man to man. Intense problems such as those Lenin was dealing with demand strongly formulated solutions. When the problem is one of ambivalence, of a mixture of feelings that keep getting in the way of each other, a system of justification is needed which precludes ambivalence, which reduces conflict to simpler and more manageable terms. Russian populism was not such a system of thought. It dealt with a set of special relationships, such as the people to the Tsar, and justified action relevant to such relationships; it did not suffice for Lenin's more encompassing needs.

Second, Lenin was looking for some assurance that revolutionary activity would not lead to disaster. The remnants of men he found in Samara did nothing to increase his confidence in the possible success of *Narodnik* activity. With his basic mistrust and the lesson learned from his brother's fate, Lenin needed mighty assurance of ultimate success. Marxism, which in the early 1890s was growing in popularity as a result of industrial unrest and the talented

[15] Cf. Ulam's discussion of the Samara period, *The Bolsheviks*, pp. 96-110.

pen of G. V. Plekhanov, met both needs; it was a total explanatory and justificatory system and it promised inevitable success. Marxists even claimed that the victory of the working class was a scientifically demonstrable fact. Here was the hardheaded realism and the instrument of analysis and justification Lenin needed, all rolled up into one and brilliantly expounded.

Lenin learned his Marxism and rejected Narodism quietly. He tried out his growing ideas only on members of the family and a few intimates.[16] He did not rush into activity based on what he was learning or attempt to refute others who were inclined to populism until he felt he had really mastered Marxist analysis. Not until his last months in Samara did he write his views in such a form as to make them accessible to others and not until the fall of 1893 did he leave Samara for St. Petersburg where participation in quasi-revolutionary activity was possible. Gandhi and Trotsky would immediately act upon the truth as they saw it. Lenin took the time to thoroughly convince himself before he sought to convince others. Similarly Lenin would never debate just for the enjoyment of intellectual engagement and the fruits of verbal victory. As early as the Samara period he did not attempt to refute the exiled populists of the area; he simply turned away (although not without some personal pain in creating the rupture).[17] Trotsky and Gandhi, by contrast, would argue their cause before anyone who would listen.

Another implication of Lenin's "silent" development as a Marxist is that he would not give the impression of hesitancy; whatever doubts he might have would be worked out privately, so that his public image was one of total confidence in his own ideas. The ideas or ideology he expounded, as we noted, had for him two crucial aspects: a justification of action and a way of or approach to action. When one envisions cogent and confident arguments being made in terms of these themes one begins to understand

[16] This discussion relies heavily on the Chapter 5 of Wolfe.
[17] *Ibid.*, p. 95.

the basis of Lenin's dominance over his followers. Lenin would claim for his ideology both rightness and righteousness, correctness and rectitude—and he would make these claims with absolute conviction and an apparent absence of doubt. For any man who was uncertain about either ends or means Lenin was sure to exert a powerful attraction, especially when events, as they did, seemed to follow the course Lenin charted for them. (Also, because he did not act until he felt he thoroughly understood the relevant theoretical and practical aspects of a problem, Lenin was less likely than his opponents to be surprised by the arguments of others or the course of events.)

This experience further exemplifies Lenin's tendency to conserve energy and time that others would expend unproductively. Instead of arguing inconclusively over unfinished ideas, he would try to master a problem himself and then produce a straightforward statement of his position. He would save his arguments for those situations where they were most likely to produce tactical advantage; and he would save his energy and strength for the struggle itself, rather than waste it on diversionary encounters.

There are essentially two reasons why Lenin learned his Marxism in this manner, a pattern of learning and action of such efficacious consequences. First, Lenin's basis mistrust, his expectation that the people in his environment would react negatively and/or dangerously towards him, led him to arm himself as plentifully as he could before exposing himself to them; and once he decided to act he would strike hard, attempt to batter down his opponent before he could effectively retaliate. This was especially true when revolutionary activity itself was involved, but it also permeated his relationships with other members of his own cause. Related to this, of course, is that from one sector of his environment—the Tsar and his minions—Lenin had much to fear. Just as for the child any thought of fighting against the father is accompanied by fear and the wish for sufficient strength to withstand apparently overwhelming might, so fighting against the Tsar led to the desire to be well-armed and cautious.

Second, Lenin acted in such a way as to avoid direct, person-to-person argument (but not controversy generally). The conflicts he was trying to rationalize in ideological terms were so intense that they had to be impersonalized as much as possible. The less the participants in debate resembled the members of the familial conflict situation, the less strain such debate entailed. By pushing conflict as much as possible into the realms of abstraction Lenin was able to reduce the tension accompanying personal ties. He could not, of course, impersonalize his intellectual world completely. The frequency with which he split with other socialists is indicative of how unbearable differences were and the commonness of reconciliation of how necessary these men were to one another, despite the ideological imperfections they saw in each other.

In 1893, as his commitment to Marxism and revolutionary action grew, Lenin became increasingly discontented with the inert environment of Samara. Anna reports that one night, after he had read Chekhov's short story, *Ward No. 6*, Lenin told her that he felt as if he, like the man in the story, were locked up. As Anna put it, "I realized that Samara was for him also a sort of Ward No. 6, that he wanted to get out of it almost as desperately as the poor man in Chekhov's story."[18]

The story itself is quite revealing of Lenin's state of mind at this time.[19] It focuses on two main characters, one the inmate of a mental ward (Ward No. 6), the other the doctor in charge of the hospital of which the ward is a part. The inmate, Ivan Dmitritch Gromov, is the son of a deceased nobleman who, after his father's death, was unable to complete his education and who gradually became overwhelmed

[18] *Reminiscences of Lenin*, p. 43.

[19] Cf. Anton Chekhov, *The Horse Stealers and Other Stories*, Constance Garnett, trans. (New York, 1921), pp. 29-109. Also see Edmund Wilson's treatment of the story in his *To the Finland Station* (Garden City, N.Y., 1953), pp. 369-71.

by persecutory phantasies. He is a man tormented by guilt feelings, but who does not know why he should feel guilty. His lack of self-control, his inability to dominate his fears, has led to his imprisonment in the mental ward. Yet, despite his madness, his mind retains a peculiar lucidity, a profound insight into the corruption and immorality of the hospital, the town, and Russia. He is, moreover, a convinced opponent of political authority, and, in a sense, the story is a parable of the fate of the resister to social and political oppression.

Here, then, Lenin found portrayed the destiny of the man who rebels, and who is guilty just because he does so. Ivan Dmitritch, like Sasha, is a rebel who was not properly prepared for the struggle into which he was thrown by his own sense of justice. He could not control his own impulses and hence was condemned to life in a dreary cell, a veritable living death. No wonder Lenin felt akin to this man, for the story posed for him exactly his own dilemma. To identify with Sasha (Ivan) meant to share their parricidal guilt and their consequent punishment. But if he did not join them in action against the oppressors, he would have to shoulder the guilt growing out of his aggressive feelings towards Sasha. Nor did acquiescence promise relief, as was graphically depicted for him in the fate of the other major character in Chekhov's story, Dr. Andrey Yefimitch Ragin.

Andrey Yefimitch is a character rather like Goncharev's Oblomov—a well-meaning but very weak-willed man of rather liberal inclination. All his life he has been unable to do what he felt was right (namely to try to reform at least some small part of society), and he justified his passivity on quasi-nihilistic philosophical grounds. He does feel dully the intellectual sterility of the town in which he lives, and hence is delighted when he discovers, quite by chance, that one of the inmates of the lunatic ward which he ostensibly supervises, namely Ivan, possesses an original and philosophic turn of mind. Fascinated by Ivan, he starts paying frequent visits to the ward. This behavior is incomprehensible to his fellow townsmen, who decide his interest in Ivan must be a sign of developing insanity and eventually succeed in having him locked up in Ward No. 6, to share the fate of the men he had previously condemned to the lifelong brutalization and dehumanization of that desolate room. And the doctor does not develop the energy or will to protest against this treatment until it is too late, until he is on the verge of death, already confined in a house of dead souls.

Thus the story did not provide Lenin with an alternative to revolt. Revolt or not, there seemed to be no escape from guilt or doom. Under the impact of this frightful prospect, in the provincial backwater of Samara, unable to act and thereby find out whether Marxism really provided a way out of this dilemma, Lenin's habitual self-control weakened, and he found himself in need of comforting conversation and escape from himself.

The very fact that Samara provided no opportunity for action is undoubtedly one of the reasons why Lenin was moved by the condition of the confined men in the story. Lenin wanted to escape the intellectually stifling atmosphere of Samara, to come in contact with people who were thinking and doing, not just vegetating amidst "the idiocy of rural life." Just as much, however, it would seem that he wanted to get away from his family. Lenin, it must be remembered, felt he bore the double responsibility for the deaths of his father and brother—whom he had wished dead in order that he might possess his mother. Now, when, in a sense, he had his mother to himself the feelings of guilt were sure to be oppressive; each day as he bathed in his mother's solicitude he would feel he was getting it only because the two elder men of the family were no longer there. He could not enjoy his love for his mother or her love for him at this close range; it was better to receive loving letters (and money when he needed it—until her death his mother remained a source of sustenance to him) and give them in turn and thus avoid a direct confrontation with his guilt.[20]

Hence in the fall of 1893 Lenin elected to go to St. Petersburg instead of following the rest of the family to Moscow, where Dmitry was to go to school. By so doing he both escaped from his family and threw himself into the center of revolutionary thinking, if not activity, in Russia. Shortly before his arrival in the capital, and during the first months there, he started to write out his views on Marxism for a reading public. "New Economic Developments in Peasant Life" and "On the So-Called Market Question," his first works, were attempts to demonstrate that Russia was a developing capitalist country and that therefore it was not exempt from the inexorable laws of dialectical development which Marx had formulated. He also wrote a long essay, "Discussion Between a Social Democrat and a Populist," which has not been preserved. In any case, as Wolfe notes, virtually all of Lenin's works until 1900 were a "discussion between a Social Democrat and a Populist."[21] Thus an analysis of his major attack on the populists, *What the "Friends of the People" Are and How They Fight the Social Democrats*, will help us to understand what he found of value in Marxism (the Social Democrats were Marxists), and why he rejected populism.

What the "Friends of the People" Are is an examination of the populist criticisms of Marxism and of the content of the populist program, as it was then being enunciated by N. K. Mikhailovsky and others in the monthly periodical, *Russkoye Bogatsvo* (Russian Wealth). In approach it is imitative of the sarcastic, somewhat heavy-handed polemical style of Marx, on the one hand, and it carries on the attack against the populists begun by G. V. Plekhanov a few years earlier, in *Our Differences* (1885), on the

[20] Lenin's writings of 1893-94 are found in Vol. I of his *Collected Works* (Moscow, 1960).
[21] Wolfe, p. 97.

other.[22] In his analysis Lenin attempts to prove that Russia is indeed a capitalist country, and that only revolutionary Marxism provides a guarantee of victory for the oppressed.

It should be noted at the outset that Lenin was careful to differentiate between two varieties of populism. Although all its forms were viewed as being in error insofar as they did not realize the necessity of Russia's passing through a capitalist phase of development, the earlier Narodism of Chernyshevsky and others, with its dialectical sophistication and activist embodiment in such things as the terrorist sections of the *Narodnaya Volya* (which Sasha and his co-conspirators claimed to represent), was treated as a glorious and heroic forerunner of Russian Marxism:

> It required the genius of a Chernyshevsky to understand so clearly at that time, when the peasant Reform was only being introduced . . . its fundamentally bourgeois character, to understand that already at that time Russian "society" and the Russian "state" were ruled and governed by social classes that were irreconcilably hostile to the working people and that undoubtedly predetermined the ruin and expropriation of the peasantry. Moreover, Chernyshevsky understood that the existence of a government that screens our antagonistic social relations is a terrible evil, which renders the position of the working people ever so much worse.[23]

Contemporary Narodism, by contrast, is viewed as betraying this heritage:

> Yes, indeed, you [the Narodniks] are besmirching those ideals!

[22] Georgy Valentinovitch Plekhanov (1857-1918) was one of the first, and most brilliant, Russian Marxists. He was the principal leader of the Emancipation of Labour group, the first organization of Russian Marxists in exile. See the discussion of his relations with Lenin in Chapter 4.

[23] Lenin, *What the "Friends of the People" Are*, in his *Collected Works* (Moscow, 1963), I, 281-82.

Faith in a special social order, in the communal system of Russian life; hence—faith in the possibility of a peasant socialist revolution—that is what inspired them and roused dozens and hundreds of people to wage a heroic struggle against the government. And you, you cannot reproach the Social Democrats with failing to appreciate the immense services of these, the finest people of their day, with failing to respect their memory profoundly. But I ask you, where is that faith now? It is vanished.[24]

In effect, Lenin is saying that not he, but the populists, are defiling the tradition of which his brother was a part. Lenin rejects the accusation that he does not "appreciate the immense services" of his brother, that he has abandoned the faith in "socialist revolution." He views himself as remaining true to the spirit of his brother's actions, even if it is now necessary to view the struggle in somewhat different terms.

The earlier Narodniks and his brother can thus be admired because they put the struggle first, because they realized that victory could only be achieved by revolution. This element of their creed can be readily assimilated into Marxism, even if their analysis of the meaning of the struggle must be rejected. But the current crop of populists have abandoned the concept of conflict while retaining the invalid theoretical framework. They have discarded the grain and kept the chaff of the doctrine. Lenin, by viewing them in this light, could condemn them with a clear conscience; his identification with his brother remained intact as long as he viewed the essence of his brother's creed as revolt rather than populist theory. And his brother's political action, after all, was exactly that—an elemental revolt of the son against the father.

As we have seen, however, Sasha's mode of action gave Lenin no assurance of success; in fact, it connoted failure. But Marxism seemed to promise a solution:

[24] *Ibid.*, pp. 263-64.

[Capitalism is progressive because] it AWAKENS THE MIND OF THE WORKER, converts dumb and incoherent discontent into conscious protest, converts scattered, petty, senseless revolt into an organised class struggle . . . a struggle which derives its strength from the very conditions of existence of large-scale capitalism, and therefore can undoubtedly count upon CERTAIN SUCCESS.[25]

Marxism thus allowed Lenin to rise above Sasha's "senseless revolt," and above his fate. By becoming a Marxist Lenin not only maintained his identification with his brother, but also conquered him. He, not Sasha, understood the dictates of Marx, the revolutionary father. He, not Sasha, would carry out Marx's program of action and thereby gain history's esteem and victory over the Tsar. In short, Marxism allowed Lenin to identify himself with both Sasha and an image of his father. In Marx Lenin found a benevolent, omniscient father, a wise and methodical teacher, a fit repository for his feelings of love and respect for his real father. And in the Tsar, the perfect embodiment of the vengeful Oedipal father, he found his dangerous opponent, over whom, however, Marx promised victory.

In many ways, this early polemical writing of Lenin's bears the marks of his more mature productions: his emphasis on revolt, on the capitalist nature of Russian society, on tsarism as the "gendarme" of European capitalism;[26] his easy assumption throughout that he is a fit spokesman for the Social Democrats (that is, Marxists); and his thorough, bone-crunching demolition of his opponents' arguments, as well as his blunt, forceful style. All these are already in evidence. But one central Leninist characteristic is missing: his discussion of organization and organizational activity is fuzzy and cursory. The Party, whose role Lenin developed in such great detail later on, here has but a nebulous embodiment. Thus Lenin at this juncture knew

[25] *Ibid.*, p. 236.   [26] *Ibid.*, p. 261.

what he was fighting for, and that he was fighting; but he did not know quite how to fight. We will examine Lenin's solution of this problem in the next chapter, in our discussion of his famous pamphlet named, after the title of Chernyshevsky's novel, *What Is To Be Done?*

As was noted earlier, Lenin expected to find in St. Petersburg a chance to throw himself into important revolutionary activity. He was evidently somewhat disappointed at what actually existed. In a famous incident, which Krupskaya records from personal memory, Lenin attended a Social Democratic gathering at which someone was arguing in favor of activity aimed at educating the workers, which would be organized through a "Committee for Illiteracy." When this was mentioned:

> Vladimir Ilyich laughed, and somehow his laughter sounded laconic. I have never heard him laugh that way on any subsequent occasion.
>
> "Well," he said, "if anyone wants to save the fatherland in the Committee for Illiteracy, we won't hinder him!"[27]

Lenin came to the capital expecting broad-scale activity and found piecemeal work. The very idea of such trivial means for such great ends must have seemed incongruous to him. In the years that followed he would look for better means, but for the time he adjusted himself to the opportunities the city presented—and threw himself into work on the Committee for Illiteracy. He did so, however, with no illusions about the ultimate effect of such activity on the possibility of broad social change.

Lenin used the work of the committee to gather information about working class conditions and worker mentality and to test his powers of communication with this group. The technique that Lenin used for getting across his ideas to the workers is described by Babushkin, a workingman who was one of his "students" at this time:

[27] Krupskaya, I, 3.

He frequently tried to provoke us to speak or to arouse us to start a discussion . . . and then urge us on, compelling each to demonstrate to the other the correctness of his standpoint on a given question. Thus our lectures were made very animated and interesting, and we began to become accustomed to speaking in public. This mode of study served as an excellent way of clarifying a given question for the students. All of us greatly enjoyed these lectures, and were constantly delighted by our lecturer's power of intellect, it being a standing joke among us that an excess of brains had made his hair fall out. At the same time, these lectures trained us to do independent work, and to find material. The lecturer would hand us lists of questions which required on our part close knowledge and observation of life in the factory and workshop.[28]

It is not surprising that Lenin was a *teacher* to the working men—teaching was the family profession. The strength of Lenin's identification with his father is shown by this incorporation of teaching into his occupation of revolutionist. Earlier he had served as tutor, mainly in languages, to other members of the family. Later others were to be struck by his professorial manner which was, at the same time, devoid of rhetorical devices and pedantry.[29] The naturalness and simplicity of his speaking—and writing—style came in part from the early absorption of his father's activities. Lenin had been emulating a teacher for so long that he could speak without consciousness of style or gesture. His manner of presentation was an organic part of his personality and by its very lack of pretension captivated his listeners and made them conscious of the intensity of his conviction.[30]

[28] Quoted in Wolfe, pp. 104-105.

[29] Trotsky, *Lenin*, pp. 32-33. Also Wilson, in his perceptive sketch of Lenin in *To the Finland Station*, refers to him as "The Great Headmaster."

[30] *Ibid.*, pp. 162-71.

One of the striking things about Lenin was his lack of personal grandiosity, of which his simplicity of speech and straightforward writing style are two examples. In other respects, too, Lenin gave the impression of extreme unself-consciousness—in the utilitarianism of his style of dress, his willingness to laugh at himself, and his embarrassment at applause. In comparison with someone as theatrically oriented as, say, Trotsky (or Gandhi, in a somewhat different way) Lenin would appear ordinary; but this very ordinariness was an indication of an extraordinary man. For the lack of self-consciousness upon which Lenin's simplicity was based is a sure indicator of a highly integrated and self-confident personality; and such a personality pattern was extremely rare among the Russian revolutionists, who, on the whole, were relatively unstable individuals. Lenin was at ease with himself, confident in his cause and in his ability to lead it. He did not need theatrical props either to reassure himself of his own importance or to attract the attention of others. He was, in other words, the one man among his contemporaries who really felt comfortable in the role of leader. Because he had salvaged from his childhood enough of his own identification with his father, he could play the role of father for others without feeling that to do so was either presumptuous or incongruous. Trotsky, by contrast, never was able to develop this feeling.

In the summer of 1895 Lenin got permission to go abroad, ostensibly for his health (he did, in fact, try a couple of cures for his chronically nervous stomach), but actually to try to establish contact with G. V. Plekhanov, P. B. Axelrod, and V. P. Zasulich, the leaders of the Liberation of Labour, a Russian Marxist group with headquarters in western Europe. His contact with Plekhanov and Axelrod in particular did nothing to shake his confidence in them; both, but especially Plekhanov, had been the major sources, aside from Marx and Engels themselves, from whom Lenin had learned his Marxism and he treated them with something approaching reverence. He accepted their advice to moderate somewhat his attacks on the Liberals,[31] and returned to Russia bent on maintaining contact with them.

Not long after his return, however, Lenin was arrested and imprisoned. During the period preceding his arrest he had become increasingly conscious of the possibility, and had made a great effort to pass on his knowledge, both of contacts and conspiratorial techniques, to others—and to appoint a successor.[32] Trotsky, in his first revolutionary efforts, would take no such precautions. Trotsky was, of course, somewhat younger than Lenin at the time of his first imprisonment, but it is nonetheless indicative of his greater involvement in himself and smaller involvement in the cause that he should have given relatively less thought to carrying on the work after his possible removal.

Although he was occasionally bothered by loneliness, Lenin adjusted well to the prison routine.[33] Political prisoners were treated relatively well by the authorities and Lenin was allowed frequent visitors and unlimited access to books. Direct communication on revolutionary matters was not possible, but secret techniques were easily devised for passing on information. Lenin was thus able to maintain considerable contact with the outside world. Soon after his arrest he began work on what was to be *The Development of Capitalism in Russia* and several other pieces as well. In fact, all three of our protagonists found prison very congenial for working; none of them gave in to the melancholia that prison often bred. All three met the challenge of imprisonment by setting themselves a routine. Lenin's consisted of exercising, careful eating, and hard work.[34] He so mastered the environment that he was able to joke, as he

[31] Haimson, pp. 106-109, also deals with some of the strategic reasons for Lenin's "softer" attitude.

[32] Krupskaya, I, II. Because she was the least known to the police Krupskaya was appointed as Lenin's successor.

[33] *Ibid.*, p. 20.

[34] See Lenin's letter to his mother of February 7, 1898, on p. 53 of Elizabeth Hill and Doris Mudie, eds., *The Letters of Lenin* (London, 1937).

left on his leisurely journey to Siberian exile, that "It is a pity they let us out so soon. I would have liked to do a little more work on the book."[35]

The routine of captivity so agreed with Lenin that by the time he reached Siberia he was even rid of his stomach trouble and tendency towards insomnia. Lenin himself attributed the change in his health to the lack of "uncertainty" about his position now that he had been arrested.[36] Manifestly, of course, Lenin's position while still at large in St. Petersburg was uncertain because he did not know if and when he would be arrested. This would be especially trying for Lenin, for he had always lived a highly ordered and organized life, with the days neatly compartmentalized for various kinds of work and the future roughly mapped out. Professional revolutionary activity, by contrast, involved a disorderly life in a constantly changing context. Moreover, it was a fight, a fight against political (and implicitly parental) authority. Hence the activity itself was to some extent guilt-inducing; some residual feelings remained that the legal authorities were also legitimate, that rebellion was wrong (although it should be stressed that this seems to have been less prominent in Lenin than in Trotsky; Lenin continued to fear and respect authority but he credited it with less rectitude than did Trotsky). Also, revolutionary activity carried with it the threat of punishment, just as Lenin's earlier coveting of his mother brought with it the threat of paternal revenge. Thus as long as Lenin was free, he would be apprehensive about being caught. Once he was caught he would find, with considerable relief, that the dreaded punishment was not so bad after all and hence bearable. At the same time he would gratify his residual feelings of guilt by bearing the punishment meted out to him. Similarly, while in prison or exile, he would be much less able to participate in revolutionary work, hence the strains attendant on that activity would be held in abeyance. Finally, prison and exile promised an

[35] Quoted by Krupskaya, I, 20.
[36] Letter to his mother, March 1897. *Letters of Lenin*, p. 27.

orderly and routinized life similar to the family life of his childhood but without the same tensions.

After spending fourteen months in prison, Lenin was exiled to Shushenskoye in Yenisseisk province, where he stayed until February 1900. While there he finished *The Development of Capitalism in Russia,* and with its completion put an end for the time being to questions of self-definition and goals. From now on, with one or two major exceptions, he was to concern himself with means, not ends. He also did a translation of Webb's *The Theory and Practice of English Trade Unions* and kept up his considerable correspondence with fellow Social Democrats both in exile and in western Russia. His family served as his primary intermediaries in this matter, as well as the suppliers of his various needs, especially books.

Before leaving Lenin, on the verge of returning to Russia and thence to western Europe, with the plans already formed in his mind for an all-Russian Marxist newspaper, some aspects of his personal life must be filled in. While he was in exile he married Krupskaya, who had been one of his earliest companions during the St. Petersburg period. Also, while in exile, Lenin avoided as much as possible the squabbles and conflicts of the other exiles. Conflicts were especially great between the young Social Democrats and the old members of the populist movements who were still in the area. Lenin's solution to this problem was exactly that which he had used earlier himself—a complete break with the older revolutionists.[37]

Finally, while still in St. Petersburg, Lenin had formed intimate friendships, perhaps the only ones of his adult life, with Martov and Potresov, two Social Democrats of his generation and men who appeared to share his theoretical orientation. As his time in exile drew to a close, he envisioned the three of them, brothers in the revolutionary cause, working together in the new organization he planned. They were to be for the younger generation what Plekhanov, Zasulich, and Axelrod were for the older; he

[37] Krupskaya, I, 38.

foresaw all six of them cooperating in the mutual effort. The next few years of his life in particular would be devoted to working out his relationship with these people, especially with Martov, his soon-to-be blood brother, and Plekhanov, the father of Russian Marxism.

Bronstein: Words and Deeds

Trotsky graduated from high school in 1896 and returned to Yanovka for a "visit." His father, not yet convinced that his son was really going to turn his back on the plans he had made for him, again tried to convince Trotsky to become an engineer. The result of this controversy between father and son was

> an acute family crisis. Everybody looked depressed and seemed to suffer intensely; my elder sister would weep furtively, and nobody knew what to do about it.[38]

Finally the tension was relieved when one of Trotsky's uncles, who was visiting the farm, suggested that the boy come to stay with him for a while in Odessa, there to decide whether to study engineering or mathematics. Trotsky was rather attracted to the latter and, in any case, was anxious to get away from the farm. Max Eastman, in reporting this decision, attributes the following thoughts to this uncle, which the man probably never had, but which do sum up the situation rather well:

> What he did see was that Leon's instinct for revolt against tyranny, born in a baby's protest against this father, could never be conquered or lulled to sleep on the original battlefield.[39]

That is, as we saw in the second chapter, Trotsky had a personality out of harmony with his father's way of life. But Trotsky's revolt against his father was not to be lulled to sleep by leaving Yanovka—it was simply transferred to another setting.

[38] Trotsky, My Life, p. 103.   [39] Eastman, Leon Trotsky, p. 57.

Trotsky returned with his uncle to Odessa, but spent only a few weeks there. During this time, as for some months after, Trotsky felt that he was "looking for something. What was I trying to find? Actually, it was myself."[40] Soon this quest drew him back to Nikolayev and Shvigovsky's garden. But the questions that were unanswered before were unanswered still. Trotsky was still stoutly maintaining his populist position with its emphasis on individuality, but it was becoming more of a strain to do so. The intensity of the conflict is reflected in a practical joke which Trotsky and Shvigovsky cooked up for Alexandra Lvovna Sokolovskaya, the older sister of two of Trotsky's friends and the only Marxist of their immediate acquaintance. She and Trotsky had been drawn to each other from the start, but their ideological positions made them bitter antagonists. Additionally, Alexandra Lvovna was several years older than Trotsky so that, as mentioned in Chapter 2, she had something of the position of maternal authority, to which Trotsky could not subordinate himself.

When Trotsky returned to Nikolayev just before Christmas 1896 he was starting to entertain stronger doubts than hitherto about his Narodnik position. He confided his thoughts to Shvigovsky, who "ridiculed him and taunted him with Alexandra Lvovna's influence."[41] He then agreed to have Shvigovsky spread the story that he had become a Marxist, making sure that Alexandra heard the news. Shvigovsky next invited Alexandra to a New Year's party in the garden house where Trotsky, after first greeting her cordially and confessing his conversion, made the following midnight toast:

A curse upon all Marxists, and upon those who want to bring dryness and hardness into all the relations of life.[42]

On hearing this speech and realizing she had been deceived, Alexandra rushed out of the garden saying that some things

[40] *My Life*, p. 103.   [41] Eastman, *Leon Trotsky*, p. 78.
[42] *Ibid.*, p. 67.

were too sacred to joke about and that she would never talk to Bronstein again.

It thus would appear that Shvigovsky delayed Trotsky's conversion to Marxism. In effect, he challenged Trotsky's masculine identity when the latter mentioned his doubts about his populist faith. To give in to a woman (and clearly Trotsky felt he would be giving in to Alexandra in accepting Marxism or he would not have reacted so strongly to Shvigovsky's idea) was to be weak and Trotsky, who was so concerned with asserting his manhood against his father, could not accept any such implication. He would thus strike back against his own desire to give in to Alexandra's position by directing a verbal assault on her. But what a peculiar form of attack, to pretend to be that which one is fighting not to become! The very choice of this ploy indicates how strong the call of Alexandra's Marxism was for Trotsky. Moreover, it is another indication of Trotsky's fundamental ambivalence towards authority, of his tendency to *identify* with what he saw as a predominantly aggressive force.[43] He seemed to take into himself part of what he was fighting against, and thereby to undermine his ability to fight determinedly against it. This characteristic was to appear often in his later life, and usually with unfortunate personal consequences. As we shall see, in particular it helps to account for his self-defeating submissiveness to Stalin and the Communist Party after Lenin's death.

Although Trotsky was still without a cause, and quite conscious of the futility of his revolutionary posturings when not joined to deeds, the return to Nikolayev signified his commitment to revolution, to fighting against authority rather than giving in to it. Then in the spring of 1897 a woman burned herself to death in the Peter-Paul fortress, in protest against a Tsarist abuse.[44] The wave of industrial

[43] Anna Freud discusses identification with the aggressor as one of the ego's defensive mechanisms with respect to the id in *The Ego and the Mechanisms of Defense*, pp. 117-31.

[44] The exact cause for this protest action is unknown.

strikes that had begun in 1896 continued into the following year, so that even Odessa, which was not an industrial center, began to feel the effects of the unrest. Trotsky, who was longing to turn his revolutionary inclinations into revolutionary action, to change an internal problem into activity directed at an external opponent, found in the grievances of the workers a basis for action. Without declaring himself a Marxist on the basis of this shift (until this time he had thought of the peasantry in a vague and unrealistic way as the source of Russia's redemption), Trotsky went in search of members of the proletariat to join him in the struggle.[45]

Trotsky and the two Sokolovsky brothers found it easy to put themselves into contact with discontented workers, one of whom, an electrician named Mukhin, became one of the leaders of their group and a friend of Trotsky's for many years. Mukhin, in fact, provided Trotsky with the first, simple, vivid image of what revolution was all about. He and Trotsky had arranged to meet in a local cafe to discuss the possibility of action and Mukhin started the conversation by telling this story of how he had gotten his message across to a group of religious dissenters:

"I put a bean on the table and say, 'This is the Czar.' Around it, I place more beans. 'These are ministers, bishops, generals, and over there the gentry and merchants. And in this other heap, the plain people.' Now, I ask, 'Where is the Czar?' They point to the centre. 'Where are the ministers?' They point to those around. Just as I have told them, they answer. Now, wait," and at this point Mukhin completely closed his left eye and paused. "Then I scramble all the beans together," he went on. "I say, 'Now tell me where is the Czar? the ministers?' And they answer me, 'Who can tell? You can't spot them now' . . . . 'Just what I say. You can't spot them now.' And so I say, 'All beans should be scrambled.' "[46]

[45] *My Life*, p. 104.　　[46] *Ibid.*, p. 105.

All men and classes are equal, that was Mukhin's message, all distinctions basically false. Trotsky was thrilled by this simple story; here was the root justification for revolution. And here, too, was justification for rebelling against his father—all men are equal and all are men. His father had by right no claims superior to his own. In the maze of Trotsky's own pseudo-sophisticated arguments this commonplace idea had been lost, although it underlay most of the literature, Marxist and anti-Marxist, that Trotsky was reading. To have rediscovered it in a Marxist context made a Marxist of Trotsky and solidified for him one of his predominant political orientations, that of the rebel against authority (or, psychologically, that of the son opposing the father). But even among revolutionists some must lead and others follow, and Trotsky had not yet come to grips with this fact. By contrast, Lenin from the start substantially amalgamated the idea of rebelling against legal authority and of being authority for those for whom one was rebelling. Trotsky, whose relationship with his father provided insufficient ground for easy identification, never mastered that combination.

In the short run, however, the problem of who was to be the leader of this small and amateurish group of rebels, which Trotsky named the Southern Russian Workers' Union, did not arise; the leadership fell into Trotsky's hands on the basis of his greater abilities and willingness to work. The other members of the group, including Alexandra, who easily forgave Trotsky now that he was sincerely working for the people, and even Dr. Ziv, who was to become a lifelong enemy, readily acknowledged Trotsky's superiority and willingly followed his directives. Trotsky's pre-eminence was further established by the force of his pen. The budding organization early acquired a mimeograph machine, or hectograph, and to Trotsky fell the duty of producing material for distribution among the workers. Trotsky describes his manner of production and the reception his writing received as follows:

[128]

I wrote proclamations and articles, and printed them all out in longhand for the hectograph. At that time we didn't even know of the existence of typewriters. I printed the letters with the utmost care, considering it a point of honor to make them clear enough so that even the less literate could read our proclamations without any trouble. It took me about two hours to a page. Sometimes I didn't even unbend my back for a week, cutting my work short only for meetings and study in the groups. But what a satisfied feeling I had when I received the information from the mills and workshops that the workers read voraciously the mysterious sheets printed in purple ink, passing them from hand to hand as they discussed them! They pictured the author as a strange and mighty person who in some mysterious way had penetrated into the mills and knew what was going on in the workshops, and twenty-four hours later passed his comments on events in newly printed handbills.[47]

Trotsky's writing had transformed him from a groping adolescent into a "strange and mighty person." The promise of gratification his intellectual abilities had had when he was still in school was richly fulfilled in the workers' reactions to his words. If he was to lead at all, it would be on the basis of his words and thoughts, for they made of him not just a man but a mighty man. Isaac Deutscher, in summing up what Trotsky learned from this first revolutionary venture, comments:

The success of this first venture demonstrated to the young revolutionary the 'power of the written word.' The town was astir with rumor; the Union, admired and feared, was a factor to be reckoned with; and friend and foe imagined it to be much stronger than it was. All this was the effect of his, Bronstein's, written word. The belief in the power of the word was to re-

[47] *Ibid.*, pp. 109-10.

main with him to the end. In every situation he would turn to it as to his first and last resort; and throughout his life he would wield that power sometimes with world-shaking effect, and sometimes with lamentable failure.[48]

Thus far, Trotsky relied almost entirely on writing. He felt incapable as an orator and apparently did badly at it:

> Word-of-mouth propaganda never gave me the same satisfaction as the printed bills did at that time. My knowledge was inadequate, and I didn't know how to present it effectively. We made no real speeches in the full sense of the word. Only once, in the woods on May-day, did I have to make one, and it embarrassed me greatly. Every word I uttered seemed horribly false. . . .[49]

The attempt at a May-day speech was not an isolated instance. In his boyhood Trotsky had been greatly embarrassed at having to read his poems to the family's company:

> [My parents would] ask me to read my verses aloud before guests. I would refuse. They would urge me, at first gently, then with irritation, finally with threats. Sometimes I would run away, but my elders knew how to get what they wanted. With a pounding heart, with tears in my eyes, I would read my verses, ashamed of my borrowed lines and limping rhymes.[50]

Also, during his first year at Nikolayev, Trotsky and his friends had given, or attempted to give, lectures on "Universal Knowledge." Trotsky attempted a couple of lectures on sociology, but he soon found he did not know enough to continue and had to give up the attempt.[51] Two themes appear to underlie these three reported failures at public speaking. First, Trotsky felt that his presentations were

[48] Deutscher, *The Prophet Armed*, p. 34.
[49] *My Life*, p. 110.   [50] *Ibid.*, p. 40.
[51] Eastman, *Leon Trotsky*, pp. 69-70. Eastman attributes this incident to Trotsky's second year in Nikolayev, Trotsky to the first.

false or the thoughts borrowed; he was, in other words, speaking someone else's lines, not his own. Thus any attention he got for his efforts was not rightfully his. There seems to be an implicit fear of getting caught in his falsehoods, of being exposed for his plagiarism. Thus when he spoke under those conditions where all attention was focused on him, where he could not just jibe at others' statements but had to produce fully formulated thoughts himself, his fear of exposure produced great strain. There was always the threat that the applause would turn into ridicule, that others would find out that his manly garb was not really his own.

In other words, public speaking reawakened the threat of being humiliated and of being ignored. Trotsky's use of words served many functions for him; they were his weapon in his war against authority and his tool for attracting attention, they satisfied his need for self-expression and helped him to build up his self-esteem. Hence any time Trotsky felt his words might let him down or betray him all the early fears which this facility allowed him to ward off became imminent.

The second theme, tightly bound to the first, is that in these incidents Trotsky felt his knowledge was insufficient. Words were the *form* of Trotsky's defense against his enemies, internal and external, knowledge the *substance*. Thus in time, as his knowledge increased, as he came to feel he had incorporated the strength of others into himself, Trotsky was less bothered by the anxieties of his youth. The growth of his self-confidence is marked by the increasingly open ways in which he could express himself: from clandestine verses as a child to essays in school as an adolescent to secretly produced but public writing as a young man to full oratorical power as an adult. His speaking ability, the last to develop, would come only after he had truly mastered the body of knowledge by which he was to live, only when he was sure of who he was. As was the case with Lenin, Trotsky worked out the nature of his adult identity in terms of his ideology.

Lenin, throughout the period of his search for a satisfactory justification for action, concentrated on the relationship of man to authority and the nature of the revolutionary struggle: who was at war with whom and why. Trotsky, although also profoundly concerned with the questions of power and righteousness, was additionally trying to work out a conception of human dignity, his own included. His problem with speaking is one indication of this. The other is that Trotsky's appeals to the workingmen of Nikolayev almost always involved some question of dignity.[52] He was constantly emphasizing that workers were entitled to the respect of their fellow men.[53] In so doing, of course, he was making an appeal for himself as well. This involvement with the question of self-respect, expressed through the demand that the class he supported be esteemed, was to stay with Trotsky throughout his life. During the period just after the Bolshevik takeover of power, when the people of Russia felt humiliated by their defeat in the war, Trotsky's speeches with their claims of the importance of the workers and peasants would serve a vital psychological function. During this period Trotsky, perhaps even more than Lenin, would be the leader of the Russian people at large.

Aside from its writing and speaking activities, the Southern Russian Workers' Union organized study groups and meetings of various kinds, as well as ways of infiltrating local factories and workshops to get and distribute information. The form of the organization, which was Trotsky's creation, was a relatively sophisticated structure of cells, each with two leaders and oriented towards the creation of ever increasing numbers. By the time it was finally deprived of its leadership by the police, it had two hundred members.

The organization was, however, not without its weaknesses. It was, for example, heavily infiltrated by the police; in fact, if the police had not been so incredulous that such a young band of conspirators could stir up so much trouble

[52] Wolfe, p. 203.   [53] Eastman, *Leon Trotsky*, pp. 83-85.

the operation would have been stopped much sooner. Additionally, no provision was made for passing on the leadership should Trotsky, Alexandra, and the others be arrested. (Lenin, by contrast, had been very concerned with the question of succession.) Trotsky's inattention to this matter seems to me to indicate that he never really expected to be arrested. He was not really convinced that the governing authority was out to get him, that its members took his activities seriously—he had never had the kind of contact with the tsarist regime that Lenin had (no one in his immediate entourage or family had suffered in any way at the Tsar's hands) and he did not quite believe in the reality of what he was doing. It was undertaken too thoughtlessly, too hurriedly, and proceeded too much like a successful school venture for Trotsky really to believe in it.

Another reason for Trotsky's inattention to the question of succession was that his conception of the organization was of Trotsky doing everything. He had no firmly conceived cause, and hence no sense of the necessity for the activity to go on even if he were not there. With time he was to develop an overwhelming loyalty to the revolutionary cause, but for the present the cause was Trotsky in action and nothing more. Again, the contrast with Lenin, who undertook no action until he was sure of the cause, is striking. Although Trotsky later came to resemble Lenin in his dedication to the revolution, he never developed Lenin's ability to act only when action made sense in terms of a specified set of goals. Activity, the escape it brought from personal considerations and the attention which was its by-product, always had an independent importance for Trotsky. Hence his efforts often lacked the economy and fine timing of Lenin's.

Trotsky and his companions did, of course, realize that there was the possibility of police interference. In fact, shortly before the organization was broken up they had decided to stop operations temporarily. They agreed, however:

not to hide in case of wholesale arrests, but to let ourselves be taken, so that the police could not say to the workers: "Your leaders have deserted you."[54]

Such a decision reflected both the inexperience of the young rebels and the degree to which they still viewed their enterprise in romantic terms. Lenin, in the St. Petersburg period, continued to work even when he feared arrest was imminent, but he never considered surrendering. Trotsky, on the other hand, throughout his life, had this peculiar tendency to throw himself into the hands of the opposition. In both 1905 and 1917 he allowed himself to be arrested when escape was possible, expecting to be given a trial at which he could defend his cause. In 1905 he was able to do this, and to escape from captivity very quickly. But the willingness to take the risk indicates that he attributed some residual benevolence to authority; at a minimum he did not expect to be killed.

There is a corollary explanation for this propensity to surrender which is psychologically congruous with activity designed to ward off guilt; that is, to some extent all three of our protagonists unconsciously desired to be punished for their activities, or rather felt that it was right that they be punished. Gandhi's use of self-suffering is the clearest indication of this motive. Gandhi fought against authority by allowing men to imprison him and against his conscience by submitting to its every demand. Trotsky was clearly somewhat less inclined to allow himself to be punished in this way, and Lenin least of all. In all three cases, however, the underlying feeling that punishment is desirable and submission proper undoubtedly existed.

The police broke up the Southern Russian Workers' Union in the winter of 1898 and Trotsky himself was arrested before the beginning of 1899. Prison came as a rude shock to him. Trotsky had always been a fastidious dresser and tremendously gregarious. In fact, his affectations of dress (whether he fancied himself a conservative or a

[54] *My Life*, p. 112.

worker he always dressed the part neatly) had been one sign of his shifting self-image, and of his lack of contentment with just being himself. (Again Trotsky differs from Lenin but resembles Gandhi in this respect.) The attention he paid to his attire, as well as the attention others paid to him, had been a vital source of pleasure, one of the ways in which he regulated his internal conflicts. Now, after a brief spell in a prison in Nikolayev with another member of his group, Trotsky found himself alone in a prison at Kherson:

> My isolation was absolute and helpless. There was no walking nor were there any neighbors. I couldn't see anything through my window, which had been entirely sealed up for the winter. . . . For three months I had to wear the same underwear and I had no soap. The vermin there were eating me alive. . . . The cell was never aired. The only way I could gauge the comparative purity of the air was by the grimace that twisted the face of the assistant warden when he sometimes visited me.[55]

If there were ever a combination of circumstances designed to break a twenty year old youth of good upbringing, this was it. But Trotsky held up under the strain. As Lenin had done under less unfavorable circumstances, he set himself regular tasks: a certain number of paces up and down his cell, or devising revolutionary songs and committing them to memory. Under the trying conditions of Kherson prison Trotsky developed self-discipline to go with his industry, perseverance to go with his inventiveness. When, after several months, his parents finally succeeded in bribing a guard to give Trotsky clean clothing, soap, and some decent food, the boy had moved much closer to becoming a man.

Trotsky's imprisonment thus had the possibility of either dissuading him from further revolutionary activity, or of confirming him in his revolutionary vocation. It did the latter, for Trotsky's need to assert his manhood was greater

[55] *Ibid.*, p. 115.

than his fear of political punishment. In fact, it was his imprisonment that transformed Trotsky's rebellion against paternal authority into a long-term commitment to the overthrow of tsarism. Just as the Tsar's execution of Sasha and the other actions of political authority against Lenin directed his rebelliousness into political channels, so Trotsky's imprisonment served to convince him that there was a malevolent authority against which revolt was justifiable.

After several months at Kherson Trotsky was transferred to a new prison in Odessa which had provision for political prisoners. There he was able to establish indirect contact with others from the organization and to do some limited research. The prison library contained a large file of religious magazines which Trotsky decided to subject to materialist analysis. Through his analysis of these materials Trotsky was able to arrive at many of the propositions he later found in the writings of "Marx, Engels, Plekhanov and Mehring," and thus to make his own what until that time had been an external body of ideas.[56] Trotsky's work on freemasonry served the same function for him that Lenin's work on Russian economics did for his intellectual development. In both cases the theories were internalized and made part of the self; in both cases an ideological identity emerged.

Towards the end of 1899 the prisoners in Odessa learned of their various administrative sentences (that is, they were sentenced without trial). Trotsky, upon learning of his, tried to get his father's permission to marry Alexandra Lvovna. His father, seeing in the girl one of the sources of his son's rebellion, hotly refused, and Trotsky had to go on to the transfer prison in Moscow unwed. There, however, he was able to convince the authorities to allow them to marry, despite the lack of parental consent.

Trotsky is strangely quiet about this marriage in his autobiography, noting only that he and a female co-worker married so that they could more effectively carry out their rev-

[56] *Ibid.*, p. 122.

olutionary efforts in Siberia. Whatever the reasons for his reticence to discuss it, it appears that Trotsky was very much in love with Alexandra, by whom he had two daughters and with whom he lived throughout his stay in Siberia.[57] His love for the revolution, however, far outweighed his personal ties; for when the opportunity to escape came in the summer of 1902 Trotsky took it, evidently without hesitation, leaving Alexandra and the two children behind to manage as they could.

During the year and a half he spent in Siberia Trotsky started to gain a reputation as a writer. Signing himself as Antid Oto (from the Italian *antidoto*) he contributed regularly to a progressive newspaper appearing in his region. Without hesitation he claimed the mantle of Gleb Uspensky, a writer of similar columns about twenty-five years earlier, and proceeded to write a series of quite brilliant sketches of life in the region, which if read carefully contained biting criticism of the ongoing regime.[58] When he escaped to Samara, his reputation as a writer had preceded him. This reputation induced Kzhizhanovsky-Claire, one of Lenin's followers, to nickname him *Pero* (or "pen") and send him on to Lenin in London. Trotsky was, in fact, eager to meet Lenin and the other founders of Lenin's newspaper, the *Iskra*. The back copies of *Iskra* available in Siberia and Lenin's *What Is To Be Done?* had aroused his excitement just before his escape, and Trotsky was eager to come in contact with what he envisioned as the united leadership of Russian Marxism.

Before leaving Trotsky on the verge of making his appearance on the stage of European Marxism, one more incident from this period should be noted. When Trotsky left Alexandra in Siberia he was already the Trotsky of history, except in name. He was well on the way to becoming an accomplished Marxist and he was already a skilled organizer and publicist. All the characteristics which were to mark his later successes and failures were developed, as I

[57] Eastman, *Leon Trotsky*, pp. 118-19.
[58] Deutscher, *The Prophet Armed*, pp. 46-55.

have tried to indicate. But thus far he was still Bronstein. In the process of escaping, however, he was given a passport in which he had to fill out the name. He chose Trotsky —the name of one of his jailors in Odessa.[59] In this simple act he revealed that ambivalence which was to be so injurious to his political fortunes. Just as he had posed as a Marxist when fighting off submission to Marxism, so now he (so to speak) posed as his jailor when trying to escape from captivity. Trotsky's fatal flaw was this indecisiveness about submitting or fighting, as shown in this case by his identification with aggressive authority. He did not call himself Lenin, a name innocent of political connotations or Stalin, a name connoting steel and hardness, but Trotsky, a name which embodied the very authority against which he was to fight.

Gandhi: The Search for Truth

Gandhi left for England in September 1888. The separation had been very painful; his mother wept copiously, his wife begged him not to go.[60] Gandhi himself, although determined to go, was torn by grief and, once the boat on which he was sailing put to sea, beset with loneliness and doubts. On board ship he kept to his cabin, living on the fruits and sweets his family had packed for him. He was too shy to eat in the dining room, where he would have to ask what dishes were vegetarian in order to avoid breaking the pledge he had given his mother. And he had never used knives or forks and hence would be in danger of ridicule on that count. His English was too limited to allow him to participate easily in conversation, even if he were not shy, and so Gandhi spent the long voyage talking to one fellow Indian passenger and a friendly Englishman who tried to convince him to eat meat.

The ship arrived in England towards the end of Septem-

[59] Eastman, *Leon Trotsky*, p. 143.

[60] Gandhi discussed the departure in the June 13, 1891 edition of *The Vegetarian*. The series of articles Gandhi wrote for this journal appear in D. G. Tendulkar, *Mahatma* (Bombay, 1951), I, 373-94.

ber and Gandhi decided to disembark in white flannels. He felt ashamed when he discovered that he was the only person so attired.[61] Gandhi had left India in order to escape the burdens of guilt; in this effort he was to some extent successful. But the England that provided relief from guilt compensated for this by supplying many occasions for shame, especially during the first part of Gandhi's stay. And he was homesick:

> I would continually think of my home and country. My mother's love always haunted me. At night the tears would stream down my cheeks, and home memories of all sorts made sleep out of the question. It was impossible to share my misery with anyone.[62]

Thus Gandhi, whose fear of ridicule made him shy, had to carry inside him all the anxieties of his first extended separation from his family.

Gandhi had left India searching for an identity, for a selfhood which would allow him to feel manly and strong, for a way to overcome the fears and guilt stemming from his childhood and youthful marriage. Not surprisingly, then, he attempted to become an Englishman, the embodiment of manhood to the subject Hindus. His inclination to do so was augmented by his desire to avoid the ridicule that would come from being uncouth, but the extremes to which he carried the effort indicate that it was the achievement of a positive status as well as the avoidance of a negative one which motivated him. He bought clothing at the most fashionable stores in London, invested nineteen shillings in a chimneypot hat, took dancing, music, and elocution courses, and spent a long time each day trying to brush his hair in acceptable English style.[63] At the end of three months he decided he could not transform himself into an English gentleman. Although he maintained his punctiliousness in matters of dress, he gave up the various lessons in proper behavior and concentrated on his regular studies.

[61] Gandhi, *An Autobiography*, p. 43.
[62] *Ibid.*, p. 45.   [63] *Ibid.*, p. 51.

By the end of this period he also convinced himself that he was a vegetarian by choice and not just as a result of the vow he made to his mother.[64] Both of these acts were tokens of failure, failure to become a man as Gandhi perceived a man ideally to be; but in another sense they were his first triumphs, for Gandhi found he could bring himself joy and a sense of accomplishment through a renunciation of manhood coupled with an affirmation of his mother's moral code. As time passed he would renounce more and more of his early conception of manhood, replacing it with a feminine orientation to life and politics.

Even during the period of his attempted Anglicization Gandhi had not abandoned his academic work. He had enrolled in the Inner Temple, one of the four Inns of Court at which one could take residency in order to qualify for the bar examination. The examination itself was notoriously easy, but Gandhi set about his course work seriously. Instead of relying on a quick reading of prepared summaries (ponies, cribs, or canned briefs as they would be called here), he went through all the basic texts, and Mayne's *Hindu Law* as well, and read his Roman Law in the original Latin. This work did not suffice to keep him busy and so he also studied for the matriculation examination at London University, which he failed once because his Latin was inadequate but which he passed with ease the second time around.[65] He passed his bar examination in June 1891, immediately prior to his return to India. Although he discusses these achievements very little in his *Autobiography*, just as he paid scant attention to those honors he won in schools in India, it is important to note that Gandhi was a conscientious worker of no mean ability, for all of his achievements in England were based on mastery of a language not naturally his own. That he could master English and other languages and subjects as well is indicative of both his abilities and perseverance.

Gandhi spends little time discussing his academic life

[64] *Ibid.*, p. 48.   [65] Fischer, *Life of Gandhi*, p. 35.

because, in the long run, he decided that the skills developed through this work were relatively unimportant. By contrast, he felt that the basis he set for himself in dietetic experimentation was of great subsequent import. As noted above, the first step was his affirmation of vegetarianism; by choosing to be vegetarian he adopted as his own one part of his Hindu—and his mother's—heritage. He first changed an external rule into an internal command. Then began a lifelong process of progressive simplification of his diet, of increasing denial of the right of the body to indulgence and gratification.

Vegetarianism was just one aspect of Gandhi's interest in diet. With time, the quantity of food as well as the frequency of eating became increasingly important. Starting from a point in childhood when he felt committed to eating all kinds of food, he gradually evolved to a position where he fasted often, ate a very limited variety of foods and frequently subsisted on one meal a day. Gandhi's primary model for this behavior had been his mother, who first imposed the claims of vegetarianism on him and had been a frequent keeper of fasts. Moreover, she, like many Hindu wives, used the fast to punish others for transgressions. When displeased with the behavior of some member of the family she would deprive herself of food. Part of Gandhi's genius lay in taking this homely practice and applying it in a political context, against the English or his own followers as the occasion demanded. In the fast, in fact, we see the highest symbolic representation of *satyagraha* or *ahimsa*, Gandhi's singular contribution to political practice.

But Gandhi in 1892 was a long way from the Gandhi of 1906 who utilized nonviolence for political purposes. Although he had come out of his shyness enough to join in the activities of fellow vegetarians, mainly English, while in London, he was still unable to speak to an audience, even a small audience of his friends from a prepared text.[66] Un-

[66] In Gandhi's last attempt to make a speech in England, some parting words to his fellow vegetarians, he chose to tell a story which

comfortable in his English environment, he had insufficient knowledge of his Indian heritage to propose a counter-model to the English way of life. In fact, he had not even read the *Bhagavad Gita*, the sacred heart of the *Mahabharata*, the greatest Indian epic poem. The *Gita* is a narration of a conversation between Rama Khrisna (God) and Arjuna, a legendary Hindu warrior, in which Khrisna defines the basic precepts of Hindu religion. Gandhi was so little conversant with his spiritual traditions that it was not until he was in England that he read the *Gita*—in Sir Edwin Arnold's English translation.[67]

Gandhi's vegetarianism, representing his attempt to come to grips with his relationship to his mother, is one reflection of the fact that change in locale had not allowed him to escape completely his feelings of guilt. In retroactive compensation to his father for his lustfulness and usurping manliness he was increasingly identifying with his mother in her passive opposition to his father. Another incident Gandhi recounts is also indicative of his continuing feelings of guilt. He was attending a vegetarian conference in Portsmouth and unknowingly ended up lodging in a house frequented by women who were not "very scrupulous about their morals." In the evening Gandhi and a friend of his were

---

is indicative of the relationship between his inability to speak and his feelings of unmanliness:

> I had with great care thought out a speech, [he reports] which would consist of a very few sentences. But I could not proceed beyond the first sentence. I had read of Addison that he began his maiden speech in the House of Commons, repeating 'I conceive' three times, and when he could proceed no further, a wag stood up and said, 'The gentleman conceived thrice but brought forth nothing.' I had thought of making a humorous speech taking this anecdote as the text. I therefore began with it and stuck there. My memory entirely failed me and in attempting a humorous speech I made myself ridiculous. (Gandhi, p. 61)

Thus Gandhi left England as he had arrived, feeling impotent and ashamed.

[67] On the relationship between "Gandhian" ideas and traditional Hindu concepts, see Joan V. Bondurant, *Conquest of Violence: The Gandhian Philosophy of Conflict* (Princeton, 1958); and Gopinath Dhawan, *The Political Philosophy of Mahatma Gandhi* (Ahmedabad, 1957).

playing bridge with the landlady. Gradually the innocent table banter took on an "indecent" tinge:

> My companion and our hostess began to make indecent [jokes] as well. I did not know that my friend was an adept in the art. It captured me and I also joined in. Just when I was about to go beyond the limit, leaving the cards and the game to themselves, God through the good companion uttered the blessed warning: 'Whence this devil in you, my boy? Be off, quick!'
>
> I was ashamed. . . . Remembering the vow I had taken before my mother I fled from the scene.[68]

This is the only time until much later in his life that Gandhi reports having sexual desire for someone other than his wife. Here the guilt he already felt about any sexual activity was compounded by feelings that he had betrayed, or could have betrayed, both his mother and his wife. In a sense the pledge his mother made him take to abstain from sex was a plea to him to save his love for her. Gandhi was disloyal to his mother and challenged his father just by making love to Kasturbai; the contemplated break with monogamy would be a compounded sin.

Gandhi, perhaps at the time and certainly later, attributed his salvation from this sin to God's intervention. In this case the voice of God was external; gradually it was to become internal so that Gandhi would talk of obeying the dictates of the "voice within." He was able, in other words, gradually to modify the internalized image of his father from a vengeful man bent on punishing him to a benevolent and basically feminine guide for his every action. The price of this change was giving up the quest for masculinity. At the same time, however, Gandhi preserved a conception of authority as powerful and dangerous. But this image, originally internal, he externalized, with enormously important political consequences. This twofold process of internalization/externalization began after Gandhi

---

[68] Gandhi, *Autobiography*, p. 71.

returned to India and developed more rapidly during his prolonged stay in South Africa.

Gandhi's return to India was practically as disturbing as the departure. His journey to England had been precipitated by his father's death. On his return to India he discovered his mother had died while he was away. The family had decided not to tell him so as to spare him the shock while he was in a foreign land. Gandhi reports that his grief was even greater than over his father's death.[69] To some extent guilt feelings must have been aroused as well, for Gandhi had gone to England despite his mother's wishes, and now she was dead. It may have seemed as if his absence were responsible for her demise. His feelings of guilt were probably ameliorated to some extent, however, by the fact that he had tried so hard to keep his vows to his mother while he was gone. His vegetarianism and sexual abstinence provided even more relief than had his father's forgiveness of his childhood theft; but his confession in the latter case and his devotion in the former were alike in allowing Gandhi to feel at least partially redeemed in his parents' eyes.

Gandhi's loss of his mother, aside from creating an additional burden of guilt for him to manage, probably augmented his tendency to identify with her. As Freud puts it:

> If one has lost an object or has been obliged to give it up, one often compensates oneself by identifying oneself with it and by setting it up once more in one's ego, so that here object-choice regresses, as it were, to identification.[70]

So it was that, for a time after his father's death, Gandhi intensified his efforts to add to his masculinity, to be as much as, if not more than, a man than his father. Eventually the strain of this attempt proved too great, and Gandhi retreated to a way of acting based on the model of his

[69] *Ibid.*, p. 87.
[70] Freud, *New Introductory Lectures on Psychoanalysis*, p. 63.

mother. Her death would thus have lent impetus to a process already well underway.[71]

Gandhi's family, especially his older brother who had financed his education, had built high hopes on his training as a barrister. With the prestige and abilities which his degree a signified, he was to build up the family fortunes and achieve a position comparable to his father's prime ministerships. In order to prepare himself for the legal practice which would result in these attainments, Gandhi spent some time in Bombay, where he hoped to get some briefs and experience before the high court. The effort was, however, disappointing. Gandhi refused to pay the bribes to the court "touts" and hence had a hard time getting cases. When he finally did get one, he found himself unable to talk in court and had to return the fee to his client.[72] His only success in Bombay was in drafting a memorial for a client and thus, despairing of practicing courtroom law and unable even to get a job as a high school teacher, Gandhi returned to Rajkot where he earned a comfortable living drafting petitions.

While he had been in England, Gandhi had come in contact with the man who was now the British Political Agent in the area. At this time Gandhi's brother was working for the ruler of Porbandar, a neighboring principality. The latter was in trouble with the political agent and Gandhi's brother asked Gandhi to see the Englishman to plead the ruler's cause. Gandhi was reluctant to presume on his fleeting acquaintance with the man, but finally agreed to see him. Much to his surprise the "sahib" would not even hear his plea and, when Gandhi persisted in talking, had him physically removed from the premises.[73] Gandhi was very insulted and distressed. He wanted to start a law suit against the official but was persuaded not to do so.

His situation had now become impossible. He had been

[71] Cf. Sebastian DeGrazia's treatment of Gandhi's identification with his mother in "Mahatma Gandhi: The Son of His Mother," in *The Political Quarterly*, XIX, 4 (Oct.-Dec. 1948), pp. 336-48.
[72] *Ibid.*, p. 94.   [73] *Ibid.*, p. 98.

a failure in Bombay and had antagonized authority in Kathiawad. Where could he now look for success? Luckily he was offered a chance to go to South Africa to do some work for a Moslem firm which had offices in Porbandar, and Gandhi, although the specific nature of his work was not spelled out for him and the pay was not particularly good, accepted. He claims he was sorry to leave his wife, who now had two children, but Gandhi left "full of zest to try [his] luck in South Africa."[74] Actually Gandhi was still plagued by jealousy of his wife, so that his sorrow at parting was at least partially offset by being able to remove himself from a stressful situation. It should also be noted that other lawyers had born insults from the British as great as or greater than Gandhi's; but Gandhi's great sensitivity to humiliation made it impossible for him to continue to work in such a situation.

Gandhi called this insult one of the turning points of his life.[75] By this he undoubtedly meant that it impelled him to go to South Africa, where his spiritual and political development crystalized. It was a turning point in another sense as well. Throughout his life, but especially after his father's death, Gandhi had been accusing himself of being both ridiculous and evil. As I have stressed, he carried a heavy load of both shame and guilt. Both of these feelings involve a mental state wherein the individual feels he really does deserve punishment or humiliation. But in the incident with the political agent, for the first time Gandhi could feel that there was little or no basis in his own action for the humiliation he had received and the violence that had been done to him. Although he had presumed to some extent on an acquaintanceship, he genuinely seems to have felt that the treatment he received was all out of proportion to the nature of his "offense." Thus action was possible. The questions of guilt and shame were no longer just internal problems; they had been partially transformed into questions of powers and rights of external authority. If at this junc-

[74] *Ibid.*, p. 103.   [75] *Ibid.*, p. 99.

ture Gandhi had developed to the point where he could have acted against the agent, and if the political situation had been one where such action would not have led to disaster, then the trip to South Africa would not have been necessary, either psychologically or occupationally. But because Gandhi could not act, yet felt that action was justified, some escape from this frustrating situation was necessary. Additionally, of course, Gandhi had not come to grips with the question of "being Indian" (which can be used as a catchall expression for the various questions of identity that Gandhi had to answer for himself) and hence escape from India provided relief on these grounds as well. It was the incident with the political agent, however, which in a small way prepared Gandhi to deal with the treatment Indians got in South Africa.

Gandhi arrived in Durban, Natal in May 1893. In short order he overcame the suspiciousness of Abdulla Sheth, the man on whose lawsuit he was to work. Sheth then decided to send Gandhi to Pretoria, where the defendant lived and the case was being considered. Thus about a week after he arrived, Gandhi purchased a first class train ticket and set off. From Durban to Maritzburg Gandhi was not bothered. At the latter city, however, where the train stopped in late evening, a railroad official gave Gandhi the choice of riding in a van compartment or getting off the train. According to this agent "coloured" men were not allowed to ride first class. Gandhi protested and was put off the train by force.[76]

Again Gandhi's dignity had been affronted and again because he was an Indian. In the long cold night at the Maritzburg station that followed the incident Gandhi pondered what to do. His first inclination was to give up and go back to India. He had gone to South Africa, after all, "only for a single case prompted by self-interest and curiosity."[77] He

[76] Gandhi, *Autobiography*, pp. 109-17; also see *Satyagraha in South Africa* (Madras: S. Ganesan, 1928), pp. 69-70.
[77] Gandhi, *Satyagraha*, p. 69.

was "merely the witness and the victim of these wrongs."[78] As the night progressed Gandhi thought:

> It would be cowardice to run back to India without fulfilling my obligation. The hardship to which I was subjected was superficial—only a symptom of the deep disease of colour prejudice. I should try, if possible, to root out the disease and suffer hardships in the process. Redress for wrongs I should seek only to the extent that would be necessary for the removal of colour prejudice. So I decided to take the next available train to Pretoria.[79]

By the time morning came Gandhi had evolved from a private citizen to a political actor. Several things were involved in this transformation. First, he again had been set upon for doing something which did not violate any of his personal moral precepts. It was not because he was Gandhi, sinful and unworthy, that he had been put off the train, but because he was an Indian. As in the incident with the political agent in Kathiawad, Gandhi was blameless by his own lights and hence free to act.

Moreover, Gandhi was now operating in a context which had less strain associated with it than his native area. Just as Lenin went to St. Petersburg to escape the family and begin his revolutionary work, and Trotsky chose the cities rather than the country as his arena, so South Africa was for Gandhi a new land devoid of the debilitating connotations of the old. Further, in South Africa Gandhi found himself to be a man of superior talents. When he arrived in Pretoria and told of his experiences, he was informed that indignity was the common lot of the Indian and that no one felt powerful or skilled enough to do anything about it. In other words, the Gandhi who in India was, by his own standards, a failure as a barrister, inferior in ability to his peers in education and caste, in South Africa was superior

[78] *Ibid.*   [79] Gandhi, *Autobiography*, p. 112.

〖 148 〗

with respect to certain strategic abilities even to those who were his employers. He found in the South African Indian community what Lenin and Trotsky found in the working class—a humble group which would grant respect and recognize power, and which was so obviously abused that one could fight for it against authority with a clear conscience. And, because the groups for which these men were fighting were not groups to which they naturally belonged, all of them could feel that their actions were disinterested and altruistic—desireless, to use Gandhi's term. They were thus able to hide from themselves their personal stake in the struggle, to relieve thereby the strain associated with the intense mental conflict they were undergoing. A problem which originally was between father and son was thus gradually transformed into one between some group of people and legal authority. Roles were changed, emotions were directed toward new objects and the conflict was impersonalized. In the next part of this chapter an attempt will be made to spell out the nature and form of this process more systematically.

When Gandhi realized that in his new environment he enjoyed a rather unusual status, his problems with speaking disappeared. Soon after he arrived in Pretoria he called a meeting of "all the Indians" and gave a substantial speech stressing the need for certain reforms within the Indian community if the Indians were to gain the respect of the British.[80] Because in fact he no longer felt as unworthy, and because ostensibly the question of his own worthiness was irrelevant, the shy, inarticulate barrister of London and Bombay was replaced by a highly vocal advocate of Indian rights.

Another aspect of the South African situation which helped turn Gandhi toward public activity was that the abuse heaped upon him, first at Maritzburg and then at several points during the remaining part of the trip to Pretoria,

[80] *Ibid.*, p. 125.

gratified his desire for punishment. Gandhi's enormous feelings of guilt could not be managed on the basis of externalization alone. It was not sufficient to see some outside authority rather than himself as evil and dangerous. He had to complement his aggressive (although nonviolent) actions against authority with aggressive actions against himself. Even Lenin and Trotsky, as was mentioned earlier, were not entirely free from this need to bear the consequences of their felt sins. Both of the Russians, however, fought against the yearning for punishment, Lenin more successfully than Trotsky, while Gandhi gave in to his desire and turned it to his political advantage.

Closely related to the last point is the fact that, as he notes, the incident represented for Gandhi a test of his courage. Gandhi had to decide whether to stay and face the situation or flee. In this sense the situation tested his courage in the conventional British sense of the word: to stand one's ground is to be a man. Similarly Gandhi had found a basis for pride, again in the conventional sense of that word, in this situation. But courage and pride were to take on distinctive forms with Gandhi. While holding on to the emotions as such, he would gradually transform their bases. His pride would become the self-respect of the man who could suffer indignities without giving way to feelings of humiliation. His courage would be "non-aggressive and internalized . . . , involving the capacity to suffer pain without retaliation, not to retreat but to stay and suffer more."[81]

Gandhi suffered further indignities and some physical discomfort on the trip from Maritzburg to Pretoria. Once in Pretoria he established contact with much of the Indian population and began to study the conditions of Indian life in South Africa. Primarily, however, he devoted his time to his client's law case, succeeding, in a relatively brief period of time, in getting both parties to agree to an arbitrated settlement out of court. When the case was settled in favor of his client he persuaded the latter to allow payments to be

[81] Rudolph, "The New Courage," p. 113.

made on an installment basis so that the loser would not be ruined by his loss.[82] In the process Gandhi learned "the true practice of law. I had learnt to find out the better side of human nature and to enter men's hearts. I realized that the true function of a lawyer was to unite parties riven assunder."[83] The essence of Gandhi's manipulation of this situation is that he turned an aggressive confrontation into a peaceful encounter. He was not comfortable in the role of prosecutor, helping one man by hurting another. Just as his shame had been too great to allow him to defend his client in an Indian courtroom, so his guilt precluded the easy performance of verbal aggression in a similar context. By removing the conflict from the courtroom, in which he was not as yet really at ease, and reorienting it from its original acrimoniousness to a newly found mutual understanding, Gandhi relieved himself of the strain that otherwise would have accompanied the performance of his tasks as a barrister. If his approach had not been successful, he might have been driven back to more conventional tasks which would have satisfied him less. But his "non-violent" solution did work, and thus it became a model for many of his subsequent actions in South Africa.

After completing his work on the case in Pretoria, Gandhi returned to Durban and prepared to go back to India. Just prior to departure, however, he discovered that Indians were about to be deprived of their right to elect members to the Natal Legislative Assembly. Gandhi agreed to stay on for a short while to help fight this action, and thus began the long career of political protest which marked Gandhi's stay in South Africa. The resolution formed at Maritzburg not to allow the railroad to treat Indians in a humiliating manner gradually became transformed into a more general drive for Indian rights.

Unfortunately, I do not have the space here to recount the events of the years 1894-1905, important as they were

[82] Gandhi, *Autobiography*, pp. 131-34.
[83] *Ibid.*, p. 134.

in Gandhi's life. During this period Gandhi spent some time in India, with Gokhale and other leaders of Indian nationalism. In India he found that his mastery of speaking was still insecure and he had to speak largely from prepared texts.[84] In South Africa, however, his talents continued to develop, and with them the scope of his activity. He gradually became, to whites and Indians alike, a symbol of the Indian community in South Africa, and frequently was in danger of physical attack both from the whites and those Indians who disapproved of his willingness to seek just compromises with authority.

During most of this period, Gandhi considered himself a loyal subject of the British Empire. He fought local abuses of authority rather than authority as such. In fact, Gandhi never managed his conflicts in quite the manner of Lenin and Trotsky. Both of the latter viewed the world in bifurcated terms, with the workers and goodness on one side and the Tsar, capitalism, and evil on the other. This dichotimization of the world was one of the ways they attempted to deal with their ambivalent feelings towards authority. By splitting their feelings up they could attempt to love unreservedly their followers and their ideological gods while hating deeply the authority against which they fought. Gandhi, too, distinguished sharply between truth and nontruth, which was his characteristic way of talking about good and evil, but he usually did not assume that any group of men was all good or truthful and another all evil. In terms of his abstractions he could be very rigid and dogmatic, and as stubborn and unbending as Lenin. But he lacked a necessary ingredient of a fully developed black-and-white view of the world: he was too trustful. Gandhi, even more than Trotsky, viewed his environment as being capable of great harmony and warmth. Lenin did not. Lenin's perception of reality was, at root, of Lenin alone in a hostile world; it was only with an effort that Lenin was able to keep his practices from leading to such a condition.

[84] *Ibid.*, p. 228.

His great tendency to split the party, which prevailed throughout the period of his life we come to next, is just one indication of this propensity towards self-isolation. It was only with great strain on his nerves, with resultant insomnia and stomach trouble, that Lenin could get himself to rely in any way on others. This does not imply that his relationships with other men were always harsh and acrimonious; they were not. They tended to become so, however, whenever Lenin found himself dependent on others. When he could feel that others were depending on him, as during the period in St. Petersburg in the 1890s, he could be cordial and charming. But when, as during most of the exile period, he was dependent on others in a multitude of ways, Lenin could be a very prickly character indeed.

Gandhi, by contrast (and Trotsky to a lesser extent), basically expected that others could be trusted to keep their word and only gradually came to develop enough mistrust of his foes so that his actions could be truly effective. The combination of his own inhibitions about aggressive actions and his feelings that, at a minimum, others were not all bad, often led him into situations where he was betrayed.

Before discussing the events of 1906, the year in which Gandhi finally developed the full form of his justification for political action, it should be noted that the years preceding it were filled not only with Gandhi's increased political activity but also, as throughout his life, with continuing spiritual experiments, revolving about such things as diet, education, and dress. One sign of his development had been his final severing of relations with Sheik Mehtab, whom Gandhi expelled from his circle after he had brought a prostitute into Gandhi's house in Durban.[85] Another was that, as he managed to control his diet and other things more to his satisfaction, he increasingly turned his attention to the question of sexual relations.

Despite occasional temptations Gandhi had remained loyal and faithful to Kasturbai throughout their marriage.

[85] Gandhi, *Autobiography*, pp. 162-63.

Although he was sometimes separated from her, when he was with her, as he was during a substantial part of the time in South Africa, his desire to make love to her was very strong. From about 1900 on he made sporadic efforts to control his passion, but separate beds and going to bed only when exhausted were insufficient safeguards.[86] Then in the early months of 1906 Gandhi broke up his household temporarily to help, as leader of a medical corps, put down a Zulu rebellion in Natal. In the process of this work it became Gandhi's conviction that "procreation and the consequent care of children were inconsistent with public service."[87] He turned his thoughts increasingly towards *brahmacharya*, the Hindu concept of self-restraint which leads one closer to God. This principle had been an important guide to his dietary experiments for some time, but he now decided to take a *vow* of lifelong celibacy. Celibacy was a major step in becoming a *brahmachari*, one not unusual among Hindus but seldom undertaken at such a young age (Gandhi was thirty-six). After taking the vow, Gandhi remained perfectly true to it.

Both the form and fact of this event demand comment. To begin with the former, Gandhi had been taking vows for years—his promise to his father never to steal again and his threefold vow to his mother before going to England are the most important early examples. They were his safeguards against forbidden impulses. Once Gandhi made a vow, action contrary to it could be interpreted as making that vow into a lie. And lying for Gandhi was a cardinal sin. His lying had been an early expression of his revolt against his father and his truthfulness a corresponding token of his submission to parental and other authorities. In other words, Gandhi took vows in order to ward off actions which would induce guilt.

It should be added that Lenin used slogans very much as Gandhi used vows, although in his case we have few examples of the kind of private promises that are so common

[86] *Ibid.*, pp. 204-207.   [87] *Ibid.*, p. 206.

in Gandhi's life. But both relied on concise dicta which provided for courses of action in both their private and public lives. For each such formulas served a vital function: they were the conscious manifestations of the mechanisms which were being used to handle intense, sharply focused conflict, the immutable hearts of the systems of rationalizations which were their respective ideologies. The political import of this form of conflict resolution is very great: because the men enunciated positions that were strongly held, simply formulated, and provided a guide to action, they were able to communicate their beliefs to a broad audience. Trotsky, whose oratorical skills were in some respects far superior to either of the other two men, would hit upon simple, comprehensible slogans when in the heat of battle; but when he had time for reflection the main lines of his ideas would be obscured in a mass of subtleties. Although he would have no trouble, until late in his life, communicating with fellow intellectuals, he would often be limited to that audience. Trotsky's life, while characterized by problems of guilt similar to those of Gandhi and Lenin in content, had not provided him with a sharply focused set of problems with which he could come to grips. As a result his ideological efforts were more diffuse, cleverer but less powerful than Gandhi's and Lenin's.

As already mentioned, in substance Gandhi's vow was a self-disciplined attempt to ward off guilt-inducing actions. For Gandhi sexual activity was inherently aggressive—it was his own sexual indulgence, after all, which he associated with his father's death.[88] For years after that event Gandhi had tried to ward off the desire to submit to his father by using the mechanism of imitating him. He had done everything in his power to be manly, but each effort had been marked by failure. Gradually he retreated from the idealized masculinity represented by his father and the British; but in this retreat he had another basis of support,

---

[88] Rudolph emphasizes what might be termed the anal-sadistic quality of Gandhi's attitudes toward sexual activity, in "Self-Control and Political Potency," p. 89.

a reserve of strength which came more and more into play. As he progressively identified less with his father, until he eventually gave up sexual activity, the quintessential mani- festation of his masculinity, he increased his identification with his mother, until, via that same act of renunciation, he brought to its logical extreme the vow he had made to his mother before leaving India for the first time. To his practices of vegetarianism, nursing, and fasting Gandhi added sexual abstinence (which was his image of what women desired),[89] and thus completed the transformation. And with the vow that marked the change came great feel- ings of release, of new energies and a new purity. Just as Lenin had freed himself from the inhibiting force of guilt through the adoption of revolutionary Marxism as his per- sonal creed, so Gandhi freed himself by taking this vow. Within a matter of months after the vow was taken Sat- yagraha was born.

In September 1906 Gandhi and others called a meeting in Johannesburg to consider possible courses of action against the newly enacted Asiatic Bill, a harsh registration act for all Indians in the Transvaal which promised to de- prive the Indians of their few remaining rights.[90] One of the resolutions passed by this meeting called for nonsubmission to the ordinance. In supporting this resolution one of the speakers swore in God's name that he would not submit to the act. Gandhi was immediately enthusiastic; here was a call to use publicly the mechanism he had recently affirmed in managing his private conflicts. Political activity could be sanctified and the will necessary for it strengthened by this means.[91]

By becoming a *bramachari* Gandhi had substantially re- duced the guilt he felt as a consequence of his father's

[89] Gandhi's insistence on his mother's saintliness and on his wife's lack of sexual desire (e.g., *Autobiography*, p. 205) point to an image of women as creatures used by men to satisfy their cravings but posses- sing no sexual desire of their own. As a man abstinence would be a close approximation for Gandhi to this state of desirelessness.

[90] Gandhi, *Satyagraha in South Africa*, pp. 156-58.

[91] *Ibid.*, p. 163.

death. Implicitly, and with passing time increasingly explicitly, he had come to think of himself in feminine terms.
He therefore no longer represented a challenge to his father's authority, but rather could view himself as one whom
his father could learn to love and respect—as he presumably did Gandhi's mother. This was the frame of mind he
was in at the time of the September meeting, more at ease
with himself and less conscience-stricken than at any previous time. Then with the vow a link was established between
the private and the public aspects of his life. Just as a vow
had marked his dedication to sexual renunciation, so the
September vow sanctified his role in politics and made clear
to him what the course of Indian action must be: feminine
(that is, nonviolent) resistance must be used against the
oppression of British masculine authority.

Soon after the meeting this new course of action was
given the name "satyagraha," or "the Force which is born
of Truth and Love or non-violence."[92] Gandhi had at last
managed to harness his energies to an absolute, one less
defined and elaborated than the Marxism of Lenin and
Trotsky, but serving a similar function of justification.
Gradually this conception of himself and his course of action would develop into a more programmatic statement
of principles and a more intricate pattern of revolutionary
means, but the crucial starting point had been found.

Thus at thirty-six Gandhi reached the point that Lenin
had reached by thirty and Trotsky by twenty-three. Each
had arrived at a conception of self which involved public
action wedded to an eternal verity. Each had become a revolutionist (although, to be sure, *satyagraha* was a different
form of revolutionary activity from Russian Marxism).
And having reached the point in the men's lives at which
they were revolutionists, it thus becomes appropriate to
try to answer the question, as systematically as we can, of
why and how they became opponents of established
authority.

[92] *Ibid.*, p. 173.

Why Does a Man Rebel?

We have now taken the three revolutionists through the period that Erik Erikson terms young adulthood or manhood. The crisis which generally emerges during this period is that of "intimacy vs. isolation."[93] Here the individual must work out the nature of his relationships with peers, especially of the opposite sex. A balance must be struck between the loss of individuality and the ability to discriminate on the one hand, and complete repudiation of intimate relations with peers on the other. With respect to this crisis, no general pattern emerges for the three men. Lenin established a close and lasting tie with Krupskaya, the sexual nature of which is unknown, while generally remaining aloof from close ties to others. Martov, Potresov, and Plekhanov are the main exceptions here, and, as we shall see in Chapter 4, these friendships did not last. Trotsky, on the other hand, had what amounts to an affair with Alexandra Lvovna and had warm relations with many of his comrades-in-arms, but these relationships were secondary to his primary emotional involvement in revolution. Gandhi, whose marriage really forced him into facing these problems very early, had a constant tension with regard to intimacy. He separated himself from his wife, children, and parental family with great frequency but always returned to them. On the whole, however, his relationship with his family was one of discomfort, marked by a tendency to withdraw. He formed, on the other hand, close friendships with many people, men and women, younger and older. In sum, Trotsky and Gandhi tended to ignore their parental and conjugal families while forming close ties with those outside the family. Lenin, to the contrary, maintained quite intimate ties with his parental family and generally stayed close to and trusted in Krupskaya, but formed few close ties with others. This division parallels that of Gandhi and Trotsky as basically trustful and Lenin as basically mistrustful.

[93] Erikson, *Childhood and Society*, pp. 263-66.

The rather chaotic conditions of the emotional ties of these three men during young manhood stems in part from the fact that they still had to deal with questions of identity, which at root are questions of how to conceive of oneself in terms of the images retained of one's elders. In each case the identity arrived at during this period involved revolutionary activity justified in terms of absolutes. Let us see if we can develop the major psychological themes (and their political implications) which resulted in what we can call, to the extent that there are a set of elements shared by the men, the revolutionary personality. At the same time there will be an attempt made to indicate the major differences among the three. In so doing we will restate in more general form what we learned about the men in Chapter 2.

The themes or variables in terms of which we will discuss the men are trust, pride, courage, industry, and confidence and drive.[94] These terms represent the values that result from the successful management of the problems of the various stages of psycho-sexual growth. Each denotes a continuum from complete or perfect possession of the value to the total absence of it, the ends of these continua never being met with in actuality. In the present case systematic categories for classifying and measuring behavior in terms of these dimensions have not been developed, and the development of such schemes will have to precede any testing of the hypotheses here put forward. Yet, admittedly on a fairly intuitive basis, it does seem possible to make some comparative statements about the men with respect to these values, and to indicate the political consequences thereof. All such statements should be regarded as hypotheses in need of testing rather than tested hypotheses, with the material thus far presented hopefully providing some presump-

[94] This list of values, which represent the favorable outcomes of the oral through adolescent phases respectively, is based on the work of Erikson (e.g., *Childhood and Society*, p. 274), but differs from his list in some respects. I do not believe, however, that there is any contradiction involved in the differences. Rather I am merely focusing on those aspects of the stages which are most important for my purposes while Dr. Erikson finds other outcomes more to his point.

tion in favor of their utility but not constituting proof of either the correctness of my interpretations of the three men or the fit of other men who would meet the definition of revolutionist proposed in Chapter 1 with the model of the revolutionary personality which will be developed here.

The first value is trust, which results from, as noted in Chapter 2, a relative minimum of frustration and loss during the oral phase of development. With respect to this value Lenin ranked lowest, Gandhi highest, and Trotsky almost as high as Gandhi. Judging from Lenin's life, those who are low in trust (or basically mistrustful) will be extremely reluctant to expose themselves to others, to leave themselves vulnerable to their environments. Hence they will act with extreme caution, will not take a position until they are sure of their ground, and because they thus make safer bets, will appear to be of sounder judgment and greater confidence, everything else being equal, than those who are basically trustful and accordingly act more impulsively and take positions more publicly and casually. In those situations where action without premeditation is necessary, however, the basically mistrustful person will be less well equipped psychologically than the trustful person. Gandhi and Trotsky, who were more trustful, both had the spontaneous responsiveness that Lenin lacked—as indicated, for example, by Trotsky's impetuous involvement in his first revolutionary activity and Gandhi's immediate recognition of the significance of the oath proposed at the meeting out of which *satyagraha* grew.

Those people who are basically mistrustful will also be reluctant to rely on others, while those who are trustful will be more willing to place themselves in others' hands. Thus Lenin was most comfortable and effective when he was in a position of control with the very minimum of reliance on others, needing only their obedience. When he was in a bargaining situation, or needed others to supply him with anything, he underwent great strain, based, one would suppose, on his assumption that others would not perform in the required manner. This will become quite apparent when we examine his reactions in the party congress of 1903 and after the takeover of power. Those who are basically trustful, by contrast, will tend to believe in promises (and hence will strike bargains) and thus are more likely to be deceived and betrayed, with probable ill consequences both in terms of their ability to survive and their hold on their followers. Needless to say, in those political contexts, such as (at least to a considerable extent) the British Empire, where honesty is accepted as one of the rules of the political game, the debilitating consequences of trust will be less than in a kill-or-be-killed situation like revolutionary Russia.

The greatest danger for the person who is mistrustful, aside from the possibility of immobilization as a consequence of his overarching pessimism (which might lead to that inactivity which accompanies extreme skepticism), is isolation. There will be a tendency towards the continual cutting off of associations, if Lenin's behavior is any guide, so that "splitting" proclivities will be one of the political hallmarks of the mistrustful. The willingness to split, however, carries with it benefits as well as risks, for it means that the individual will be less bound by sentiments of loyalty or a feeling for the need to cooperate than his fellow who has faith in his brothers. He will have, in other words, greater maneuverability. He will also tend to view the world in more rigidly dichotomized terms than will a more trustful man, for he tends to view his fellow men as potential betrayers rather than potential friends. This mistrust will, as indicated by the tendency to split, also permeate the person's view of his fellow revolutionists. It is easier for the more optimistic man to blur the distinctions between enemies and friends, for he believes that basically the people in his environment want to respond favorably to him. In terms of the dichotomized world view which is characteristic of revolutionists, however, the problem of guilt and its management is apparently more important than that of trust.

The second value, which results from overcoming the feeling of shame which originates in the anal phase, is pride.

With respect to pride, and the self-assurance and naturalness of manner which results from it, Lenin ranks highest,
Trotsky second, and Gandhi last. Pride was not the major
issue for Lenin at any discernable point in his adolescence
or adult life. Trotsky worked out a solution to his feelings
of shame fairly early, by his verbal humiliation of others,
with the final pattern of conflict management not really set
until he arrived in Europe and had more or less mastered
Marxism. Gandhi was concerned with pride until his victory
over humiliation in South Africa. His basic feelings of
shamefulness, however, were so great that he had to allow
himself to be humiliated, as he had to allow himself to suffer pain, in order to keep a reasonable harmony between
his view of himself and what he perceived to be others' views
of him. Both Trotsky and Gandhi had the good fortune to
be living in times when a politicized solution to a personal
problem of shame would have wide appeal. Unfortunately
for both, but especially for Trotsky, each outlived the period of crisis which gave him power on the basis of that
solution.

Because Trotsky and Gandhi, or in more general terms
the person troubled by shame, suffered from the consequences of ridicule and other unfavorable forms of attention, they had a residual fear of humiliation which inhibited
their speaking and made them sensitive to insult, although
Trotsky superbly overcame the former problem and
Gandhi the latter. On the whole, however, the person lacking in basic pride or self-respect will be less able to bear
acrimony, more likely to react by trying to humble the of-
fender, than the person who is secure in his self-esteem. At
the same time this person will crave attention and, unless
he can disguise his craving under an elaborate shield like
Gandhi's assumed modesty, he will therefore be in danger
of offending others by his apparent egotism and desire for
applause. He probably will also have, however, the advantage of being more sensitive to the responsiveness of an
audience than a less uncertain man, but here other variables, such as the person's capacity for empathy (which

seems more likely to be an attribute of the self-respecting person) may tend to equalize the situation.

The next phase, the genital, has a nascent courage as its favorable outcome, but because this phase is replayed so strikingly in adolescence it will be discussed in conjunction with the latter. It should be mentioned again here, however, that one of the short-run outcomes of the mastery of this phase is the capacity of the individual to sublimate his hostilities into socially useful forms. The industry of the latent period, which serves as the basis for later devotion to tasks and achievement, depends on successful management of the conflicts of the preceding phase. All of our subjects performed well in this period, although Gandhi, whose feelings of guilt were more severe, did not do quite as well as the others.

Adolescence, as noted in Chapter 2, is the period when relations with the older generation must at last be defined and decisions about life's work made. In the case of our subjects these problems, which Erikson terms the crisis of identity, extended well into their young manhood, so that these two periods, as well as the genital phase, can be discussed concurrently. The successful mastery of the conflicts of this period leads to courage, the ability to act in a manly fashion without being overwhelmed by anxiety and guilt; confidence, a sure sense of one's own individuality and purpose; and drive, the ability to work devotedly to reach goals and fulfill ambitions. Each of the three men achieved mastery in these terms although, to be sure, there was some variation in both the form and content of the achievement among them. In order to discuss this very complex process as simply as possible it seems best to present a generalized model of the genesis and nature of the revolutionary personality, which is based on our three cases but does not fully describe any of them.

Before turning to an elaboration of this model, however, a note on its principal intellectual antecedents seems appropriate. These are the works of Harold Lasswell on political personality and the studies of the so-called "authoritarian personality," the most influential model of political personality which psychoanalytically oriented work has given to the social sciences.

The fundamental hypothesis of Lasswell's work, first presented in *Psychopathology and Politics*, is that for political men *private motives* are *displaced* on *public objects* and *rationalized* in terms of the *public interest*.[95] If this were not the case, it would make little sense to study personality and politics, for the implication would be that political activity is, in terms of the thought processes and emotions used in it, sui generis. It is possible, of course, that personality and politics are connected by the use of mechanisms other than displacement and rationalization, but some such link must exist unless political participants are people who live in two unconnected psychic worlds, that of their childhood and private life and that of their public life. Lasswell presents about twenty cases in the work mentioned above and others in *Power and Personality*, and I have now added three more. All of these, it seems to me, support the argument that the private and public lives of an individual are interrelated, and that the motivations of political men develop out of and are substantially explicable in terms of their prepolitical lives. By this I do not mean to argue that personality does not change after childhood—we have seen some of the ways in which it does—nor that political goals *qua* political goals are without motivating power. It is asserted that there are limits to change, especially after adolescence,[96] and that there are always private motivations underlying any drive to political achievement.

It should be mentioned that the distinction between public and private, as Lasswell uses it and as we used it in defining politics and revolution, creates an overly rigid distinction between the sectors of an individual's life.[97] It is

[95] Lasswell, *Psychopathology and Politics*, pp. 261-62.
[96] See Bellak, pp. 12-14, for a treatment of this.
[97] A discussion of the usefulness of this distinction can be found in Lucian Pye's article, "Personal Identity and Political Ideology," in Dwaine Marvick, ed., *Political Decision-Makers*, (New York, 1961), pp. 291-92.

useful at a minimum, however, to differentiate that set of relationships which is an individual's family life from the set which is his nonfamily life. Moreover, in many cases it is helpful to distinguish between a person's political and nonpolitical activities, grouping all nonpolitical activities under the heading private and political activities under public. But this separation is only made for purposes of analysis.

To elaborate Lasswell's formula somewhat, he found that political activity was, in motivational terms, a derivative of an individual's private life, an attempt to work out in a less emotionally supercharged context problems which would be psychically injurious if expressed within the family. Moreover, he found that people involved in political activity tend to rationalize, consciously and often systematically to explain and justify their involvement in terms of some more general, less personal object like "the public interest." He did not, however, specify what emotions and familial objects would be dealt with in this way, except with respect to his cases as such. In the model to be used here I will attempt such a specification, on the assumption that a sub-type of political actor should have a specifiable set of attributes which differentiates it from other types but does not put it outside the general set of attributes denoted by the type political man.

The other personality model which has most influenced the present effort is that of the authoritarian personality. The classic work on the subject is T. W. Adorno *et al.*, *The Authoritarian Personality*, first published in 1950. It had been preceded by the work of Max Horkheimer and his associates, mainly neo-Freudians, in Germany in the 1930s, out of which grew what in many ways was its theoretical model, Erich Fromm's *Escape from Freedom*. In this work Fromm proposed the model of the sado-masochist in politics, a person highly involved with questions of domination and submission. In elaborating this model, and in the process subjecting it to substantial, if not definitive, testing,[98]

[98] The most thorough review and analysis of the study are the essays

Adorno and his associates developed a set of characteristics which such a person seemed likely to have. For example, the authoritarian personality was viewed as being moralistic and condemning, extra-punitive (always blaming others), distrustful, suspicious; he feels victimized, views the world as a hierarchy, tends toward hero worship, fears emotional involvement, is exploitive, manipulative, and status conscious.[99] His attitudes toward his present self are self-glorifying (or alternatively "ego-alien-self-contempt"), he highly values such masculine traits as determination, energy, industry, independence, decisiveness, and will power, and his ego ideal corresponds to his self-image.[100]

Many of the traits listed here do seem to be attributes of our three cases, but several do not. None of the men was extra-punitive, only one (Lenin) was really distrustful, only Trotsky tended towards hero worship and Lenin was not status conscious. Again Lenin and Gandhi were not self-glorifying, nor was Trotsky in the usual sense of the term. Gandhi's self-image did not match his ego ideal, and he eventually repudiated that ideal with its masculine attributes. A central concern with domination and submission does exist, along with feelings of victimization, in all three cases, but there are differences in their problems and in the solutions to those problems. Hence we must use a somewhat different construct to define and explain the revolutionary personality.

The starting point in constructing our model is the assumption, based on the analysis of the early lives of our three cases, that the question of why a man becomes a revolutionist can only be answered by taking account of the state of mind of the individual before he becomes a rebel. In this respect the root psychological condition appears to be a particular kind of relationship with parental authority, specifically with the father. That relationship is a highly

---

in Richard Christie and Marie Jahoda, eds., *Studies in the Scope and Method of "The Authoritarian Personality"* (Glencoe, Ill., 1954).
   [99] Adorno *et al.*, pp. 405-06.   [100] *Ibid.*, pp. 422-23.

ambivalent one, an intense focusing of love and hate on the same person. Because the father is the provider of certain rewards in the individual's early life (affection, approval, and so on, to say nothing of material comforts), and because the individual comes to identify with his father to a substantial extent in the process of forming a conception of his own masculine role, the potential revolutionist has strong feelings of love and admiration for his father. (All three of our men had this favorable side in their relationships with their fathers, something which is lacking in the case of the authoritarian personality.) Moreover, it is the individual's father who served as the basis for his own superego development, so that his conception of right and wrong, of justification, comes largely from what he senses to be his father's standards in these matters. This was particularly marked in the case of Lenin, but the elaborate extremes Trotsky and Gandhi went to in trying to change their moral conceptions away from the models provided by their fathers points to a strongly developed identification in those cases as well.

But the father is also a withholder of privileges and, to a large extent, in possession of the most important love object of a person's early life, his mother. As a result the individual develops strong feelings of aggression towards the father. The result of this combination of love and hate is tension at holding disparate feelings towards one object and guilt, anxiety and fear as a result of the internalization of the father's standards of rectitude, uncertainty about the consequences of the emotions felt, and the conviction that the father will punish the individual for his illicit thoughts and desires, respectively. To some extent, of course, this combination of feelings, Oedipal ambivalence, is common to most men. But in the person who is to be a revolutionist both love and hate are felt unusually strongly, so that the individual is being psychically torn apart by intense internal conflict between his basic drives and the stern strictures of his superego. Although we have not in the present instance developed indices for the measurement of ambivalence, the argument is that our three cases showed signs of this intense struggle. Until indices are developed, and revolutionists and nonrevolutionists are compared with respect to ambivalence, this point must remain hypothetical.

Moreover, we have found that this ambivalence is intensified rather than reduced during adolescence, and, due to death or separation, cannot be dealt with in the familial context. If the individual is to avoid neurotic involvement, an arena for working out this conflict must be found. If the person's ego is strong enough, presumably because he has received adequate support and love from the people in his environment, and if his problems coincide with certain possibilities for action inherent in his environment, the individual may be able to deal with this situation. Psychologically the revolutionist is a man who has been able to deal with these conflicts in the context of public activity in his milieu.

How, then, does the individual meet this internal crisis? Several things seem to be involved.[101] First, as we have seen in all three of our cases, he will try to turn the conflict from an *internal one* into an *external one*, from a conflict within himself to a conflict between himself and others. The occasion for this must be set by the individual's perception of reality, typically through experiencing some aggressive action by another person or group of people which allows the individual to jump to the (unconscious) position: "Aha, it is not I who am the aggressor but this outside force which is acting hostilly towards me." That is, there must be a precipitant or catalyst of revolutionary involvement. In Lenin's case his brother's death and the incident with the ferryman, in Trotsky's the rise of industrial unrest during his adolescence coupled with his imprisonment, in Gandhi's the incidents with the political agent in Kathiawad and the trainmen in Maritzburg served this purpose of ex-

[101] The discussion which follows deals primarily with the defenses the revolutionist seems to use against his undesired affects and drives. For the motives and mechanisms of defense see Fenichel, *Psychoanalytic Theory of Neurosis*, pp. 129-68.

ternalizing the conflict. In addition, such incidents serve as the basis for a period of toughening which follows hard upon revolutionary involvement, a period of imprisonment or extreme risks of one kind or another which tends to make or break the individual. This time, that of Lenin's and Trotsky's imprisonments and Gandhi's being physically abused in South Africa, is one of great psychological stress, out of which the individual emerges as a committed and confident rebel or a defeated man. This is also a period during which self-discipline is strengthened.[102]

In talking about toughening we have jumped ahead of the revolutionist's development somewhat. At the point of the occurrence of the outside incident the conflict is externalized, but the individual is still plagued by a generalized ambivalence with respect to these new objects, which are beginning to displace the original objects of his emotions. To relieve strain the individual next tries to *split the complex of ambivalence* into its respective parts by focusing all feelings of love onto one object or set of objects and all feelings of hate onto another object or set. The world is dichotomized into friends and enemies, good and bad. Toward friends, at first a brotherhood of which one is a part and eventually a sort of revolutionary family of which the leader is the father, one tries to feel only love, and deep love at that. Thus Trotsky overflowed with fellow-feeling for the other members of the Southern Russian Workers' Union, Gandhi devoted himself unstintingly to his fellow *satyagrahis*, and Lenin formed deep friendships with people like Potresov and Martov. Both Lenin and Trotsky, who in contrast to Gandhi had a choice in the matter, even married fellow revolutionists, thus joining sexual love to the love of revolt.

The revolutionist thus forms love relationships with other

---

[102] The period of toughening seems to me to be comparable to what Erikson terms the moratorium which great men go through, a period of great doubts about oneself and one's future which must be resolved before going on. He treats this idea in many places, but see, for example, *Young Man Luther*, pp. 100-104.

revolutionists. Moreover, he *projects* onto members of the brotherhood the feelings of love he has for them; in other words, he views them as loving him. In the process of projecting these feelings of love onto his fellows, however, the revolutionist also projects his residual feelings of hatred toward his peers. This is particularly true if sibling rivalry has been important in the person's development, but for the leader-to-be it is true because he will eventually tend to view the other rebels as children, people to be guided, and will thus see in them the same feelings of aggression he had towards his own father. Except when this is exacerbated by the kind of mistrustfulness characteristic of Lenin, however, this residual ambivalence does not create unmanageable problems.

By displacing his conflicts in this way (we will turn to the displacement of hate for the father below), the revolutionist is able to deny to himself the psychological roots of his conflict. "It is not I who am being abused by authority, who is in danger from it and hates it, but these poor oppressed people whom I have voluntarily undertaken to help." He and his fellow revolutionists speak not for themselves but for others, and for people lower and less powerful than themselves. Thus Lenin and Trotsky supported the workers and Gandhi spoke first for the underprivileged Indians in South Africa and then for the Indians, especially the Untouchables, in India.

It should be noted that the party or revolutionary brotherhood is seldom peopled predominantly by members of this represented class or reference group. However, there must be some minimal representation of this group in the party if the leader is to maintain contact with this source of his internal strength and external adherency. Alternatively, of course, if the revolutionist has enough freedom regularly to come in contact with the population for which he speaks, the need for members of that population in his immediate entourage is diminished.

The other half of the individual's basic ambivalence is his hatred for his father. Just as all love ideally was turned towards the brotherhood, so all hate ideally is directed against encroaching authority. It becomes justifiable and possible to hate this symbolically bad father, to act against him to protect oneself and one's charges. Again displacement and projection are at work, for the revolutionist not only hates this surrogate father but views such authority as hating him—although, as in the case of love for his fellows, there must be some basis in reality for these emotions, at a minimum as a result of a self-fulfilling prophecy, if the revolutionist is to be something other than a lone rebel against the political system of which he is a part. Again, the separation of emotions is not perfect. There are residual feelings that authority is benevolent and that it is right to submit—these are feelings which must be warded off just as hate must be controlled within the brotherhood. This phenomenon we saw particularly in Trotsky and Gandhi.

Additionally, the revolutionist will try to use up whatever excess of guilt he has, once the above measures have been taken, either by submitting himself to some authority to be punished or by inflicting some, possibly symbolic, punishment on himself.[103] Thus revolutionists, especially leaders, will often be ascetics, like Gandhi and Lenin. This asceticism, as well as the revolutionist undertaking to assist in what may well be an unpopular cause, helps to ward off envy which success might otherwise bring. When asceticism is less pronounced, as in Trotsky's case, envy develops more easily, although in that instance there were other aspects of Trotsky's personality which contributed to strained relations.

One of the characteristics of the revolutionist's view of authority is that authority appears to be very strong, almost omnipotent. Quite apart from the fact that such authority may in fact have great power, the origins of this view can be found in the fact that political authority is a surrogate for the father and hence is perceived as having some part of

---

[103] See Freud's discussion of self-punishment in "Dostoevsky and Parricide," in his *Collected Papers*, Vol. V, James Strachey, ed. (New York, 1959), 229-31.

the father's imagined omnipotence. To offset the power of this evil father the revolutionist chooses a benevolent father to protect himself, first in terms of personal leaders and then, if an individual rises to full leadership himself, in terms of an impersonalized equivalent of the leader/father which is either the central figure in or the originator of the person's ideology or revolutionary religion.

The introduction of the term "ideology" directs us to the fact that revolutionists assuredly do not think of their activity in the terms that have been used here. Rather they think, especially the leaders, in terms of highly developed systems of rationalization which serve to mitigate residual internal conflict by further masking the underlying psychological nature of the revolutionist's activity. The authority embodied in the ideology, which is this system of rationalization, serves as the source of superego justification for the individual, as well as providing inner assurance of success. Trotsky's and Lenin's adoption of Marxism and Gandhi's reliance in his ideology on Rama (or God or Truth) are examples of this.

For the revolutionary follower this justificatory system has a concrete embodiment in the leader. The leader, by contrast, whose superego is stronger and who is in less need of outside support, is free to hear authority speak as he wants it to speak. Eventually, in fact, he may virtually merge what are for him the root aspects of the ideology into his superego, so that he becomes a living embodiment of rectitude and correct action. Lenin and Gandhi came very close to this position; Trotsky did not to nearly the same degree. Such achievement is based on a stronger identification with the father (or in Gandhi's case his mother) than Trotsky possessed.

One of the characteristics of the ideology the leader either creates, activates, distorts or simplifies is that it must be totalist, must account for all possible relations of man to man. If it does not, there is room for ambivalence and doubt. Any person who denies the validity of the system, or any event which the system has not been made to explain, is taken by the revolutionist to mean that his faith is misplaced *or* as a sign of his lack of faith. In the latter case, to prove his loyalty to the creed, he must eliminate those people or things which challenge the ideology.

Moreover, because this system of rationalization is so intimately tied to the individual's view of himself, it must be clung to unalterably. The root characteristics of the ideology serve as the conscious justificatory formula for the individual, the token of his management of intense and disruptive feelings. Any challenge to that formula is also a challenge to the tight control the individual has established over himself. Shatter the formula in the person's mind and you shatter his personality as well. This brittleness, however, does not necessarily extend to questions of means. As we shall see with Lenin in particular, only ends must definitely be viewed as unchanging—any means can be used to achieve them. Means involve merely transient relations with other people and are not a key attribute of the self. But ends, as we have seen, are a matter of self-definition, of identity. For followers, however, those who are more like the authoritarian personality, the sophisticated rationalizations of the leaders may not be possible. There may have been insufficient support in their environment to provide the basis for the sophisticated ideological thinking of the leaders, with its important side effect of channeling emotional energy and tension into words and abstractions and thus leaving concrete relations relatively relaxed and flexible.

In the next chapter we will trace the evolution of these men into revolutionary leaders. For this purpose we will concentrate on Lenin's and Trotsky's lives from 1900-1905 (but will take them briefly up to the Revolution of 1917 as well). In Gandhi's case we will have to forego discussing the rest of the period in South Africa and pick up his life on the verge of his return to India, following his actions from then until the beginning of the Second World War.

adulthood 1

Thus far in our discussion it has been possible to maintain, at least in form, a more or less continuous narration of the events in the lives of our subjects. From this point forward, however, all three men are so heavily involved in political activity that full coverage of the significant events in their lives is impossible in a study of this scope. Even in the earlier sections of the work we were just sampling behavior, but until we got to the analysis of Gandhi's stay in South Africa we at least sampled it rather heavily. It thus becomes necessary to select for analysis events of the men's adult lives which will be useful for both understanding the men and inferring some of the psychological attributes of leadership. In other words, the events chosen hopefully will be indicative of major themes in the men's personalities and politics.

There is a danger of distortion in the process of selecting these events. If atypical and insignificant events in the men's lives are chosen, no analysis of them will yield a picture of what the men were typically like or what their primary motivations were. Of course, to the extent that our task is only the construction of a personality model and hypotheses related to it, we need not be concerned with the representativeness of events. Strictly speaking, in fact, there would be no need to include the kind of empirical material used here. But, as it is hoped that this study sheds some light on the motivations of the three revolutionists in particular and thereby gives some presumption as to the usefulness of the model for understanding revolutionary leaders in general, we must be concerned with selecting for analysis events which are typical and/or important determinants of the men's behavior. Although in the present case it has not been possible to use fully rigorous or unambiguous criteria of inclusion or exclusion, an effort has been made to choose events which are of manifest political significance, illustrative of leadership behavior or the lack thereof and psychologically significant for the men themselves. The focus accordingly is on the effort of the three men to build up a revolutionary following or organization, to sever the submissive or equalitarian ties with superiors and peers respectively and to develop an effective doctrine of revolutionary means.

Lenin: The Tactics of Revolutionary Leadership

By the time Lenin's period of exile in Siberia ended in February 1900 he had resolved most of his doubts about the goals of the revolutionary struggle and the suitability of Marxism as the tool for understanding the Russian experience. He also had decided what *means* were most suitable for carrying on the struggle at that particular time. He saw two related functions that had to be performed if revolutionary work was to be carried on effectively:

> our principal and fundamental task is to facilitate the political development and the political organization of the working class.[1]

In order to carry out this work he had proposed the creation of the newspaper in which the above lines were to appear. It was to be called *Iskra*, the "Spark," and was to serve as a propaganda organ for the Social Democrats throughout Russia. The organization which would have to be created to handle its distribution and supply it with information was to serve as the nucleus of the revolutionary party that was to topple tsarism. This was Lenin's bold

[1] Lenin, "The Urgent Tasks of Our Movement," written in September 1900 and published in *Iskra* in December 1900, in Lenin's *Collected Works*, IV, 369.

[175]

plan, to unite all of the revolutionary potential of Russia around *Iskra*, which in turn was to be under the direction of Lenin and his "brothers," Martov and Potresov. They would work cooperatively with the older Marxists, Plekhanov, Axelrod, and Zasulich, all of whom Lenin respected, but control of the organ and hence of the organization was to be in the hands of the three younger men. The difficulties that emerged in running this enterprise, and the death of the "old" *Iskra* after the Second Congress of the party in 1903 we will examine below in connection with Lenin's evolution into full leadership stature. Here we will examine Lenin's principal tactical piece of this period, *What Is To Be Done?* (written in the winter of 1901-1902), in order to get some grasp of what Lenin believed about propaganda and organization, and why.[2]

The fundamental premise of *What Is To Be Done?*, as indeed of Lenin's Marxism generally, is that the revolutionist, and especially the Russian revolutionist, lives in a dangerous world. Accordingly, one of Lenin's tasks in the work is to demonstrate that other writers underestimate the inherent violence and prolonged nature of the revolutionary struggle. He condemns the Economists (the revisionists and evolutionary socialists) on the one hand and the terrorists on the other for failing to understand the nature of revolutionary politics, misjudging the capacities of the masses and misconstruing the relationship between the *spontaneous* activities of the masses and the *conscious* direction of the revolutionary organization.[3]

As was mentioned in Chapter 3, Lenin thought he had found in Marxism both a guarantee of revolutionary success and an activist creed. He did not really perceive the

[2] There is a considerable literature on this period in Lenin's life and writing. A few of the most important works are: Leopold Haimson, *The Russian Marxists*; Nathan Leites, *A Study of Bolshevism*; Donald W. Treadgold, *Lenin and His Rivals* (New York, 1955); Adam Ulam, *The Bolsheviks*, pp. 160-216, and Bertram Wolfe, *Three Who Made a Revolution*.

[3] Lenin, *What Is To Be Done?* (New York, 1943), pp. 72-75.

disjunction between them.[4] He desired to hold to both ideas, and hence blinded himself to the contradiction between determinism and voluntary action. He now found, however, that not everyone saw in Marxism this combination of ideas, that the advocates of spontaneity did not see the need for political activity and that the advocates of consciousness were, if you will, not Marxists at all, but terrorists dedicated to symbolic, and rather sporadic, gestures of protest. In other words, revolutionary politics was coming perilously close to confirming Mikhailovsky's position. The tenuous unity of Marxist theory was crumbling in the face of the differing needs, both psychological and political, of the various antitsarist factions. And because these differences were starting to find institutional embodiments in the forms of competing revolutionary journals and organizations, it became necessary for Lenin to give careful attention to the attempts to fragment Marxism. Both the unity of his personality in its ideological expression and the possibility for unified Russian action were at stake.

In fact, Lenin did not, nor could he resolve the difficulties involved in the contradiction of spontaneity and consciousness. Instead he avoided the issue by creating an ideology of organizational activity. He made the idea of the vanguard serve the dual psychological functions of guaranteeing success and of demanding active revolutionary commitment.

Lenin begins his argument for an organization of professional revolutionists by characterizing tsarism as "the most powerful bulwark, not only of European, but also . . . of Asiatic reaction."[5] Overthrowing tsarism is seen as incomparably more difficult than defeating the Western European regimes, and therefore the "Russian workers will have to undergo trials immeasurably more severe [than other workers]; they will have to take up the fight against a monster. . . ."[6] Because its task is the hardest, however,

[4] Cf. Lenin, *What the "Friends of the People" Are*, p. 159.
[5] Lenin, *What Is To Be Done?*, p. 30.
[6] *Ibid.*

and the consequences of its victory so great, for victory would lead to the fall of capitalism generally, the "Russian proletariat [is in] the vanguard of the international revolutionary proletariat. We shall have the right to count upon acquiring the honourable title already earned by our predecessors, the revolutionists of the seventies. . . ."[7]

Lenin, as we know, had every reason to think that the Tsar was a "monster"; after all, Sasha had lost his life in fighting him. In order to assuage his feelings of guilt over Sasha's death, however, Lenin could not foresake the combat. He felt obliged to carry on the tradition of the earlier revolutionists. Moreover, he had a strong feeling that it was up to him alone, in ideological terms to the Russian proletariat, to lead the fight against world capitalism. With Sasha gone, the fight was between Lenin (and his fellow revolutionists) and father Tsar. There could be no substitutes, no falling away from the challenge. Sasha's memory must not be betrayed.

But, as we saw in Chapter 3, Lenin could not merely accept his brother's perceived terroristic stance. To do so would be to court death—futilely. For even the terrorists admitted that the government could not be made to fall by terror alone, that terror would only serve an "excitative" function, would arouse the people to spontaneous activity.[8] In other words, Lenin argued that, while the terrorists were very much heroes in one sense, commensurate in bravery and manliness with their forefathers, in another they were fools, for the sparks they sought to ignite would dissipate harmlessly into the unorganized and unself-conscious mass. For all their boldness, they were not men enough, not controlled enough, to cope with the overwhelming power of tsarism.

Nor did Lenin feel the problem could be avoided by flying to spontaneity in the Economist's sense of the term The Economists, in a way, denied the struggle itself. Holding firm to the Marxist doctrine that political conditions

---

[7] *Ibid.*   [8] *Ibid.*, pp. 74-75.

were a superstructure erected upon the basis of the organization of the means of production, they argued that the workers should concentrate on the bread-and-butter issues of employer-employee relations and fight only for immediately realizable gains; that the workers could develop for themselves sufficient organization to carry on the struggle, and that in the long run tsarism would evolve into a more humane system.[9] Lenin compared this position to a story about a sixteenth-century publisher, Johann Ballhorn, who:

> published a child's reader in which, as was the custom, he introduced a drawing of a cock; but this drawing, instead of portraying an ordinary cock with spurs, portrayed it without spurs and with a couple of eggs lying near it. On the cover of this reader he printed the legend, "*Revised* edition by Johann Ballhorn."[10]

In short, Lenin accused the Economists in particular and Marxist revisionists in general of attempting to emasculate the party, of depriving it of its "spurs" and leaving it unprepared for combat. The party must be a fighting cock, not a hen, if it was to avoid having its neck wrung.

Thus the terrorists through their undisciplined masculine assertiveness would strike at tsarism ineffectually, while the Economists, with their passivity, their reliance on spontaneity, did not realize that there was a battle to be won. And, in one way, Lenin conceded that they were right, for he believed that the masses, unless thoroughly indoctrinated, were capable of only "trade union consciousness," that their energies would be used up in futile attempts at specifically economic reform and the political struggle would not be attempted. The Tsar and his police would continue unhampered in their oppression.[11] Hence neither the terrorist nor the Economist solution was satisfactory to Lenin, despite the logical consistency of each, either psy-

[9] *Ibid.*, pp. 31-67, *passim.*
[10] *Ibid.*, p. 66. Cf. Haimson's treatment of spontaneity and consciousness, pp. 117-41.
[11] *Ibid.*, Chapter III, *passim.*

chologically or politically. The question was, indeed, "what
is to be done?"

As mentioned earlier, Lenin's program for escaping from
this dilemma was to create a revolutionary newspaper,
which would be under central supervision and would cir-
culate throughout Russia. Around this newspaper would be
built a core organization of professional revolutionists, well
trained men who would be supported out of party funds.
And around these men would be the various nonsecret organizations of political and economic protest, which the
members of the revolutionary vanguard were to penetrate
and, if possible, control. As one author puts it, Lenin
sought to create an "organizational weapon," a body of men
who would work with passion and control for the overthrow of the forces of reaction.[12]

Lenin's organization was to serve two underlying functions: it was to protect him from the blows of a dangerous
foe and it was to make him stronger, more masculine, for
purposes of attacking the aggressor. Out of the available
human material Lenin would attempt to create a machine,
a leviathan, a reliable instrument of political warfare.

But Lenin had little faith in the inherent dedication and
skill of either the proletariat or the intelligentsia. Both were
likely to fall into deluded ideas about the spontaneous nature of the struggle, or to fall victim to Oblomovism, what
seemed to Lenin to be the natural carelessness and lethargy
of the Russian mind. In order to make the organization invulnerable to the dangerous natural impulses of the men
who were to compose it, it was necessary to professionalize
them, to create of them a new kind of man.[13] They must be
men who would not be carried away by feelings of either love
or hate for the enemy, men of perfect emotional control.

[12] See Philip Selznick, *The Organizational Weapon* (Glencoe, Ill.,
1960). Lenin's statement of these principles is in *What Is To Be Done?*,
pp. 105-42.
[13] Lenin, *What Is To Be Done?*, p. 116; Cf. Leites, *Study of Bolshevism*, pp. 187-208, for an analysis of the Bolshevik need to defend
against impulse.

The idea of a *professional* organization has two other important meanings as well. A professional organization meant that its active members were to be supported out of party funds. This caused others to suspect Lenin of un-democratic designs, of wanting to have control over the lives of those who would be working for the party.[14] Lenin's defense against this accusation is to dismiss the charge as irrelevant—there can be no question of control among like-minded comrades.[15] In fact, Lenin's defense amounts to no more than the promise that he will be a benevolent father to his revolutionary children, that no follower will be abused despite the fact that the party was a command or-ganization under the control of the leader. And Lenin, by and large, honored this promise during his lifetime. Others did not after his death.

The other meaning of a professional organization is that Lenin viewed revolutionary activity as, in fact, a profession. Revolution was not a game for sportsmen or an after-hours hobby, but a full-time job. This position reflects not only Lenin's deadly seriousness about the struggle, and his in-tense concentration on the issue of overthrowing tsarism, but also his need to view his activity as an occupation, as a respectable way of life. There was nothing of the nihilistic rebel about Lenin. Like Marx, his life remained markedly bourgeois in many respects. In short, one would guess that Lenin thought of his career as revolutionist as in some ways analogous to his father's as educator: each was a hardwork-ing head of an organization, following the proper line as dictated by some higher agency. Only the father's directives came from the Tsar, Lenin's from the sacred scriptures of Marxism.

In addition to being professional, Lenin's organization was to be small, centralized and secret. Each of these meas-ures, of course, would augment Lenin's control—and make the organization, and Lenin, less vulnerable to the tsarist police. Lenin also wanted the organization to be all Rus-

[14] Lenin, *What Is To Be Done?*, pp. 125-30.
[15] *Ibid.*, p. 131.

sian.[16] The war was between the Social Democrats and the Tsar; hence strictly local efforts were to no avail. The only course of action carrying some intimation of success was to arm oneself for combat against the Tsar, the bulwark of reaction, by solidifying the party and instilling greater consciousness of the "objective" condition into the workers, the proletariat. It was for this latter purpose that a newspaper was vital, a propaganda organ which would make the workers aware of the conditions in Russia generally, and teach them the proper response. Lenin, like his father, sought to educate the lower classes—but, again, Lenin had very different goals in mind.

Lenin thus wanted to build an organization which would reduce the probability of defeat.[17] Even when all the above safeguards had been adopted, he did not feel confident that *his* organization would overthrow the Tsar (although he did believe that in the long run the victory of the proletariat was inevitable). The world was still dangerous, the Tsar was still an enormously powerful foe. The Narodniks, too, as Lenin notes, had a well-designed organization (in their early revolutionary days), but they had been easily defeated.[18] It is only when you combine organization with the correct Marxist line, when you bring Marxism properly to bear on a given choice, that you reduce to an absolute minimum the risks of engagement. In other words, guiding all actions by theory, by the one right line for the moment, was assurance of success and reaffirmation of one's unity with the fatherly strength of Marxism. Hence theory (that is, the rationalized formulas which express the resolution of basic conflict) had a special importance for Lenin, and the question of what is the right line, rather than what is a good line, would be the starting point, implicitly or explicitly, for all of Lenin's writings. And because he spoke for the correct line, and with the conviction which comes from fiercely held beliefs, his appeals had a persuasiveness which others, less certain and hence less clear and forceful, could not

[16] *Ibid.*, pp. 133-42.   [17] *Ibid.*, p. 127.   [18] *Ibid.*, pp. 125-26.

match. Wolfe gives a quotation from Pokrovsky, which reflects the great power of Lenin's conviction:

> There was above all, his enormous capacity to see the root of things, a capacity which finally awakened in me a sort of superstitious feeling. I frequently had occasion to differ from him on practical questions but I came off badly every time. When this experience had been repeated about seven times, I ceased to dispute and submitted to Lenin even if logic told me that one should act otherwise. I was henceforth convinced that he understood things better and was master of the power denied to me, of seeing about ten feet down into the earth.[19]

To enunciate workable principles of leadership, of course, is not necessarily to be able to make them work. Pokrovsky's comment indicates that Lenin was, in fact, the leader that his program called for. He could not, however, be such a leader as long as Plekhanov was recognized as his superior and Martov and Potresov as his equals. This web of personal relations had to be broken before Lenin could realize the power and the risks of primacy. The break took place between 1900 and 1904.

Immediately upon his arrival in western Europe in July 1900 Lenin had occasion to quarrel with Plekhanov. The latter had just split the united Russian socialist movement on the continent because he found it impossible to work with revisionists and opportunists. Lenin, just coming from Russia and aware of how fragile the movement was, was distressed at the thought of losing any source of support. He was counting on a united movement, which the *Iskra* group would end up controlling after convincing all others of the rightness of its views. (As we shall see in the next section, Trotsky's reaction to Lenin's splitting of the movement in 1903 was similar in some respects to Lenin's at this earlier time.) Lenin went with Potresov to Geneva to visit Plekhanov and was eventually joined by Axelrod and Zasulich.

[19] Cited in Wolfe, p. 363.

In the course of the visit Plekhanov rejected flatly Lenin's proposal to attempt a reconciliation with the more revisionist wing of the movement, treated with scorn Lenin's proposed draft of a declaration of purpose for the soon to be published *Iskra* and outmaneuvered Lenin and Potresov in such a way as to end up with two seats on the *Iskra* editorial board to one apiece for Lenin, Martov, Potresov, and the two older revolutionists mentioned above. In the end, however, Lenin did manage to arrange matters so that the actual editorial and organizational work would be under his management.[20] Before that end was reached, however, Lenin came close to breaking with Plekhanov and, while the break did not quite come about, relations with Plekhanov were toned down. Lenin's description of these events is, as Wolfe remarks, the most "psychologically revealing" thing Lenin ever wrote.[21] As such it is worth quoting "How the 'Spark' Was Nearly Extinguished," as the commentary was called, at length.[22]

In the following part of the narration Lenin describes his and Potresov's emotions at discovering that Plekhanov had outsmarted them:

As soon as we found ourselves alone . . . we broke into a flood of angry expressions. . . . My "infatuation" with Plekhanov disappeared as if by magic, and I felt offended and embittered to an unbelievable degree. Never, never in my life, had I regarded any man with such sincere respect and veneration, never had I stood before any man so "humbly" and never before had I been so brutally "kicked." That's what it was, we had actually been kicked. We had been scared like little

[20] See Krupskaya, *Memories of Lenin*, I, 58.
[21] Wolfe, p. 151.
[22] It might be mentioned that Lenin did not settle upon the name "Lenin" until 1901. Although the meaning he attributed to the word is unknown, it is interesting that the word has no inherent meaning. Unlike Trotsky, Lenin did not borrow his name from another man, and unlike Trotsky, he resumed the use of his original family name, along with his pseudonym, once he gained power.

children, scared by the grown-ups threatening to leave us to ourselves, and when we funked (the shame of it!) we were brushed aside with incredible unceremoniousness. We now realised very clearly that Plekhanov had simply laid a trap for us that morning when he declined to act as co-editor; it had been a deliberate chess move, a snare for guileless "pidgeons." . . . And since a man with whom we desired to co-operate closely and establish most intimate relations, resorted to chess moves in dealing with comrades, there would be no doubt that this man was bad, yes, bad, inspired by petty motives of personal vanity and conceit—an insincere man. . . . Our indignation knew no bounds. Our ideal had been destroyed; gloatingly we trampled it underfoot like a dethroned god. . . . We had received the most bitter lesson of our lives, a painfully bitter, painfully brutal lesson. Young comrades "court" an elder comrade out of the great love they bear for him —and suddenly he injects into this love an atmosphere of intrigue, compelling them to feel, not as younger brothers, but as fools to be led by the nose, as pawns to be moved about at will, and, still worse, as clumsy *Streber* [careerists] who must be thoroughly frightened and quashed! An enamoured youth receives from the object of his love a bitter lesson to regard all persons "without sentiment," to keep a stone in one's sling.[23]

There are many more pages to his intriguing document, which essentially concludes with the following sentence:

Outwardly it was as though nothing had happened; the apparatus must continue to work as it had worked till then, but within a chord had broken, and instead of splendid personal relations, dry, business-like relations prevailed, with a constant reckoning according to the principle: *si vis pacem, para bellum.* (If you desire peace, prepare for war.)[24]

[23] Lenin, "How the 'Spark' Was Nearly Extinguished," in *Collected Works*, IV, 340-42.
[24] *Ibid.*, p. 348.

Politically this piece records the growth of a man from a position of following to one of leadership; psychologically it is the drama of the son casting off the authority of the father.

Until this time Lenin had treated Plekhanov with, as he says, "sincere respect and veneration." In the process of his selection of a revolutionary career Lenin had chosen Plekhanov as the righteous and benevolent counterpart to the Tsar. Along with the now almost legendary Marx, Plekhanov was to be guide, protector, and moral authority for Lenin's revolutionary activity. Marx and Plekhanov on the one hand and the Tsar on the other were thus a split psychic reconstruction of Lenin's ambivalent image of his father: Plekhanov was the father/leader, the Tsar the father/enemy. The former would protect the humble revolutionary children from the attacks of the latter; operating under Plekhanov's aegis Lenin hoped to avoid Sasha's fate.

But Plekhanov, the "good father," turned out to be only human. Instead of acting warmly and protectively toward his followers he "resorted to chess moves" to get his own ends. The imagery used here is indicative of the degree to which Lenin saw the situation in familial terms. Not only does he refer to himself and his companions as children, but Plekhanov is accused of using chess moves—and chess had been the game his father taught him. And, like his father, Plekhanov seemed intent on gaining control over an object that both he and Lenin desired. Just as his father was the possessor of his mother, so Plekhanov would be, if Lenin were unable to stop him, the master of *Iskra*. And just as Lenin had eventually beaten his father at chess, thus symbolizing his growth to manhood, so he was in 1903 to beat Plekhanov in the adult chess game of revolutionary politics.

The basis for the later victory over Plekhanov was set here. Lenin "dethroned" Plekhanov in his mind, he no longer owed him, as before, an almost filial loyalty. As a result he was freed from that debilitating feeling that someone else was rightfully the father, the feeling that so hindered Trotsky in his efforts to lead. He had learned that there was no man on earth who could adequately play the role he had assigned to benevolent paternal authority. Only the impersonal and idealized Marx, or rather the legend and writings of Marx, would be viewed and invoked as a superior moral force, to be relied upon and guided by. Toward men the attitude would be a redoubled mistrust, a constant alertness to ward off all efforts to rob one of one's manliness and life. Relations with others would be "dry, business-like," instead of cordial and intimate.

At least with respect to superiors, Lenin had thus learned to control his inclinations toward affection and trust. He would no longer be "used" by others, taken in by their insincerity.[25] As Wolfe puts it:

> It is not too much to conclude that, from the disillusionment which ended his "youthful love affair," the thirty-year old Vladimir Ilyich suddenly matured from Ulyanov to Lenin. Indeed, behind the whole "lovers' quarrel" was the fact, never consciously formulated, that Ulyanov was beginning to feel within himself the capacity to lead the movement, if necessary, without his master.[26]

Another aspect of the encounter was that Plekhanov won his victory over Lenin not only by being smarter but by being harder, by being willing to chance a split, not only with the economists but also with Lenin and the other young men who held the future of Russian Marxism. By the end of the meeting Plekhanov had backed away from his intransigence a bit, but only after he had won his victory. Lenin, who admired the control that Plekhanov on the whole demonstrated, hence had a model for his later actions: on the basis of firm conviction of one's own rectitude and correct understanding of the dictates of the Marxist faith, one must stand firm against opposition, be it agres-

---

[25] Haimson in particular stresses this aspect of the incident (cf. p. 140).

[26] Wolfe, p. 152.

sive or seductive, even to the point of risking a split with those who would follow a different course. In 1904, in the aftermath of the split between the Bolsheviks and Mensheviks, Plekhanov, who had originally sided with Lenin in upholding the "hard" line of centralization, professional party membership and the narrowed *Iskra* board (Axelrod, Zasulich, and Potresov were to be removed, leaving Lenin, Plekhanov, and Martov in control), wavered and went over to the Mensheviks. For Lenin this represented a betrayal, but it also was a mark of his triumph over his former master; for in this crucial situation Plekhanov, not Lenin, had been moved by sentiment to abandon a position he theoretically was convinced was right. Lenin was henceforth the "hardest" of the Social Democrats.

Thus as early as 1900 Lenin was laying the emotional basis for a position of being without superior in the movement, one of the essential criteria of leadership. The other criterion is that of being without equal and, by 1903, Lenin, psychologically and to a considerable extent politically, had accomplished this as well, in a sense despite his overt wishes (as the incipient break with Plekhanov had been against his expressed desires). The basis for this result was the severing of intimate ties with his "blood brothers," Martov and Potresov.

Lenin's bond with Potresov had gradually been weakening and his contact with him diminishing, but until the 1903 Congress Lenin and Martov had been working in close tandem in the London offices of *Iskra*, with Lenin generally asserting his leadership through the definiteness of his ideas and his willingness to undertake the vital but arduous day-to-day organizational work. As early as 1902, however, a difference in temperament was beginning to make itself felt. Trotsky reports:

> Martov, his closest companion in arms, was already beginning to feel not quite at his ease. They [Lenin and Martov] were still addressing each other as "ty" (thou), but a certain coldness was beginning to creep

into their mutual relations. Martov lived more in the present, . . . Lenin, on the other hand, although he was firmly intrenched in the present, was always trying to pierce the veil of the future. Martov evolved innumerable and often ingenious guesses . . . whereas Lenin waited until the moment when he needed them. . . .

* * *

One can say of Lenin and Martov that even before the split, even before the congress, Lenin was "hard" and Martov "soft." And they both knew it. . . .[27]

Martov's softness represented a danger for Lenin, the possibility of inadvertent betrayal from diffusion of ideas and an inability to view the struggle in "realistic" life-or-death terms. But Lenin's attachment to Martov was great and so, in his proposal to reorganize the *Iskra* board, presented to the Second Congress, Lenin tried to keep Martov as part of his triumverate (Plekhanov was to be the other member). Martov refused to serve, however, without Potresov, Zasulich and Axelrod.

Lenin's desire to reduce the membership of the *Iskra* board in order to make it more efficient was just one aspect of the program Lenin tried to get enacted by the Congress. He also wanted the first paragraph of the party program, which defined membership standards, to reflect this emphasis on tight central control and a professionalized organization. Here, too, Martov wanted a different position taken, one which would allow for more spontaneous participation by the masses.[28] Lenin lost to Martov on this point, but later won on the question of the editorial board, after certain groups, unwanted by both Martov and Lenin, were expelled from the Congress. Taking the name Bolshevik to signify that his was the majority faction of the

[27] Trotsky, *My Life*, pp. 150-51. This description is also found in Trotsky's *Lenin*, pp. 27-29.

[28] See in particular Wolfe, pp. 230-48, Haimson, pp. 165-81, and Leonard Schapiro, *The Communist Party of the Soviet Union* (New York, 1959), Chapter 2, for discussions of the Congress.

party, he left the Martovites with the name Menshevik and the split was realized. Within six months Plekhanov went over to the Mensheviks and Lenin was isolated from the rest of the top leadership of the party. Although he tried for reconciliation with the others, Lenin would not abandon his position to achieve it and hence, when the others refused to yield, he even resigned from *Iskra* rather than continue to work in the ambivalent and tension-ridden atmosphere which had enveloped the party.

The break with Martov and the consummation of the split with Plekhanov was an enormous strain on Lenin. He had to take an extended period of rest in 1904 in order to settle his nerves.[29] But his conviction of his own righteousness and of his correct understanding of the objective demands of the situation remained unshaken. His only wavering was in regard to his personal relations with Plekhanov and Martov, especially the latter. In giving up his "brotherhood" with Martov he was sacrificing a great love to the demands of the cause. Having impersonalized and abstracted his relationship with authority by eliminating his discipleship to Plekhanov, he now removed the last intimate and concrete manifestation of the abstract party, or brotherhood. In so doing he gave himself enormous latitude in dealing with other people, for his emotional involvement in others was from this time on to be minimal.[30] He had eliminated the danger of love and had kept his emotions under control, at least as reflected in his political activity. He had, in a sense, met his own implicit criteria of what a member of the vanguard must be—a hard, convinced, and dedicated leader of an elite.

We must pass over the years from 1904 to the First World War and the advent of the revolution, important though they were. There is space only for a brief note on *Imperialism*, Lenin's influential analysis of the war as a manifestation of the breakdown of capitalist society. Writ-

[29] See Krupskaya, I, 106-16, for Lenin's wife's description of the Congress and the toll it took on his nerves.
[30] Cf. Ulam, p. 194.

ten in 1916, *Imperialism* was meant to answer any questions about the adequacy of Marxism in light of contemporary developments—primarily the working class support for their nations rather than for the international cause of the proletariat after the outbreak of the conflict. Lenin himself had gone through a period of depression and, presumably, doubting, in 1914[31] and *Imperialism* evidently stilled his own doubts as well as those of his followers (or rather the research for it did, as it had in *The Development of Capitalism in Russia*). The form of the book betrays its intimate connection with Lenin's root notions of revolution —and therefore with the identity he had built for himself on the basis of linking himself with the revolutionary cause. The work is highly statistical, as his earliest works had been, an attempt to deal with the facts and objective reality in the manner of Marx, the master himself. Only in those areas where he found his ideology, his rationalized conception of himself and his world, challenged, did Lenin resort to detailed statistical analysis. His early works, his works on agricultural questions (the dominant status of agriculture in the Russian economy did not bode well for revolution in Marxist terms and hence constantly had to be re-examined) and *Imperialism* are the major works of this kind, and each reflects a fundamental concern of Lenin's Marxist identity. The book, then, is an affirmation of Lenin's calling in the face of an apparently recalcitrant reality. Lenin was soon to demonstrate that Russian reality at least was more pliable than many had assumed.

Trotsky: Permanent Revolution

When we left Trotsky, making his way from Siberia to Lenin and the headquarters of *Iskra* in London, he was already a Marxist and a revolutionist; he was not yet a leader. During the period which we now enter, from his arrival in London to the outbreak of the Revolution, he had three essential tasks to perform if he were to develop into a leader of Lenin's caliber. First, Trotsky had to work out his

[31] Wolfe, p. 635 and Possony, p. 163.

relations with equals and possible superiors within the revolutionary camp. Here the results of his efforts were marred by ambivalence, as were all of his attempts to come to grips with authority. Second, and closely related to the first, he had to create a usable organizational basis for himself, as Lenin did so assiduously in building up a faction loyal to himself during the prerevolutionary period. In this attempt Trotsky failed; in a sense, he was never really conscious of the need. Third, he had to develop his Marxism into a workable theory of revolutionary action. Although his theory of "permanent revolution" differed in important respects from Lenin's theory of the vanguard, in many ways it was not incompatible with the latter; it had, however, some additional strengths and weaknesses which made it an even more powerful guide to immediate action but failed to provide the means for prolonged struggle.

During his first two years in western Europe Trotsky established a pattern of relationships with the other prominent Social Democrats which was to last in various guises until 1917. This was a pattern of uneasy alliance with the Mensheviks and other "soft" elements against Lenin and the "hards," an alliance which was frequently broken as Trotsky strayed off into positions of relative isolation.

At first, however, Trotsky's relations with Lenin were extremely good. It was Lenin who had arranged for Trotsky to come to London and introduced him to the city as well as to the current work of *Iskra*.[32] Moreover Trotsky was attracted by Lenin's ideas on the revolution—even while in Siberia Trotsky had argued a position similar to Lenin's on the need for centralization in the party and related issues.[33] And as yet being committed to Lenin's view did not imply being opposed to the other members of *Iskra*; in 1902 Lenin differed from Martov and the others not so much in the elements of his thought but in the weight he attributed to various of those elements and the way he com-

[32] Trotsky tells of his early experiences with Lenin in *Lenin*, pp. 3-11.

[33] Deutscher, *The Prophet Armed*, pp. 45-46.

bined them. These were the differences which were to become clear in 1903, when the "softs" discovered the voluntaristic idea of the vanguard was not mere obeisance to the traditions of Russian revolutionism but a vital part of Lenin's thinking. Trotsky envisioned himself as a follower of *Iskra* as a whole. He blinded himself as much as possible to internal squabbles,[34] and viewed Lenin and the others equally as teachers and guides.[35] And the other members of the board, with the exception of Plekhanov, viewed him in reciprocal terms: he was their student, the brilliant youth who would be trained to be a good Iskraite.[36] To further this training Trotsky was taken to live with Martov and Zasulich and fell very much under their influence. Although his relations with Lenin remained very good until the Second Congress, he was much more involved with the others. All in all it must have seemed like a dream come true to Trotsky: he was loved by people whom he could respect, his articles were being published in *Iskra*, he was speaking for *Iskra* both in London and on the continent—and with extraordinary success. He had found an even more congenial Shvigovsky's garden, an idyllic family in which he was able to rebel against authority, in the form of tsarism and capitalism, while remaining the favorite son and the star pupil. Instead of contracting the range and intensity of his personal ties, as Lenin did, Trotsky was radically expanding them. He was creating a situation in which his feelings of self-esteem and rectitude were dependent upon the continued existence of the complex and fragile social structure which was *Iskra*.

In early 1903, four months after Trotsky's arrival, Lenin proposed that the "youth," as Trotsky was called by some, be elevated to the *Iskra* editorial board. In his letter to Plekhanov urging this course, Lenin cited Trotsky's "rare abilities," "conviction and energy" and emphasized that it would be a convenience in voting to increase the board

[34] Trotsky, *Lenin*, p. 24.
[35] Deutscher, *The Prophet Armed*, pp. 63-64 and 88.
[36] *Ibid.*

from six to seven members.[37] Krupskaya and Trotsky both surmise that, in making this move, Lenin was mainly working to put an end to the deadlocks which developed when the board split in opinion between young and old members.[38] This is undoubtedly part of the story and the fact that Plekhanov vetoed the proposal lends weight to the supposition—Plekhanov, as we know from his relations with Lenin, was something of a "hard" and would therefore reject any change in operations which might weaken his personal power. One still has to explain, however, why it was Trotsky instead of any one of a number of other revolutionists who were in contact with Lenin at the time (Krupskaya's memoirs are full of the comings and goings of an extensive circle of revolutionists) whom Lenin selected in this effort.

It seems clear that Lenin felt that Trotsky was an extraordinary young man, one of unusual brightness and revolutionary fervor. Trotsky certainly must have appeared to be an ardent "Leninist," with his eagerness to act, his facile absorption of Lenin's line and his apparent commitment to centralized organization. His youth, which others may have held against him, probably had a positive attraction for Lenin; here was what every leader needs, a brilliant disciple in whom one could place a degree of faith, whom one could train to be a firm member of the revolutionary vanguard. Trotsky, it appears, had no knowledge at the time that Lenin was attempting the "co-optation" to the board.[39] Hence he and Lenin must have perceived the situation as the Second Congress opened in rather different terms. Lenin thought of Trotsky as a loyal disciple whose interests Lenin was trying to promote; Trotsky saw himself as a disciple of *Iskra*, loyal to all members ideologically,

[37] Cited in Trotsky, *My Life*, pp. 152-54.
[38] *Ibid*., p. 155; Krupskaya, I, 85.
[39] It is unclear exactly how much Trotsky knew of the maneuvers to get him on the editorial board. Trotsky, who discovered the letter from Lenin to Plekhanov only in later years, claims that he was ignorant of everything going on behind the scenes (*My Life*, p. 154).

but personally loyal first to Martov and Zasulich, then to Lenin and not at all to Plekhanov.

During the early stages of the 1903 Congress Trotsky sided with Lenin on a large range of questions, speaking very effectively for Lenin's positions. His closeness to Lenin's stance is indicated by the fact that new arrivals at the Congress were often sent to Trotsky for indoctrination[40] and that Trotsky soon earned the nickname of "Lenin's cudgel."[41] But he split with Lenin over paragraph one of the party platform, which Lenin wanted to see as an affirmation of a "narrow" or professional party membership, and even more violently over Lenin's plan to bring the *Iskra* board down to three members. At first Lenin did not react harshly to Trotsky's stand, as he did to Martov's. He spoke to him in conciliatory and fatherly tones at the sessions of the Congress and spent long hours with him when the Congress was not meeting attempting to "bring over Trotsky," to make his young (now former) follower understand the logic and necessity of his position.[42] But Trotsky only became more intransigent in his anti-Leninist views. When the Congress closed Trotsky was on the side of the Mensheviks.

Why did Trotsky, who apparently had held views similar to Lenin's and who had been so closely aligned with Lenin during the early phases of the Congress, now side with the group which was "soft" then and was eventually to be condemned by Trotsky to "the dust heap of history"? Deutscher, Eastman, and Trotsky each addresses himself to this question—in a sense, an unfair question because it is largely in retrospect that the differences in orientation implied by the split became clear.[43] In another sense, however, it is an important question, for the differences in mood, in feeling, were commented upon at the time and were in fact the principal determinants of the divergent

[40] Wolfe, p. 229.   [41] Krupskaya, I, 99.
[42] Deutscher, *Prophet Armed*, p. 81.
[43] *Ibid.*, pp. 88-97; Eastman, *Leon Trotsky*, pp. 170-81; Trotsky, *My Life*, pp. 161-64.

courses the two parties took during the revolution and after.

Eastman claims that Trotsky sided with Martov and the others because "he had faith in his friends."[44] This, in fact, is the major argument that both Deutscher, and Trotsky himself, advance. And it would seem to touch on an important aspect of the situation: Trotsky had to choose between Lenin and Plekhanov on the one hand and Martov, Zasulich, and Axelrod on the other. His contact with the latter had been closer and his antipathy for Plekhanov was great. Trotsky had not freed himself from the web of personal involvement as Lenin was in the process of doing and hence he reacted against Lenin, who was breaking up the emotionally comfortable world that Trotsky had found in *Iskra*. Lenin and Plekhanov embodied an arrogant authority bent on depriving Trotsky of people whose love he prized. But the major unconscious reason for Trotsky's becoming a revolutionist in the first place had been to escape from a situation which had just such elements, to escape from the presence of his father who had deprived Trotsky of his mother's love when he most wanted it. This time, however, Trotsky did not find it necessary to flee from the situation (although his later meanderings in Austria and the Balkans before the outbreak of the First World War probably were analogous to the earlier flight); he could side with the abused party and feel that he was not acting for himself but for people being abused by authority, in this case fellow revolutionists.

There is another reason for Trotsky's siding with the Mensheviks, at the Congress and throughout the next decade or so (siding with the Mensheviks but never quite becoming one). Deutscher hints at it in the following passage:

> Trotsky's inclinations, his tastes, his temperament revolted against the prosaic and business-like determination with which Lenin was setting out to bring the party down from the clouds of abstraction to the firm

[44] Eastman, *Leon Trotsky*, p. 174.

ground of organization. Trotsky's present protest was little different from that which, as a boy of seventeen, he had, with so much ill-temper, thrown at Sokolov-skaya, the first Marxist he had met: 'A curse upon all of you who want to bring dryness and hardness into all the relations of life!'[45]

Trotsky, in a set of comments which bridges the themes of pain at the dissolution of the revolutionary family and an unwillingness to face, as he put it, the "harsh, imperative and demanding principle" of revolutionary centralism,[46] states:

> My whole being seemed to *protest* against this *merci-less* cutting off of the older ones when they were at last on the threshold of an organized party. It was my *indignation* at his attitude that really led to my part-ing [with Lenin] at the second congress. His behavior seemed *unpardonable* to me, both *horrible* and *out-rageous*.[47] (Emphasis added.)

At the time, in fact, Trotsky wrote anti-Lenin tracts which were much harsher and anguished than the above in their denunciation of Lenin's hardness. When Trotsky wrote *My Life*, in which the above lines appear, he had consciously accepted the "demanding principle" of revolutionary cen-tralism; unconsciously, however, he never quite did, and in that fact lies much of his appeal and his tragedy.

Lenin's hardness, as we have seen, was premised on his basic mistrust and his view of the world as dangerous and the class enemy as deadly. In order to survive in this world he created organizational safeguards for himself, sacrificed personal ties and dedicated himself singlemindedly to the struggle. Trotsky, although more of an activist than his fel-low Mensheviks, shared their essential faith in others. Ad-ditionally, he did not view the enemy with quite the fearful respect and hatred that Lenin did. Because he did not view

[45] Deutscher, *Prophet Armed*, p. 97.
[46] Trotsky, *My Life*, p. 161.   [47] *Ibid.*, p. 162.

the struggle in such harsh terms, and because his own experiences with the masses, in the Ukraine and then in 1905 and 1917, led him to have confidence in their revolutionary spirit, Trotsky could not understand the need for eliminating Zasulich and the others in 1903, even if they were not efficient, nor could he grasp the kill-or-be-killed nature of the intra-party struggle after the takeover of power. Although Trotsky ultimately did come to understand the nature of the struggle somewhat better, he never fully realized that disciplined organization was the key to victory in the Russian context. Hence relations with superiors, equals, and followers remained ill-defined and debilitating. In brief, Trotsky always relied on the power of the word, on his ability to convince others of his correctness and prerogatives by the force of his verbal production alone. He was thus not motivated to create an organizational instrument for the advancement of his policies, nor ruthlessly to break off relations with those who could not be molded to his purposes.

Trotsky's alliance with the Mensheviks was fundamentally unstable, for in a crucial respect he was even farther from them than Lenin was. Trotsky's faith in revolutionary action and his youthfulness combined to make him very impatient. He was convinced that the final struggle was coming soon. In this regard he was even closer to the populist tradition in Russian politics than Lenin, who in turn was much closer to it than the Mensheviks. His idea of "permanent revolution" was predicated on the imminence of the conflict, as we shall see, and his eager response to the revolutionary events of 1905 is another indication of the centrality of immediate action in his mind. The Mensheviks were content to let history run its course; Lenin sought to act as a catalytic agent for the historical process; and Trotsky was convinced that stages of historical development could be skipped under certain conditions. So ran the continuum of activism. In 1917 Lenin was to accept implicitly Trotsky's notion of passing over the bourgeois

democratic phase, and Trotsky grew to realize the importance of party.

For several years after the 1903 Congress, while his relationship with Martov and the others fluctuated widely,
Trotsky maintained close ties with Parvus, who befriended
him on many occasions and provided many of the basic
ideas of permanent revolution.[48] Although it was formally
a relationship of peers, Trotsky, by far the younger, was
rather in the position of disciple or student, although a
difficult student with his own ideas and given to independent action.[49] At the same time he had trouble working with
those people who were his peers and only moderate success at building up a group of followers. To the extent he
was successful in this latter task, it was only with other
exiled intellectuals, not with Marxist workingmen and
others inside Russia itself. Until Lenin's death, this was the
characteristic pattern of Trotsky's relations with others. His
half-rebellious, half-admiring ties to his father and his frequent humiliation by the peasant boys (now transformed
into a tendency to humiliate others); his mocking yet dutiful attention to his school teachers coupled with betrayal by
his schoolmates; now his uneasy following of the older
Mensheviks and Parvus and his inability to function with
his equals; and later his assertive obedience to Lenin and
his complete failure to build a faction loyal to him—this
pattern is indicative of the fundamental ambivalence of
Trotsky's attitude towards authority and the weaknesses
inherent in his own particular mastery of the expression of
aggression problem.

While the Russian revolutionary exiles were myopically
involved with their factional disputes, events in Russia were
pressing ahead without them. The disasters of the Russo-
Japanese war, labor unrest, and "Bloody Sunday," the day
on which the Tsar's troops fired on a peaceful delegation

[48] Parvus (A. L. Helfand) was a Russian Jew who lived in Germany
and was a highly respected contributor to Marxist periodicals.
[49] Deutscher analyzes the relationship in Chapter IV of *The Prophet
Armed.*

of St. Petersburg workers led by Father Gapon, were rapidly creating a situation conducive to revolutionary action.[50] Trotsky was one of the first to recognize the possibilities for action, and by February was in Kiev and in early spring in St. Petersburg. In order to escape arrest, he was forced to flee to Finland during the summer, but returned to the capital in October. Throughout the autumn he was the effective leader of the Petersburg Soviet, speaking endlessly and setting out the guidelines for all tactical decisions. He also found time to write intensively, producing a wide range of propaganda designed to appeal to as many levels of Russian society as possible.[51] On December 3 Trotsky and the other leaders of the Soviet were arrested.

At the trial which followed Trotsky defended his principles and actions brilliantly and aggressively, and won for his trouble another term of exile in, this time, a not-so-pleasant area in northern Siberia. He managed to escape even before he arrived, however, and was back in western Europe by 1907. While in prison, he had examined the events of the past year, concluded that they marked a turning point in his life and the course of Russian history (Trotsky always identified his personal life with more general events) and produced a full-blown statement of permanent revolution.[52] Before turning to that doctrine, however, there are several things which should be noted about 1905 itself.

First, Trotsky was enormously stimulated by his participation in the events of the period, as he had been earlier in his work with the Southern Russian Workers' Union and as he was to be later during the Russian Revolution and its immediate aftermath. Trotsky had adopted revolution as a form of activity in which to lose himself and thus avoid facing certain problems. During quiet periods those problems, in surrogate form, continually arose; he had to deal

---

[50] Wolfe deals with the events of 1905 from the perspective of Lenin and Trotsky in Chapters XVII and XVIII.

[51] Deutscher, *Prophet Armed*, Chapter V, *passim*.

[52] Trotsky discusses his reactions to the events in *My Life*, pp. 183-85.

carefully with peers and attempt to interpret events without being able to act upon his interpretations. He lacked Lenin's ability to wait for the appropriate time for action by preparing carefully for any eventuality. Away from the immediate stimulation of the event, Trotsky dissipated his energies in diverse journalistic enterprises instead of remaining narrowly oriented towards the one goal of revolution in Russia.

Moreover, the source of this stimulation was Trotsky's production of words in a context where those words had great power. Verbal prowess had been his first expression of self-esteem and masculine assertiveness and now masses of people were paying attention to him as a result of that skill.[53] 1905 was thus a massive confirmation of the utility of the technique he had chosen to enunciate his manhood and independence. His faith in words, especially his own words, was thus reinforced.

In addition, as it became more and more obvious that arrest could not be far off, Trotsky, instead of fleeing, allowed himself to be arrested.[54] Here again his behavior was similar to that of his first revolutionary efforts. Trotsky still regarded authority as partially benevolent, for he did not expect to be killed for his insurrectionary activities. He did expect a sentence of hard labor, however, although in fact he received a milder one. Ostensibly he did not flee because his trial presented an opportunity to enunciate his revolutionary position. Although for a person who valued the effects of his words as highly as Trotsky did this was undoubtedly an important reason. One is led to suspect that, as we surmised earlier in connection with Trotsky's reactions to the threat of arrest in the Ukraine, his imperfect mastery of the problem of guilt impelled him to seek punishment. Again Trotsky's critical streak of ambivalence is displayed. Unlike Gandhi he could not incorporate the need for punishment into an effective political tool—and if he

[53] Deutscher, *Prophet Armed*, p. 128.
[54] Trotsky, *My Life*, p. 180.

had tried his fate would have been Sasha's; and unlike Lenin he could not control his tendency to submit sufficiently to move out of danger's way when necessary, even at the cost of temporary loss of popularity with the masses. As it turned out this ambivalence was an asset in 1905; Trotsky, through his trial and escape, was able to solidify his prestige without significant suffering. In 1917 during the July Days, when he again allowed himself to be arrested, he placed himself in greater jeopardy; but on balance Trotsky's ambivalence towards authority worked to his advantage in these situations (although only because the officials of the regime did not strike as strongly as they might have—Trotsky placed the initiative in their hands, not his). After the Revolution, however, when the authority was Stalin's instead of that of a crumbling tsarism, this same attitude would be the principal psychological cause of Trotsky's defeat.

Finally, as mentioned earlier, the experiences of 1905 shored up Trotsky's faith in the spontaneous revolutionary inclinations of the masses, and thus they reinforced his tendency to discount organization. Formally, he never took an antiorganization position. At most he protested, as in 1903, against what he felt were abuses of intra-organizational power. But such things as his emphasis on intuition in politics, of a "subconscious sense which, although it may be developed and enriched by theoretical and practical work, must be ingrained in the very nature of the individual,"[55] is a far cry from the distrust of human nature on which Lenin's demand for organization is based; and Trotsky's pointed comments on the ineffectiveness of the Bolshevik organization in 1905 when deprived of Lenin's direction indicate his essential commitment to nonorganizational forms of revolutionary activity.[56]

While he was still in prison in 1906 Trotsky wrote *The Balance and the Prospects—the Moving Forces of the Revolution*, in which he systematically outlined the theory of

[55] Trotsky, *My Life*, p. 185.　　[56] *Ibid.*, p. 176.

permanent revolution.[57] Like Lenin, he argued that the Russian proletariat was the vanguard of the international socialist revolution, but his ideas differed from Lenin's in certain vital respects. First, he saw in Russia conditions which would enable the proletariat to come to power as a result of the first successful antitsarist revolt. Because of the peculiarly Russian mixture of primitive social and economic differentiation and a highly developed state apparatus, there would be no need to pass through a period of bourgeois control of the state. He argued that

> It is, therefore, not excluded that in a backward country with a lesser degree of capitalistic development, the proletariat should sooner reach political supremacy than in a highly developed capitalist state. . . .
>
> * * *
>
> It is our opinion that the Russian revolution creates conditions whereby political power can . . . pass into the hands of the proletariat before the politicians of the liberal bourgeoisie would have the occasion to give their political genius full swing.[58]

For the proletariat to keep power, however, two conditions must be met. First, the proletariat must win the support of the peasantry, the majority of the Russian population— "once in power, the proletariat will appear before the peasantry as its liberator."[59] Second, the Russian proletariat would have to be supported by proletariats of western Europe, who would seize power now that the bulwark of Russian autocracy had been broken down.[60] This idea he shared with Lenin—but he held it with more faith and fervor than the latter. Thus the Revolution, when it came, would

---

[57] Unfortunately no good English translations of this work exist. Hence we will rely on Trotsky's "Prospects of a Labor Dictatorship," in *Our Revolution*, Moissaye J. Olgin, ed. and trans. (New York, 1918), which is the most extensive translation available of *The Balance.*

[58] Trotsky, "Prospects of a Labor Dictatorship," pp. 84-85.

[59] *Ibid.*, p. 98.   [60] *Ibid.*, p. 93.

be permanent: it would not stop at its bourgeois phase in Russia and it would not stop at Russia's borders. To survive it would have to spread to Europe and result in the creation of a socialist world.

The strengths and the weaknesses of this ideological perspective are clear. It promised the socialist utopia soon, and told the Russian worker that it was his to achieve. These were its main strengths; it was a suitable prophecy of process for a revolutionary situation. But for its socialistic promise to be fulfilled the Russian proletariat would have to win the support of the peasantry and the progressive elements in western Europe; either there must be world socialism or the revolution would be crushed. (In point of historical fact the revolution was not crushed when Russia was isolated, but the fruits of the revolution which Trotsky foresaw, a dictatorship of the proletariat followed by a classless society of equality and freedom for all, were nipped in the bud.) What themes in Trotsky's personality help us to account for this perception of the situation, so radically different from those of Lenin and the Mensheviks alike?

In Trotsky's view, the inevitable laws of history, in this case as manifested by the possibility of somewhat altering the prophesied pattern of development, were subordinated to the initiative of a particular set of workers and leaders. Trotsky was a participant first and a Marxist second, and so his doctrine bore the stamp of his emphasis on activity. For Lenin the danger had been inactivity, a falling into Menshevism as a result of his caution and reliance on paternal Marxism. His need to identify with his brother, however, provided the necessary activating ingredient. For Trotsky the danger was action without direction; but his intellectual prowess and his need to relieve the tension of the revolutionary struggle helped to insure that doctrine would not be ignored.

Marxism for Lenin had been both a guide to action and a definition of the end-state of the struggle, although he had to infuse the doctrine with voluntaristic elements to make

it effective. For Trotsky, despite his affirmation of the usefulness of Marxism as an analytical tool, the doctrine essentially seemed to represent the utopia to which he aspired. In the post-capitalist world, as he was to put it in
Literature and Revolution in 1924:

> Man will become immeasurably stronger, wiser and
> subtler; his body will become more harmonized, his
> movements more rhythmic, his voice more musical.
> The forms of life will become dynamically dramatic.
> The average human type will rise to the heights of an
> Aristotle, a Goethe, or a Marx. And beyond this ridge
> new peaks will rise.[61]

In other words, one aspect of the permanence of the
Revolution was that the socialistic world would be realized
soon. Trotsky's struggles, against his feelings of guilt and
authority, would thus be ended; he was much less successful at managing his feelings of ambivalence than Lenin
(or Gandhi) and hence needed to view the end as near. At
the same time his optimism—his faith in the favorable outcome of events in Russia as well as in the revolutionary potential of western Europe—allowed him to have confidence
in the imminence of world revolution. While Lenin viewed
his environment balefully, fighting hard to preserve the endangered life of his cause and himself, Trotsky faced the
world eagerly, expecting that any moment it would be transformed into the society of his dreams. Trotsky's optimism
would provide him with great resilience during the days of
the revolutionary struggle, but it would leave him ill-pre-
pared for the grey struggle for power within the Krem-
lin. Lenin would have, by contrast, far less need for
readjustment.

The doctrine of permanent revolution did not attract immediate attention; the revolution of 1905 was already wan-
ing by the time Trotsky's manuscript was published. But in
the years to come it was to be the main element of "Trot-

[61] *Literature and Revolution* (Ann Arbor, Mich., 1960), p. 256.

skyism" and Trotsky was to defend it, with only some significant changes in emphasis (more caution, for example, was introduced into his later statements of his position) until the end of his life.[62]

During the period after the 1905 revolution Trotsky participated on and off in Menshevik affairs, and was involved in various publishing and journalistic ventures. He built up no firm organizational affiliations and he did not, patiently and single-mindedly, prepare for the advent of a new revolution. Despite his frequent quarrels with the Mensheviks, he refused to break with them completely. The period in general was marked by a diffusion of interest, a tendency to move away from the affairs of Russian Social Democrats (preferring the more congenial company of urban European Marxists), and a lack of renunciation of those pleasures and interests which had no direct bearing on the revolutionary struggle. One of the reasons Trotsky appealed and still appeals to intellectuals, of course, is the very universalism of his interests, his responsiveness to diverse intellectual stimuli. But this very openness meant that he was less prepared to lead than Lenin, whose narrow field of interest gave him a rather prosaic appearance in comparison but also the power that comes from total involvement in one set of problems.

There is another aspect of Trotsky's lack of renunciation: there was nothing of the ascetic about him. He did not give up personal ties, intellectual and asthetic pleasures or even stylishness of dress for the cause. This "indulgence" had the important side effect of making Trotsky more of an object of envy than Lenin, whose simplicity and personal unaffectedness helped to ward off feelings of personal animosity, and it also reflected a certain lack of commitment to the root aspects of the revolutionary identity he had chosen for himself. Lenin and Gandhi were so involved in and dependent on their beliefs that they had little need or room for the supplementary props of personal friendships or sweeping intellectual prowess. These qualities, as much

[62] See, for example, his *Permanent Revolution* (Calcutta, 1947), first published in 1930.

as we admire them in Trotsky and may crave them for ourselves, are a sign of political weakness, not strength, in the revolutionary leader.

Gandhi: Satyagraha *as Revolution*

Gandhi went home to India in January 1915. His passive resistance movement in South Africa had yielded substantial success and he returned to his homeland something of a hero. He had yet, however, to test the efficacy of his ideas or of *satyagraha*, his means of political action, in the Indian context. Nor did he have either an organizational basis for action in India or a clearly defined set of relations with Indian nationalist leaders, the great mass of the Indian people—or the servants of the British raj. But before trying to indicate the nature of his Indian experience in these regards, it seems wise to try to spell out in somewhat greater detail than we have done hitherto the characteristics of Gandhi's ideology.

The basic text of Gandhism, *Hind Swaraj*,[63] is in the form of a dialogue between Gandhi and an advocate of violent action in the service of India's liberation. This "Reader" holds a position which was very common in India throughout the first half of the twentieth century—he is a westernizer, an advocate of western, especially British, civilization for India as a counterweight to British domination.

As Gandhi puts his position:

[63] There is no one text of Gandhism which is fully comparable to Lenin's *What Is To Be Done?* or Trotsky's *Balance and Prospects. Hind Swaraj* (Indian Home Rule) is the closest approximation. Gandhi wrote it as a series of articles in 1909, the purpose of which was to pose an alternative position to the one advocated by those in favor of using violence against the British. The advocate of violence is encountered as the "Reader" in the work and is gently led to the realization of the importance of *Ahimsa*, nonviolence, by the helpful "editor." Although written soon after the advent of Satyagraha, *Hind Swaraj* was long considered the handbook of nonviolence. Gandhi himself wrote, in an article in *Aryan Path* in September 1938 that "after the stormy thirty years through which I have since passed, I have seen nothing to make me alter the views expounded in [*Hind Swaraj*]."

We may get [self-government] when we have the same powers [as the British]; we shall then hoist our own flag. As is Japan, so must India be. We must own our own navy, our army, and we must have our own splendour, and then will India's voice ring through the world. . . . If the English Parliament be the Mother of Parliaments, I certainly think that we should copy the English people, and this to such an extent that, just as they do not allow others to obtain a footing in their country, so we should not allow them or others to obtain it in ours.[64]

As Gandhi, as "Editor," says, the "Reader" wants:

English rule without the Englishman. You want the tiger's nature, but not the tiger; that is to say, you would make India English. And when it becomes English, it will not be called Hindustan but *Englistan*.[65]

Importantly the solution to the problem which the "Reader" poses is the same in essence as that which Gandhi earlier had attempted in his effort to resolve his problems of lack of masculinity. In London and earlier, Gandhi had tried to be like the English in order to be a man; he was unable to master the task and reverted to his mother's Hinduism, thereby arriving at a workable identity for himself. Now he finds Indians at large chasing after the same counterfeit, from his viewpoint: British/masculine identity. He sets out to prove to them that neither self-respect nor courage, and certainly not "*Swaraj*," can come from such an attempt: the result would be as incongruous as "Englistan."

Gandhi first tries to demonstrate that, even if Indians were capable of becoming English, there is nothing to be gained from Anglicization. Politically he asserts that the English Parliament, which is so much esteemed, is a "sterile woman and a prostitute," for it brings forth nothing good and is always being abused, first by one master, then by

[64] M. K. Gandhi, *Hind Swaraj* (Ahmedabad, 1938), p. 21.
[65] *Ibid.*

another.[66] The immediate implication would seem to be that the ideal in government would be a fertile "woman" capable of ruling herself; the abusive father must be eliminated. Lenin and Trotsky, too, wanted to eliminate a brutal authority, but they quickly came to believe, however reluctantly, in replacing such authority with a benevolent paternalism. In Gandhi's thought there is no room for the father as father; masculinity and femininity, ruler and ruled, must be merged into one, into *Sat*, simple truth or love.

For Gandhi, the general evil, of which the English Parliament is only a part, is modern civilization.[67] This civilization, to Gandhi, is strictly a process of increasing material gain, coupled with progressive spiritual loss. "This civilization is irreligion," he says, and its effect has been to weaken men, so that in Europe men "lack real physical strength or courage."[68] It is a "Satanic Civilization," a "Black Age," a disease which must be cured.[69] Although he hedges on this sometimes, Gandhi basically rejects western civilization in particular and materialism, including thereby the human body, in general. All such things are *maya*, illusion; truth and permanence rest in the soul. The differentiation between *sat* and *maya* is a root idea of Hinduism; many Indians believed in it. But few felt compelled to hold the belief as strongly or to make it as much a part of their lives as Gandhi, whose renunciation of the physical—of sex, food, clothing and possessions—was one of his most striking characteristics. As I argued in the preceding chapter, the linchpin of this web of asceticism was the renunciation of sexual desire, the rejection of masculinity as too dangerous and difficult and the affirmation of feminine passivity as not only godly and true but as courageous and estimable as well.

If, the Reader then asks, the British are so afflicted and so weakened, how have they been able to conquer and hold India? The Editor replies: "The English have not taken

[66] *Ibid.*, p. 22.
[67] *Ibid.*, pp. 24-27.
[68] *Ibid.*, p. 26.
[69] *Ibid.*, p. 27.

India; we have given it to them."[70] The English hold India because the Indians have sold out their heritage for a figurative mess of pottage. Out of their hunger for material well-being they have allowed the English to gradually control—and divide—them. All the signs of English rule in India are viewed as tokens of evil. The British provide peace but at the price of making the Indians "emasculated," "cowardly," and "effeminate."[71] They built railroads which allow them to spread their rule farther and facilitate the spread of disease and other evils ("Good travels at a snail's pace," claims Gandhi, and hence has no need of the rails). British rule has led to strife between Moslems and Hindus which Gandhi claims did not exist before; it has accentuated litigation through the introduction of western courts and law and this has contributed to communal enmity; and by the introduction of doctors it has caused Indians to weaken in self-restraint (for relief from their corporeal sins is always available).[72] Thus the Indians, in chasing after material well-being, have left themselves victimized and degraded. A purified return to the old traditions of Hinduism is needed, a return to "good conduct," to the simple and spiritual practices of India which make her the most civilized country in the world.[73] India, in other words, must follow the path to redemption that Gandhi has followed. In so doing it will make of itself a people worthy to be led, worthy to have Swaraj. This also had been the theme of Gandhi's appeal to the South African Indians—through self-purification and restraint to victory.

After admitting that there are imperfections in the Indian traditions, such as child marriage, which must be eliminated along with the subservience to British ideals, Gandhi goes on to argue that India's self-realization will in fact yield Swaraj. India is enslaved only because its westernized segments, of which the Editor and the Reader are two representatives, have betrayed their heritage. The great mass of the Indian people are as yet uncorrupted. Thus

[70] *Ibid.*, p. 27. [71] *Ibid.*, p. 31.
[72] *Ibid.*, pp. 34-42. [73] *Ibid.*, pp. 42-47.

if we [the westernized ones] become free, India is free.
And in this thought you have a definition of Swaraj. It
is Swaraj when we learn to rule ourselves.[74]

Swaraj is thus an individual matter; each man must learn to
rule himself. When he does, his example will convince
others, even the English. And once the English have been
converted by the example of the Indians, there will be no
need to expel them from India, for they will be "Indian-
ized." Hence, too, violent struggle will not be needed. Individual self-restraint will be sufficient to secure India's
liberation.[75]

In a sense, Gandhi here provided the Indian intellectual
with an extreme form of the voluntaristic elitism which was
so crucial in Lenin's thought, while at the same time providing an analogue to the Marxist concept of the historical
process. The eternally spiritual nature of the Indian peasantry gives the same assurance of victory that the inevitable
course of class development does. But, as in Leninism, elite
action is needed to activate the potential of this great force.
Unlike Lenin, Gandhi stated that the individual could act
without the concurrence of others and, unlike Lenin,
Gandhi claimed that the "elite" was inferior, not superior,
to the masses. But both viewed the struggle in terms of an
elite which would utilize a larger population in securing
utopian ends. In Lenin this combination stemmed from his
identification with his brother and his need for the security
of paternal strength. In Gandhi it resulted from the need to
achieve a masculine identity which was less conflict-ridden
than one based on the full assumption of masculine activity,
but one which nonetheless would provide an opportunity
for the expression, no matter how disguised, of those feelings of assertiveness and aggressiveness which were so de-
structive when internalized.

The Reader in *Hind Swaraj* is not yet totally convinced
by the Editor's arguments. The British have always ruled
by "brute force," he says. Is not brute force necessary to

[74] *Ibid.*, p. 47.   [75] *Ibid.*

counter brute force? Are not the English like a thief in a house, who must be driven out by any means?[76] The Editor's reply is that ends and means cannot be separated. If the goal is Swaraj as he has defined it, and the Reader by now has agreed to that end, then the means must be compatible with it. "I am not likely to obtain the result flowing from the worship of God by laying myself prostrate before Satan."[77] Thus if Swaraj is to be obtained at all, only peaceful means must be used. In this, obviously, Gandhi differs radically from Lenin and Trotsky. Each of the latter argued that violent means could be used to gain idyllic ends. Neither of them had the inhibitions about the expression of aggression that Gandhi did, nor did they identify with their mothers as Gandhi did with his. None of these men believed in uninhibited aggressiveness; Gandhi and Lenin in particular believed that lack of emotional control, whatever the nature of the emotion, was dangerous. But Lenin, who was basically mistrustful and who had a firmer identification with the masculine figures in his life, felt that love was more dangerous than hate, passivity more of a risk than activity. Gandhi, who was more trustful and more feminine, reversed the formula: hatred and aggression were more likely to lead to unhappy consequences than love. Both held to these formulas with great intensity, and both tried to transform their environments in terms of their ideas. But Gandhi's effort was based on love and femininity, which gives his actions their peculiar saintliness.

In the course of dealing with the Reader's argument for brute force, Gandhi turns to the question of how to treat a thief:

> Now we shall take the example given by you of the thief to be driven out. I do not agree with you that the thief may be driven out by any means. If it is my fa-

[76] *Ibid.*, p. 51; it should be kept in mind as this section of *Hind Swaraj* is analyzed that Gandhi stole as a child and that his confession of his theft to his father resulted in a lessening of his internal tension (pp. 78-80).

[77] *Ibid.*

ther who has come to steal I shall use one kind of means. If it is an acquaintance I shall use another; and in the case of a perfect stranger I shall use a third. . . . Again, I fancy that I should pretend to be sleeping whether the thief was my father or that strong armed man. The reason for this is that my father would also be armed and I should succumb to the strength of either and allow my things to be stolen. The strength of my father would make me weep with pity; the strength of the armed man would rouse in me anger and we should become enemies. . . .[78]

It is striking that the first example of aggression that Gandhi takes up, one which is an intentional analogy to British–Indian relations, is of how he would act if his father had come to rob him while he was in bed! One is immediately reminded of Gandhi's adolescent fears of spirits which would come to harm him when he and Kasturbai were in bed together. These spirits, the British and the hypothetical thief are all manifestations of the same fear of his father, the fear that his father will come and deprive him of something precious. In his adolescence, however, his father was viewed as bent on punishing him for his sexual presumption; as I argued, Gandhi's feelings of guilt were very strong. Now, although the dread of the father is still apparent, father is a thief and hence morally inferior. Gandhi feels "pity" for him. He goes on to say that one should, without objecting, give the thief all one has, for then the thief, moved by this selfless action, will repent, return one's goods, beg one's pardon and become one's servant.[79] By a willingness to lose one's masculinity, one will not only regain it but have one's father as a servant. Underneath the selfless femininity of *satyagraha* is the undying hope that one's masculinity is not gone after all, that even one's father will accept it some day, and that, in fact, the father will recognize the moral superiority of the son.

[78] *Ibid.*, p. 52.   [79] *Ibid.*, p. 54.

The Reader, who is becoming more acquiescent as the pages pass, now asks that passive resistance be enlarged upon. The Editor responds:

> Passive resistance is a method of securing rights by personal suffering; it is the reverse of resistance by arms. When I refuse to do a thing which is repugnant to my conscience, I use soul-force.[80]

The Reader acknowledges some of the strengths of this method. He admits that subservience to laws with which one does not agree is unmanly, that by passively resisting them one can object to such laws without bringing widespread violence and that, if the objector has chosen an unjust cause, the only one to suffer thereby is himself. But, he says, does all this not make passive resistance a technique for the weak, who cannot defend themselves anyway? Surely arms are to be preferred when one is strong. The Editor replies:

> This is gross ignorance. Passive resistance, that is, soul-force, is matchless. It is superior to force of arms. How, then, can it be considered only a weapon for the weak? Physical-force men are strangers to the courage which is requisite in a passive resister. . . . What do you think? Wherein is courage required—in blowing others to pieces from behind a cannon, or with a smiling face to approach a cannon and be blown to pieces? . . . Believe me that a man devoid of courage and manhood can never be a passive resister.[81]

Thus Gandhi claims that passive resistance is more manly than violent resistance. He has, as Susanne Rudolph argues, redefined courage, infused it with feminine attributes and the glorification of suffering.[82]

Gandhi, as the Editor, then describes the path to Satyagrahi. It is, naturally enough, exactly that course of action that Gandhi has been following in South Africa: one

[80] *Ibid.*, p. 57.   [81] *Ibid.*, pp. 59-60.
[82] Rudolph, "The New Courage."

must abstain from sexual intercourse, seek poverty, follow truth and cultivate fearlessness.[83] If Indians would but be like Gandhi, if they would base their pride on humility and the willingness to suffer ridicule and their courage on the renunciation of aggression, then India would have Swaraj.

After his return to India, Gandhi did not immediately involve himself in political activity. Gopal Krishna Gokhale, one of the leading moderates in Indian politics and the man whom Gandhi considered to be his "political guru" or teacher, had commanded him to spend a year observing the Indian scene before engaging in political activity.[84] The command was congenial to Gandhi, who felt the need to reacclimate himself to Indian conditions. Before that year was out Gokhale had died. Henceforward Gandhi recognized no living guru. Like Lenin, his activity was to be guided strictly by his own interpretation of the truth. He would obey the "still small voice" inside him in all things. Thus Gokhale's death eliminated the possibility of clashing with any Indian nationalist whom Gandhi would feel compelled to obey.

Gandhi did not claim superiority to any of the other leaders of Indian nationalism. Rather he claimed inferiority; he was the humblest, the lowliest of them all. The important thing, of course, was not whether he had pretensions of being the highest or the lowest, but that he said he was one or the other. Either would give him a unique status and in India, with its traditions of the holy beggar and the need of its people to find a counter-identity to that proposed by the British, Gandhi's sincere posture of humility and lowliness could serve as the basis for actual leadership. Because his ideas had such enormous appeal, and because he personally developed such a hold on the emotions of the other nationalists and the country as a whole, as a result of his confidence, serenity, and personal asceticism, he had no trouble building an organized following. Although he followed a rather changing course of political

[83] Gandhi, *Hind Swaraj*, p. 61.
[84] Gandhi, *Autobiography*, p. 383.

activity throughout his career, cancelling demonstrations when he felt violence would result and even leaving national politics entirely when he felt such action was appropriate, and despite the fact that he never sought the formal positions of leadership in the Congress Party, the national organization of Indian politics, until the advent of independence Gandhi was usually able to get the Congress to follow the course of action he proposed. And, like Lenin, he sought to train a body of men and women who would be totally loyal to the cause, who would be perfect Satyagrahis as Lenin's followers were to be perfect Bolsheviks. Although he never advocated the kind of centralism and control which was so vital a part of Leninism, he nonetheless sought to transform the lives of those around him in such a way that the same end was accomplished. His primary instruments in this task were the *ashrams*, variously located throughout India during this period. The *ashram* was a communal settlement under Gandhi's direction and devoted to the purification of its members. Through spinning, vegetarianism, sexual renunciation, prayer, and other forms of service and asceticism, the members of the settlement were to become servants of Truth.[85] When in 1930 Gandhi felt the need for absolute reliability in his followers, it was to the Sabarmati *ashram* that he turned for recruits.

The nucleus of Gandhi's organization in Indian politics, then, consisted of ashramites and certain Gandhian leaders of the Indian National Congress (such as the Nehrus and the Patels). The Congress itself was often the instrument of Satyagraha, but Gandhi's authority was never wholly or even primarily derived from his control of the party. The Congress had turned to him in 1920 when Gandhi proposed noncooperation with the British and no other forms of resistance were proving effective.[86] At that time, Gandhi reorganized Congress, transforming it from a forum for nationalist lawyers into a mass organization. For Gandhi the primary function of the organization was to bring Indian

[85] Nanda, *Mahatma Gandhi*, pp. 139-40.
[86] *Ibid.*, pp. 181-86 and 207-14.

leadership into contact with their natural source of strength, the great mass of the Indian people. He proposed to the Congress his personal remedy for all ills: abandon the Englishman's legalistic debating and root your strength in the support of common men and women of India.

Gandhi was not highly dependent on the party, for he could often establish contact with the broad mass of the people without the intervention of any organization. Because he attached a high importance to symbolic acts, and because newspaper coverage insured that his own symbolic acts would be widely reported, Gandhi could afford to maintain only informal contact with the Congress. Moreover, he could sustain his pre-eminence in Indian politics without splitting the nationalist coalition: whenever he felt the Congress was not ready to support his actions, he simply acted as an independent agent. Unlike Lenin, Gandhi had an underlying optimism and a faith in token acts of truth. He could thus be confident the Indian people would follow him even without Congress support and that eventually the Congress would return to him. As a result Indian revolutionary politics were far less acrimonious than their Russian equivalent.

From 1915 to 1930 Gandhi led several different attempts to force concessions from the British. None of them had yielded any great success and by 1930 Gandhi had finally lost faith in the British intentions to give India home rule. He was now intent on securing Indian independence. Moreover, he felt the people were ready for, and he was prepared to use the full force of, *satyagraha*, to lead a movement of mass civil disobedience. But as 1930 dawned he was uncertain what form that civil disobedience was to take.[87] He was even prepared to put off civil disobedience if Britain would grant "the substance, if not the outward form, of self-government" by meeting eleven demands, including prohibition of alcoholic beverages; reduction of land taxes, military expenditures, and civil service salaries; enactment of a

[87] Tendulkar, *Mahatma*, III, 3-6.

protective tariff against non-Indian cloth; and discharge of political prisoners. Among these was the demand that the tax on salt be eliminated.[88] By February the salt tax received increasing attention in Gandhi's public statements and, at the same time, Gandhi started to issue instructions about how to carry on civil disobedience and what to do when he was arrested. Then on March 2, 1930 he wrote a letter to the Viceroy in which he reiterated what he felt to be the primary British abuses and outlined and justified the course of action he was about to undertake:

> My ambition is no less than to convert the British people through non-violence, and thus make them see the wrong they have done to India. I do not seek to harm your people. I want to serve them even as I want to serve my own. I believe that I have always served them. I served them up to 1919, blindly. [In 1919 Britain passed the oppressive Rowlett acts which stirred Gandhi into his first attempt at *satyagraha* in India.] But when my eyes were opened and I conceived non-cooperation, the object still was to serve them. I employed the same weapon that I have, in all humility, successfully used against the dearest members of my family. If I have equal love for your people with mine, it will not long remain hidden. It will be acknowledged by them, even as the members of my family acknowledged it, after they had tried me for several years. If the people join me, as I expect they will, the sufferings they will undergo, unless the British nation sooner retraces its steps, will be enough to melt the stoniest hearts. . . . But if you cannot see your way to deal with these evils and my letter makes no appeal to your heart, on the eleventh day of the month, I shall proceed with such co-workers of the ashram as I can take, to disregard the provisions of the salt laws. I regard this tax to be the most iniquitous of all from the poor man's standpoint. As the independence movement is essentially

[88] *Ibid.*, p. 13.

for the poorest in the land, the beginning will be made with this evil. . . .[89]

When the Viceroy was unmoved by Gandhi's letter, Gandhi announced that he and a band of ashramites would march from the ashram to Dandi, a deserted seacoast town about two hundred miles away. Civil disobedience was not to begin until, from Dandi, Gandhi gave the signal, the nature of which was not stated.

On March 12 Gandhi and seventy-eight followers started walking towards Dandi, on what Gandhi termed a "sacred pilgrimage."[90] From then until April 6, when Gandhi picked up a few grains of salt from the Dandi beach and thereby broke the law, the eyes of the nation followed his every move. Thus his simple, symbolic gesture, which told India what it must do, came after a long period during which the tension and curiosity rose.

On May 4 Gandhi was arrested. He had been expecting this punishment and had warned his followers not to demonstrate against it but to continue their breaking of the salt laws. This they did, extending civil disobedience to the non-payment of taxes, complete boycott of foreign cloth, and other actions which were part of the Gandhian program. Finally, to relieve the pressure, the British released Gandhi in January 1931, and in February Gandhi and the Viceroy negotiated a truce between Indians and British. As Fischer observes, Gandhi "came as the leader of a nation to negotiate 'on equal terms' with the leader of another nation. The Salt March and its aftermath had proved that England could not rule India against or without Gandhi."[91] Gandhi had laid the cornerstone for Swaraj: the British were forced to recognize that the Indians could take effective action against them and the Indians realized that they had a strength and power hitherto unsuspected, much as Gandhi had claimed they did in *Hind Swaraj*.

How was it, then, that Gandhi originated the Salt March?

[89] *Ibid.*, pp. 22-23.   [90] *Ibid.*, p. 32.
[91] Fischer, *Life of Mahatma Gandhi*, pp. 281-82.

As with any complex event, several themes are interwoven in it. First, it should be noted that the effectiveness of the march depended on the discipline and response of the Indian people—ashramites, Congressmen, and peasants alike. Gandhi had spent fifteen years teaching and training them and winning their respect and love. The fruit of this effort, which had been motivated by Gandhi's need to bring his world into harmony with his personal values, was the obedient and self-sacrificing response of the Indian people.

But why did Gandhi choose the salt tax from among his list of grievances as the first object of Satyagraha? Two things seem to be involved here. First, as indicated in his letter to the Viceroy, above, he believed that of all British oppressions the salt tax was the most offensive because it struck the poorest people hardest. And Gandhi conceived of himself as the servant of the poor (or the leader of the poor—to Gandhi, the two functions were identical), just as Lenin and Trotsky viewed as their constituency a class of people lower than themselves. By undertaking to serve or lead the lowliest self-esteem is raised; we saw this earlier in Gandhi's life when the weakness and ignorance of the South African Indians gave him the confidence to act for them. Second, the tax on salt constituted an oral deprivation, a restriction on eating. Gandhi himself seldom used salt, but the great mass of the Indian people did. The fact that he did not use it made it all the easier for Gandhi to object to the tax: he was acting not for himself, but for others.

Gandhi's choice of a campaign against the tax does not indicate that he was an advocate of increased use of salt. He was opposed, in fact, to the use of condiments in general. Rather he objected to any authority telling others, symbolically himself, what they could and could not eat (his desire for a prohibition had a strong basis in the Hinduism he had taken as his own). Gandhi saw eating as a question of personal choice. Just as he objected to his parents' ban on meat-eating when he was a boy, so now he resisted the British regulations. Once the ban was removed, then Indians themselves would be free to use it or not as they saw fit.

Another line of interpretation, which is consonant with the view I have been developing of Gandhi's personality, is suggested by Ernest Jones' contention that one of the two basic symbolic significances of salt is human semen.[92] If it had this unconscious meaning for Gandhi, then we may understand his depriving himself of condiments, including salt, as a form of sexual abstinence, involving a regression to an issue of the oral phase. In the context of the Salt March, Gandhi's taking of salt from the British can thus be seen as reclaiming for the Indian people the manhood and potency which was properly theirs. The British had denied the Indians their manhood by monopolizing the manufacture of salt; Gandhi, in order to break that monopoly and restore the virility of the Indian people, risked punishment and death.—an altruistic act, for as just noted, Gandhi himself had renounced the use of salt (that is, was celibate).

Finally, why did Gandhi walk to the sea at Dandi rather than break the law without undergoing the strain of the long march? The obvious motivations here are two: first, the length of the march would draw attention to the act. Second, it would make the action more religious, make of it, as Gandhi himself put it, a "pilgrimage." Both of these motives are indicative of the private motivations which lay behind the choice.

The long march focused attention not only on Gandhi's cause but on him and his actions as well. In this manner it gratified Gandhi's need for observation and approval. Trotsky, too, had this need to be watched and approved. In each case the desire for applause grew out of early feelings of being ridiculous. Gandhi's fear of ridicule by his schoolmates and Trotsky's humiliation by the peasants at Yanovka are examples of the sources of those feelings. Each man, as we have argued, had to overcome feelings of

[92] Ernest Jones, "The Symbolic Significance of Salt," in his *Essays in Applied Psycho-Analysis* (New York, 1964), II, 43-44.

shame, and each chose the mechanism of exhibiting himself in a context where praise was likely to result.

The march was also a form of suffering, self-sacrificial in and of itself, as well as in its goal. And it was a gesture of respect both to the Indian people and the authority he was about to challenge, the long march of penance of a humble worshipper. Probably part of the motivation for such an action was to ward off the anger of the authority. Most importantly, however, the march and the act of disobedience in which it culminated represented the desire to be punished—and forgiven—by those in power. (As was mentioned in discussing *Hind Swaraj*, the attribution of morality here has been reversed. The British will see the evil of their ways through the noble self-sacrifice of Gandhi and the others. Just as Gandhi had sought punishment and forgiveness from his father when, as a boy, he had stolen from his brother, so now he sought suffering and redemption from what was, in effect, an act of stealing, only this time justified in terms of Hindu rights and the assertion of Indian freedom and manhood. As in *Hind Swaraj*, the British, who had replaced his father as the embodiment of authority, are conceived by Gandhi to be more of a thief than he.)

From 1931 to 1940 Gandhi busied himself primarily with social reform projects of one kind or another. He labored long and hard for the *Harijans* (Children of God), as he called the Untouchables, and devoted himself to the improvement of rural economic conditions and the increased use of the spinning wheel. His overtly political activity, however, was sporadic until the outbreak of World War II. In the next chapter I shall examine the period from 1940 until the end of his life, a period which saw the realization of Gandhi's dream of Indian independence, but in a form and with side effects that horrified him.

The Psychological Bases of Revolutionary Leadership

In Chapter 3 an attempt was made to indicate the psychological basis for involvement in revolutionary activity. In this section we will return to the model presented in that context with a different but related question in mind: in psychological terms, what enables a revolutionist to gain a position of leadership in the movement of which he is a part? That is, what enables him to assume a role which possesses the potential of allowing him to secure the obedience of others in seeking his goal of the attainment of power? This potential, of course, is varyingly realized—depending on the psychological needs of prospective followers and other factors, just as the leader's success in getting power is contingent upon a large number of variables.[93] In the present case, however, we will direct our attention only to the leader himself. It shall be assumed that the development of a revolutionary organization, and primacy within it, and ideology are significant aspects of revolutionary leadership. The effort will be to explain the evolution of these elements in terms of their connection with the psychic needs of individual leaders.

Before turning to the model, it ought to be mentioned that the ability to lead is related to what Erikson considers to be the psychological "crisis" of adulthood. Once the identity crisis of adolescence and intimacy crisis of young manhood have been met, the individual is ready to confront the question of "generativity," of producing and caring for offspring.[94] For the revolutionist this crisis takes on a different, a political, form. Because the individual conceives of his identity in terms of his political goals, he approaches the question of generativity, of fatherhood, in terms of the necessity to guide others in the performance of political tasks. His own children, if he has any, are not

---

[93] The psychology of followership has been explored by many writers. Among the most relevant works are Adorno *et al.*, *The Authoritarian Personality*; Hadley Cantril, *The Psychology of Social Movements* (New York, 1941); Erich Fromm, *Escape From Freedom*; William Kornhauser, *The Politics of Mass Society*, especially Chapter 4 and Part III; Seymour Martin Lipset, *Political Man* (Garden City, N.Y., 1963), Chapter 4; Eric Hoffer, *The True Believer*.

Much of this literature is based on Freud's *Group Psychology and the Analysis of the Ego*.

[94] Erikson, *Identity and the Life Cycle*, p. 97.

viewed as having any special claim to affection. In fact, both Trotsky and Gandhi tended to neglect their children and/or to subject them to unusually rigorous demands.[95] "Children" warranting attention and affection are found elsewhere, in the form of the maligned classes or peoples the revolutionist chooses to defend and the revolutionary followers he seeks to lead. Leadership, in this sense, is a surrogate fatherhood which is made possible by the successful mastery of earlier conflicts. In order to explain the ability to lead, then, we must return to the psycho-genesis of the revolutionist.

To sum up briefly what we have already discovered about the revolutionist, he is a person whose childhood was marked by unusual ambivalence towards paternal authority and consequently a large amount of guilt which, as long as it remained locked up inside of the person, produced debilitating effects. In two of the three cases the intensity of the guilt was amplified by a traumatic incident, the death of the father, during adolescence. In the third case, Trotsky's, the father did not die, but Trotsky's early separation from him when he went away to school, which accentuated their lack of compatibility when they were together, served a similar function of preserving an exaggerated image of the father's sexual primacy. This separation was not exactly the same as the father's death, however, and consequently Trotsky's feelings of guilt were somewhat less intense than the other two men's, he could bear more ambivalence in

---

[95] Fischer, *Life of Gandhi*, pp. 212-14, discusses the relationship of Gandhi and his children. Trotsky, as was mentioned, abandoned his first wife and his two children in Siberia and developed a very ambivalent relationship with Leon Sedov, one of his two sons by Natalya Sedova. Lenin had no children.

The conflicts the men had with their children are related to their conflicts with their fathers. They appear to see in their children, especially their sons, themselves re-embodied, and thus attribute to the children the same ambivalent feelings they had towards their fathers. Male children represent a challenge to the father in any case, but when the man has harbored particularly aggressive feelings against paternal authority his child appears even more dangerous than he would normally.

his relationships, and he was less driven to seek a narrow and difficult road to personal redemption. Lenin and Gandhi, by contrast, carried the heavy burden of guilt for their fathers' deaths—and in the mastery of those feelings a potential for leadership which Trotsky lacked.

One characteristic of the revolutionary leader, then, as opposed to plain revolutionists, is that he is forced to come frontally to grips with the question of his relationship to his father. His feelings of ambivalence are too strong, his guilt is too great, for him to continue in the role of his father's son, no matter how disguised that role might be. He aspires to be the father himself, not just to fight against him as does the revolutionary follower. He must redefine the relationship of man to man if he is to justify his actions to himself. The basis for such an effort lies in his inner resources and the potential of his environment.

The first step towards becoming a revolutionary leader is to become a revolutionist, to become a member of a revolutionary brotherhood under the leadership of another man. At this point all the defenses which the revolutionist uses to ward off guilt and anxiety are brought into play. The aggression which had been directed against the self is partially redirected against an external authority, onto which the revolutionist also projects this aggressive feeling. The conflict is now external and less self-destructive, but still difficult to manage because of the ambivalence involved in feelings with respect to the new object. Consequently, occasion is found to split the emotions into distinct love and hate components, all hate (ideally) being directed against authority, all love to one's fellow revolutionists, one's leader and the population for whom the revolt is ostensibly undertaken. A substantial but far from complete impersonalization of relations also takes place, which manifests itself in the tendency to attribute higher significance to ideas than to people. The revolutionist looks for and finds, concretely and abstractly, a model for himself in his new role, an ideal standard of behavior and a justification for action. The leader provides him with the standard for right action and the leader's ideology with the justification for it.

At this point the individual is archetypically a member of a "primary group," to use Freud's term, bound by ties of love in two ways, by identification with his revolutionary peers and idealization of the leader.[96] In fact, none of the three men fully developed this tightly bounded relationship, which is based on a more striking regression to a childlike state than any of them underwent.[97] In each man there were strains with both peers and superiors almost as soon as the group membership had been formed. Gandhi, in fact, at least in South Africa, created a movement where none had existed before, just as Trotsky essentially did in the Ukraine. Later, however, both had to adjust to working with organizations of which they were not initially the leaders. Thus each of the three men, to a greater or lesser degree, had to go through a stage of development where he was one of a band of brothers. This was possible for them because some identification with actual brothers existed—Lenin's with Sasha, Trotsky's with the other children whom he describes as equally neglected by his parents, and Gandhi presumably with his older brother, who was one of his models in his experiments with meat-eating and who financed his education. But revolutionary brotherhood was not sufficient for any of them. A brotherhood does not hold together of its own accord; even its ties of identification are induced by the emotional bond of each member to the father. And these were men who could not bear to be under the direction of any authority. In order to assert their manhood, it was necessary to be authority themselves, at least with regard to those whom they deemed to be on their side. The very stance of revolutionist, of course, implies to some extent that the individual still feels himself to be a rebellious son against a very strong father. The way in which an individual does or does not manage to relinquish this directly insurrectionary part of his identity when he succeeds

[96] Freud, *Group Psychology*, p. 80.   [97] *Ibid.*, p. 82.

in gaining power is the subject we will turn to in the next chapter.

But what is the process through which the individual evolves from revolutionist to revolutionary leader? Essentially it is one of clarifying, in a particular way, relationships with other individuals and sets of individuals: the potential leader must define his status with respect to leaders in revolutionary activity, his revolutionary peers, the followers of the cause, the population for whom he speaks and the enemy, incumbent authority.

If a revolutionist is to be *the* leader of his movement, he must eliminate any other person who might occupy that position. None of the three men we are studying, it should be noted, thought of himself as aspiring to leadership. Each, to the extent that he consciously conceived of himself as a leader, felt that the position had been thrust upon him by the force of circumstance—one aspect of which was that he happened to perceive the truth, the correct way of acting, when others did not. In a sense, of course, this kind of self-evaluation is correct: these men succeeded or failed as leaders in part due to the fit of their aspirations, tactics, and ideas with the needs of prospective followers. There is, as was mentioned in the Introduction, a circumstantial element in any situation. But psychologically Lenin, for example, was deceiving himself when he claimed that the break with Plekhanov was because the latter was not following the right line. As he himself inadvertently revealed in "How the 'Spark' was Nearly Extinguished," Lenin found himself uncomfortable and malcontent as Plekhanov's follower the first time Plekhanov tried to assert the prerogatives of leadership. Consciously Lenin may not have aspired to be the leader of Russian Social Democracy, but unconsciously he could not bear to be anything but the leader. Gandhi, in apparent contrast, claimed not only that he was not a leader but that he was the lowliest of men. In making the latter claim, of course, he gave the game away: the important thing is not that one finds himself superior to his fellows but that one establishes a status of being different from all others. Gandhi's oft-proclaimed statement that he was the humblest seeker after truth had the same effectiveness as Lenin's implicit boast that he was the only correct interpreter of Marxism. *Each achieved a unique position,* and as long as others were willing to recognize as legitimate and estimable the basis upon which this uniqueness rested, Lenin and Gandhi were assured of a following. Trotsky, until the days of the Fourth International, never achieved such a position.

The conditions out of which the need and the psychological resources to be the leader arise appear to be as follows. As has been argued, the revolutionist generally is a person with severe conflicts over masculinity. He is a person on the one hand whose Oedipal hatred of his father has not been dissipated and on the other who feels unusually guilty about asserting his masculinity. In the leader this pattern is accentuated because the individual has a more grandiose image of his own masculine powers and more intense feelings of guilt. The sense of power grows out of some apparent manifestation of the strength of one's sexual desire, such as the hoped for death of the father in the cases of Gandhi and Lenin. But because the Oedipal wish is so literally fulfilled, a great guilt builds up which can be assuaged only through the most radical measures, by sexual asceticism in particular and a thorough self-denial in general. Trotsky's conflicts, as has been mentioned, were less severe—and Trotsky was that much less a leader.

The asceticism of the leader is a corollary to his tendency to submit to authority, to take punishment upon himself. Even Trotsky found enjoyment in being in prison, while Gandhi positively delighted in it and Lenin half-regretted leaving it. In Lenin and Gandhi this tendency, rigidly controlled in the former case and exploited in the latter, expressed itself in all aspects of their lives; in Trotsky, the involvement in revolutionary activity was not as nearly total and his yearning for punishment not as broadly expressed. His lack of personal asceticism reflects this lower intensity of commitment and had the side effect of making him more of an object of envy than the other two men.

The leader's propensity to suffer provides an indication of his view of authority relationships: either one kills the father via the assertion of one's masculinity and courage or one is punished by him. Moreover, the image of both the father's and one's own powers is preserved larger than life, maintained at the level of development of the Oedipal conflict and its rebirth during adolescence. Thus one cannot feel that another man can safely be left in a position of superiority to one's own position nor can any other man adequately fulfill the leader's requirements for the power and knowledge a father must have. The former attribute underlies opposition both to other revolutionary leaders and to legal authority; the latter helps account for why it is that no man can be the leader's ultimate teacher—as Gandhi put it, one's spiritual guru.

The fact that submission is impossible, except as it is expressed in asceticism, does not mean that dominance is possible. Another factor must be added in order to account for the individual's ability to actually fill the father's role, at least with respect to his fellow revolutionists. There must be a firm identification with the father, manifested in the individual's strong sense of recitude and ability to assert himself without undue hesitation, if he is to conceive of himself as a father for others. Lenin, whose professorial proclivities were so often noted, obviously had a significant model for his own behavior in his father, a teacher. Gandhi, whose development was particularly strained and unusual, had this kind of identification with his mother, which helps account for many of the specific techniques he used and the reliance on passivism and suffering which generally characterized his activity. Trotsky found less that was useful in the model of his parents' behavior and hence was less able to envision himself in or play a leadership role. And he did not eliminate loyalties to superiors as Lenin and Gandhi effectively did.

Although the revolutionary leader sets up a situation in which he owes allegiance to no man, he does not eliminate the idea of loyalty and submission as such. A purified loving and loved image of the father (as discussed in Chapter 3) is retained, an abstraction which fulfills the function of justification and lessens the strain of standing alone. In essence, the father's standards of rectitude, although in somewhat distorted form, are embodied as the individual's superego, as they are in any man; but they are held to with an unusual firmness and rationalized much more elaborately than is normally the case. The leader thus approaches much closer than other men to having a self-sufficient moral system, one which relies on the dictates of no other man. To some extent, of course, the leader is dependent on others for approval and support. He needs at least some minimal amount of reassurance from his inferiors that he is speaking truth and acting wisely; but Gandhi and Lenin, and even Trotsky in his later years, were unusually self-reliant in this regard as well. Thus the leader impersonalizes relations with superiors, making of himself an autonomous agent whose commands follow directly from his contact with Truth, with an internalized and (ideally) wholly benevolent father—which Lenin represented as a careful analysis of Marx and current realities, Gandhi as his response to the small voice within.

Relations with peers are similarly impersonalized, abstracted: Lenin severed relations with Martov while positing a doctrine of organizational brotherhood; Trotsky broke with the Mensheviks repeatedly, as in 1905, all the while preaching the need to end factionalism and make of the party a cooperative brotherhood; and Gandhi, who claimed that all men were his brothers, would not admit that anyone was as lowly as he and was never willing to sacrifice principle to friendship.[98]

The reason for the impersonalization of relations with peers rests partially in the primacy of the leader's commit-

[98] The question of brotherhood was never as important for Gandhi as it was for the other two.

ment to filling a father role. His underlying model for the world of human relations is one family, not many families, and in one family there can only be one father. Additionally, however, there is the consideration of relations with peers as such. Lenin became involved in revolutionary activity in part as the result of an identification with his brother, and Trotsky began his rebellion in Shvigovsky's garden, which was a substitute for the sibling relations of the Bronstein family at Yanovka. (Trotsky's claim that his parents neglected the children, it will be remembered, applied to all of the children, not just to him.) Gandhi, who was the youngest child in his family, did not really have an analogous experience. He was the leader from the start in South Africa and never regarded himself as the equal of the other leaders of the Congress Party in India: he always spoke of them somewhat reverently as his superiors while at the same time commanding their loyalty and obedience. He would break with others when agreement could not be reached and act on the basis of his widely acknowledged superiority while proclaiming his inferiority, but there were few splits in his life of the intensity of those in which Lenin and Trotsky were involved.

For two out of the three men, then, the two that were most involved in party activity as such, identification with one or more siblings served as the model for the political brotherhood. But such an identification is heavily charged with ambivalence, at a minimum because one's natural envy of siblings who partake of parental affection has to be overcome and repressed when such identifications are formed. The implication which follows from this is that there will always be tension, of varying amounts, in a political brotherhood and that, under special conditions, brotherhood will be repudiated behaviorally while being retained in the abstract. Whether it be from a special situation, like Lenin's, or from a combination of no real model for a brotherhood combined with an overwhelming involvement in conflicts associated with masculinity, as in the case of Gandhi, for the revolutionary leader equality with others exists only in theory. Needless to say, these different bases of brotherlessness result in somewhat different end products. Lenin was intensely concerned with the question of peer relations and he glorified equality just as much as he extolled central control. The two are, in fact, linked in the idea of democratic centralism, which Lenin was able to make work after 1917—but only on the basis of his actual primacy within the party elite. Eventually Lenin paid the price for his democratic inclinations: by relinquishing absolute authority he allowed Stalin to control the succession to power after he became ill. Trotsky, who was also torn between the rights of the brothers and the rights of the father, finally was impaled on the horns of the dilemma neither he nor Lenin was able to resolve. Whatever the defects of this formula, however, it was invaluable during the early phases of the struggle, enabling Lenin to speak in the name of democracy while acting in an authoritarian manner. In Russia, with its opposing populistic and authoritarian traditions, some such combination was needed. In India, where the struggle could be carried on in the open, there was less of a need for a tightly bound brotherhood and hence Gandhi, who preached a brotherhood so encompassing that it was meaningless as a basis for political organization, was not handicapped as much as he would have been in another context.

As is probably apparent by now, the question of relations with peers slides off easily into that of relations with inferiors. In fact, parity relations are an unusual thing in any political context and tend to be largely ephemeral in the face of the need to make decisions—when such decisions must be made quickly. The people who survive as leaders in such situations are the ones like Lenin and Gandhi, who can act on the basis of their own authority. The Martovs, those who cannot rise above the position of brother, are doomed to ineffectiveness in revolutionary situations.

Turning, then, to the relations of the leader to his followers, it should first be noted that a large degree of impersonalization is involved here, as well as in the relations outlined above, but not to the same extent as in the former cases. All other relations involve great strain for the leader, forcing him to work in a situation too closely analogous for comfort to that of his childhood and youth. But when he is the leader himself, when he can act as a father to his revolutionary children, the gratifications outweigh the strains, if there has been a sufficient basis in his experience for performance of the leadership role. As a leader he is finally the one who is powerful and righteous, whom the "children" love, fear, and respect and who ultimately will enjoy, in some impersonalized way, possession of his mother.

Ideally, then, the relationship is one of unbounded love of the leader for his followers and of his followers for him. In fact, residual ambivalence remains, making necessary some impersonalization and safeguards. The tension exists because, just as the leader is one who, psychologically speaking, tries to become his own father, so also the leader projects onto his followers the ambivalent feelings he had toward his father. Thus he is able to view them as loving him, but he also finds in them the seeds of disloyalty and hatred. As he asserted his manhood against his father, so his followers will desire to challenge his authority.

Additionally his followers, and even more importantly the reference group for whom he speaks, will be viewed as having childlike weaknesses. For example, Gandhi, who it would appear had severe problems during his anal phase, directed the major part of his first public address to the Indians in South Africa to the subject of personal cleanliness. At the same time the leader sees in his followers an idealization of his own childhood self-image: the people are viewed as all powerful, just as the young child views himself as omnipotent (feelings which are truly moderated only with successful mastery of the Oedipal crisis).

The leader thus has substantially ambivalent feelings toward his followers. He manages these emotions in two ways. First, a degree of impersonalization is involved. Followers are transformed into the idea of an organization, personal relations into rules. Both Gandhi and Lenin were constantly outlining rules and impersonal procedures of one kind or another to overcome the weakness and untrustworthiness of the human material with which they were working. Unlike the cases of the relations with peers and superiors, however, this process must be limited; one can be a leader without owing allegiance to any other leader on earth and still be politically effective, but one cannot lead a movement to gain power without having concrete, living followers. Because the leader is highly motivated toward gaining power and because the rewards from relations with inferiors are considerable, it is possible for the leader to cut the process short of total impersonalization.

The second mechanism for managing the strain is by maintaining centralized control over the party, both in theory and in practice. The greater the control from the center, the less the danger the sons will overthrow the father; the greater the control, the more rewards there are available in terms of the compliance of others with the leader's wishes; and the greater the control, the more the leader can feel that the results of his activity are his own achievement. In this last regard, to be sure, the leader has somewhat conflicting goals: he wants the rewards of fatherhood without having to share them, but he wants others to carry the blame for acting against the father in the first place. Thus one would suspect that all revolutionary leaders will posit ideologies which implicitly or explicitly contain some combination of elite voluntarism and populistic inevitability or objectivity, the former to serve as the repository for the yearnings toward fatherhood and its privileges, the latter to relieve the burden of guilt associated with revolutionary action as well as to guarantee success.

An additional motive for the organized control of followers is the leader's fear of the enemy, of legal authority. Once properly instituted, the party serves as a means of protecting the leader from the opposition (at the same time that the leader envisions himself as being the defender and support of his followers).

The revolutionist, it will be remembered, views the authority against which he fights as a powerful and evil father figure, whom it is legitimate to resist on the basis of a justificatory system born out of the individual's need to establish a rightful claim to manhood. For the leader, whose ambivalence toward the father is even greater as the result of the traumatic events of childhood, this authority is viewed in highly impersonalized terms—the Tsar is transformed into capitalism or Russian tsarism, British Political Agents and Viceroys into the British system of colonial government.

The revolutionist's goal is to overthrow authority and reconstitute it on his own terms. As we shall see in the next chapter, the revolutionist's faith in himself is put to a severe test once power is attained, for the goal of the struggle is essentially the end of internal conflict and the achievement of certain psychic rewards, the need for which arose out of the early and personal conflicts of the individual and which is out of line with the probable consequences of winning governmental power. But until power is attained, the individual need not face up to the improbability of his goals, the inherent contradictions in his identity. His task rather is to develop a way of activating the potential for revolutionary action which has evolved out of his revolutionary self-definition. He must either subscribe to or create a doctrine of means which is compatible with the ends in terms of which he justifies himself. One of the attributes of the leader is that his personal experience, both its trauma and its rewards, provides the basis for utilizing an ideology of means. This is not to say that nonleaders never develop such ideas nor that leaders create them out of whole cloth. Only if the potential for this kind of creation is linked to the kind of experience which is conducive to leadership is the tactician also a leader. And certainly a leader may take over in part or as a whole the idea of another man, as long as they are not alien to his personality. But the person who in fact is able to lead other men must have a cause and an apparently workable program to put in the service of the cause.

Each of the men we are studying evolved an effective doctrine of means. Lenin's turned around the idea of the vanguard, stating essentially that in a world of conflict the proper program of political activity was "to keep a stone in one's sling," always to be armed against one's supposed friends as well as one's enemies. For this purpose an elite, command organization was needed. Lenin (and Trotsky) insisted, however, on the separability of means and ends, and hence justified the use of violence or anything else if it would further the cause. Trotsky's doctrine was similar to Lenin's in some respects, but placed more emphasis on the activation of the inherent powers of the masses who, with proper leadership, would move swiftly to the realization of revolutionary goals. Although there are logical difficulties in combining these doctrines, as there are within each of them, they were joined in practice in 1917 and produced the desired effect of mobilizing the masses and supplying at least the broad outlines of the techniques which were used in securing power.

Gandhi, in contrast to Lenin and Trotsky, believed that ends and means were inseparable and hence precluded the possibility of utilizing violence. Satyagraha asked of its followers that they disobey laws in which they did not believe, but nonviolently. Through self-sacrifice the enemy would be converted, the courage and honor of the Satyagrahi recognized and one's goals achieved. Gandhi's doctrine is thus widely divergent from those of the other two, but it is like them in having action at its heart and in being directed toward the achievement of revolutionary goals. Gandhi is by definition a revolutionist, but not therefore the same kind of revolutionist as Lenin or Trotsky.

What, then, accounts for the choice of means? Psychologically, revolution is the expression of aggression towards authority, the potential for which develops in each individual in the manner we have discussed. Hence the question of means is the question of how that aggression is going to be manifested. In the case of Lenin and Trotsky it was enunciated quite openly. The enemy was defined as evil and force was to be the instrument of his removal. Several things seem to have contributed to this open expression of hatred. First, Lenin and Trotsky established male identities, one component of which involved physical prowess and/or the willingness to use force. Lenin had the example of his brother's attempt to use violence politically, which served to justify the means and provide, through identification, a feeling that Lenin was right in using it. Trotsky undoubtedly valued highly the physical prowess of his father, which had sadistic overtones, and also was trying to rid himself of his Jewishness, with its reputation for Eastern effeminacy.

Second, and related to the first, both men were less guilt ridden than Gandhi. The clean split of the world into good and bad halves is one sign of this, the fact that their identity as men was relatively secure is another. Therefore they could act aggressively with fewer inhibitions than Gandhi. Finally, they had more fear of punishment than Gandhi did (although Lenin far more than Trotsky). The enemy was fearful and dangerous and any means were justified to defend oneself against him.[99]

Turning to Gandhi, one finds that in all three respects he differs from the others. As mentioned, Gandhi's experience made his burden of guilt heavier than either of the other two men's, which was part of the reason for his relinquishing his masculine role and modeling himself on the behavior and standards of his mother. And because his feelings were so extraordinarily mixed, he was not able to split his emotions as cleanly as did the other two. He was more persistent in thinking of himself as evil and in attributing residual goodness to his enemies. Finally, confession of sins had always led to redemption for Gandhi—confessing his theft to his father led to his father's forgiveness, each of his subsequent imprisonments led to increased veneration from his people and even admiration from his captors. More-

[99] The choice of means is developed more systematically in the author's "Violence or Non-Violence: A Psychoanalytic Exploration of the Choice of Political Means in Social Change," Princeton University Center of International Studies Research Monograph No. 20, October 1965.

over, Gandhi's greater guilt meant that he had a greater need to be punished and hence he built a technique based on violence upon himself. Lenin and Trotsky, while not free from this masochistic desire, on the whole managed to repress it.

Each of the men, then, developed means which allowed him to express hatred of authority without incurring debilitating levels of guilt. Thus at any given intensity of hatred for authority, the higher the level of active guilt, the less violent the form of opposition. Gandhi, who carried the largest burden of guilt, was the least able to express aggression uninhibitedly and violently. Trotsky, who was in some ways the least guilt ridden of the three men, did not manage to externalize his guilt feelings to a sufficient degree and hence was not as uninhibited about using violence as Lenin. The latter had strong feelings of guilt but managed to reduce their active force to an unusual degree and accordingly felt quite free to use violence. Of course, if there is less antagonism toward authority, as there is in the case of the nonrevolutionary politician, then there will also be a lessened proclivity to use violent means.

With respect to means, the leader is one who utilizes a sharply focused and highly activist ideology. Thus, as we would expect, Lenin with his emphasis on building up an organization and expressing ideas in terms of slogans, and Gandhi with his penchant for vows and his ability to turn his personal experience (with such things as diet and stealing) into public programs were more effective leaders than Trotsky. Trotsky's doctrine captures the spirit of revolutionary excitement and his oratorical skills in enunciating it made the utopia seem very near indeed to the St. Petersburg workers; but Trotsky seldom was able to steer a clear and unambiguous course when not under the immediate pressure of insurrectionary activity. Again the pervasive ambivalence of his development, instead of the sharp and traumatic experience of Gandhi and Lenin, seems to provide the crucial distinction.

We are now ready to explore the final phases of the men's lives, and to turn our attention to another question: what are the psychological attributes of the revolutionist's successful assumption of governmental power?

CHAPTER FIVE

adulthood 2

Lenin's, Trotsky's, and Gandhi's experiences with the assumption and exercise of governmental power will be discussed in terms of three major questions. First, how did the men act during the period of the takeover of power itself? Second, how did they react to the problems of consolidating their power and administering the state? And third, what attention, if any, was given to the matter of succession? As in the earlier chapters an attempt will be made to outline and explain the general configuration of similarities among the men without thereby disguising or explaining away the differences.

Lenin: The Utilization of Power

Lenin was in Zurich, Switzerland when tsarism fell in February 1917. Only a month before he had told a meeting of young people that "We of the older generation may not live to see the decisive battles . . ." of the inevitable socialist revolution,[1] and he obviously did not anticipate the swift turn of events that brought the Provisional Government to power. He reacted swiftly to the news, however, writing to fellow Bolsheviks inside and outside Russia and making fevered attempts at finding a way back to the motherland. Krupskaya reports:

> Ilyich burned with eagerness to go to Russia. . . . From the moment the news of the revolution came, Ilyich did not sleep, and at night all sorts of incredible plans were made.[2]

[1] V. I. Lenin, "Lecture on the 1905 Revolution," in his *Selected Works* (Moscow, 1960), I, 842.
[2] Krupskaya, II, 200.

The problem was that none of Russia's allies in the First World War would admit Lenin, nor at first would Germany. He was thus stranded in Switzerland for about a month. Finally arrangements were made with Germany for the safe transport of Lenin and his fellow exiles by train through Germany to Sweden and from there to St. Petersburg.[3]

As noted above, Lenin did not expect the imminent fall of tsarism. The mighty authority against which he had been struggling for so many years seemed to crumble without much resistance. How, then, was he to explain to himself his years out of power, how justify his life to this point? His personality was based on the need to fight a practically omnipotent foe and now the enemy had fallen—in the face of attacks by the much-despised Russian liberals. In the first of the "Letters from Afar," written for the Bolsheviks in St. Petersburg within a week after Lenin had received the news of the fall, Lenin turns to this subject:

> How could such a "miracle" happen, that in eight days . . . a monarchy that had maintained itself for centuries, and continued to maintain itself during these years of tremendous national class conflicts of 1905-1907, could utterly collapse?[4]

The answer is that a "combination of a whole series of conditions of worldwide historic importance was required for the tsarist monarchy to collapse in a few days." He then goes on to enumerate the conditions: the weakening of tsarism from past conflicts with revolutionary forces, the emergence of the bourgeoisie, the heightening of class con-

[3] Lenin's utilization of the German offer to transport him to Russia gave rise in 1917 to the report that he was a German agent. Although he did rely on the Germans for transportation, and also apparently for funds, none of the investigators of this period produce evidence which in any way substantiates the claim that the "sealed car" was the token of Lenin's subservience to German masters. See Fischer, *Life of Lenin*, pp. 108-13; Possony, *Lenin: The Compulsive Revolutionary*, pp. 202-15; David Shub, *Lenin* (Garden City, N.Y., 1948), pp. 180-85.

[4] Lenin, *Collected Works* (New York, 1929), XX, Book 1, 27.

sciousness throughout the world and most of all the war, marking, according to his previous analysis, the death throes of capitalism. In this manner Lenin absolves himself of responsibility for either the Tsar's continuance in power until 1917 or his demise. Greater forces are at work, hence Lenin has neither betrayed his identity by not acting more resolutely nor does he now bear the guilt for eliminating the father of the Russian people. The almost all powerful Tsar has fallen to the even more powerful forces of history and his chair was now empty.

In other communications, as well as the one cited above, Lenin attempted to steer the Bolsheviks through the chaos of February Russia, but the organization he had been carefully building did not respond adequately without his personal supervision.[5] It was effective enough, however, to provide Lenin with an impressive welcome when he arrived at the Finland Station in St.Petersburg:

> But at long last [Lenin's train] arrived. A thunderous *Marseillaise* boomed forth on the platform, and shouts of welcome rang out. We stayed in the imperial waiting rooms while the Bolshevik generals exchanged

[5] N. N. Sukhanov (Nikolai Nikolayevich Himmer), an internationalist Menshevik who recorded many of his observations on the events of 1917 in *The Russian Revolution*, 2 vols., Joel Carmichael, ed. and trans. (New York, 1962), explains the ineffectiveness of the Bolsheviks before Lenin's arrival in terms of the lack of second-rung leaders of high quality in the party, so that all Bolsheviks relied on Lenin alone for decisions and direction:

"But in the Bolshevik Party Lenin the Thunderer sat in the clouds and then—there was absolutely nothing right down to the ground. . . . There could be no question of replacing Lenin by individuals, couples, or combinations. There could be neither independent thinking nor organizational base in the Bolshevik Party without Lenin." (I, 291).

In making this point Sukhanov explicitly states that he is describing the Bolsheviks before Trotsky joined their ranks. But Trotsky was an atypical Bolshevik phenomenon. On the whole the party was as Sukhanov described it, for Lenin, as we saw in Chapter 4, could tolerate no peers or near-peers in the party. He was comfortable and behaved with assurance only in situations where he was clearly the dominant authority.

greetings. Then we heard them marching along the platform, under the triumphal arches, to the sound of the band, and between the rows of welcoming troops and workers. . . . Lenin came, or rather ran, into the room. . . . Running to the middle of the room, he stopped in front of Chkheidze [a member of the Provisional Government] as though colliding with a completely unexpected obstacle.[6]

Chkheidze made a sermonish speech, warning Lenin not to try to disunite the democratic forces in the country, to which Lenin responded:

Dear Comrades, soldiers, sailors, and workers! I am happy to greet in your persons the victorious Russian revolution, and greet you as the vanguard of the worldwide proletarian army. . . . The worldwide Socialist revolution has already dawned. . . . Germany is seething. . . . Any day now the whole of European capitalism may crash. The Russian revolution accomplished by you has prepared the way and opened a new epoch. Long live the worldwide Socialist revolution![7]

A triumphal procession then followed Lenin to the house where he was to stay. There, to his fellow Bolsheviks, he repeated in more detail his first words of greeting, words sounding very much like Trotsky's idea of permanent revolution, an idea which had previously been anathema to Leninists. Until this time Lenin had advocated the view that the revolution in Russia would be bourgeois in character; now he argued that the revolutionary forces of peasants and workers, with the Bolsheviks at their head, must push through to control of the organs of state. He was willing to find in the Provisional Government Russia's bourgeois political phase and to rely on European socialists to come to the support of the Bolsheviks before the inherent contradictions of socialist government in an economically

[6] *Ibid.*, I, 272.   [7] *Ibid.*, I, 273.

backward country manifested themselves. As he said at the Second Congress of Soviets in June:

> The citizen Minister of Posts and Telegraphs . . . has declared that there is no political party in Russia that would agree to take the entire power on itself. I answer: There is. No party can refuse to do this, all parties are contending and must contend for the power, and our party will not refuse it. It is ready at any moment to take over the Government.[8]

What, then, accounts for the change in Lenin's attitude —his eagerness to take power immediately and his increased reliance on European socialists? Several factors seem to be involved. First, the fact that the Tsar had fallen meant that the authority Lenin most feared, and was potentially most guilty about replacing, was gone. He did not, especially before the July days, perceive in the Provisional Government anything other than the groping and uncertain liberalism of which he had been contemptuous since his brother's death. Moreover, his feelings toward the liberals were almost purely aggressive; there was little of the strain which characterized his opposition to tsarism. The claim of the liberals and moderate socialists that they were now governmental authority was thus met by derision and fierce antigovernmental propaganda. Lenin's world-view had at its root a split image of paternal authority: a good and a bad father, Lenin-Marx and the Tsar. With the Tsar gone there was only one legitimate claimant to the father's, the ruler's, chair, and that was Lenin. Certainly the weak bourgeois would not be allowed to stand in the way.

Another element involved here is that the moderates did control, more or less, the armed forces of the state, against which Lenin was fighting. Although the foe was weaker than had been anticipated, he was still capable of inflicting great damage. Hence the reassurance that opposition to the government was not an isolated action but part of the inevitable course of history, and therefore extremely

[8] *Ibid.*, II, 380.

likely to have a favorable outcome, was needed. In times of danger Lenin would call forth the spontaneous uprising in Europe to reassure himself and his followers. When affairs were more manageable this idea, while always formally espoused, was less prominent in his thinking.

The reliance on the European proletariat could never be done away with completely, however, because too much of Lenin's system of justification, the ideological manifestation of his image of himself and his internal conflicts, was bound up in the classic Marxist formulation that revolution would come first where economic, and therefore class, development had progressed furthest. In order to give himself the reassurance of Marxist inevitability, Lenin had become a Marxist; in order to maintain the identification with Sasha, Marxism had to be stretched and blended with Russian populistic elements. A set of stresses was built into Lenin's socialism which thus impelled him to ever greater activism—and ever greater reliance on forces he could not control. The more Marxist he became, the more voluntaristic he had to become to maintain the guilt-relieving tie with Sasha. The more he relied on direct, controlled action and violence, the more Marxist he had to become so that the tie with his father would not be broken. Neither the primacy of the Russian proletariat nor the ultimate importance of the European masses could be given up. Lenin had to make them coexist.

In July of 1917, after an abortive Bolshevik uprising, the Provisional Government sought the arrest of the Bolshevik leaders and Lenin went into hiding. Sukhanov, who was very much anti-Bolshevik and whose comments on Lenin accordingly must be treated with circumspection, discusses Lenin's action as follows:

> I've already said . . . that in the given circumstances the shepherd's flight could not help but be a heavy blow to the sheep. The masses mobilized by Lenin, after all, were bearing the whole burden of responsibility for the July Days. They had no means of ridding

themselves of this burden. Some remained in their factories or in depression or unthinkable confusion of
mind. . . . And the 'real author' abandoned his army
and his comrades, and sought personal salvation in
flight!

Why was it necessary? Was he in any real danger?
Absurd, in the summer of 1917! . . . Lenin risked absolutely nothing but imprisonment.

Lenin of course may have prized not his life or
health, but his freedom of political action. But in a
prison of the time could he have been more hampered
than in his underground retreat? He could unquestion-
ably have written his fortnightly *Pravda* articles from
prison, while from the point of view of the political
effect the very fact of Lenin's imprisonment would
have had an enormous positive significance. His flight
had only a negative one.[9]

Although in retrospect it was easy enough for Sukhanov to
play down the dangers inherent in imprisonment, his ques-
tioning of Lenin's action is supported by the fact that Trotsky and others did not go into hiding, did court arrest, and
were able to operate quite effectively from prison, certainly
with fewer restrictions than Lenin did from his retreat.
Why, then, did Lenin flee?

Trotsky sheds some light on Lenin's decision. He reports
that after the July attempt had failed he saw Lenin, who
commented to him, " 'Now they will overthrow us. . . . Now
is their given moment.' His basic thought was to begin the
retreat and, as far as it turned out to be necessary, to go on
illegally."[10] Krupskaya reports that Lenin considered putting in an appearance after the order for his arrest. In preparing to go out he said to Krupskaya "Let us say good-
bye . . . we may not see each other again."[11] (He was subsequently prevailed upon not to expose himself.) It would
thus appear that, despite Sukhanov's estimation (and, implicitly, Trotsky's as well), Lenin feared for his life. The

[9] *Ibid.*, II, 471.   [10] Trotsky, *Lenin*, p. 77.
[11] Krupskaya, II, 233.

elaborate measures he took to conceal his whereabouts, his careful provision for adequate protection and the fact that he turned the manuscript for *State and Revolution* over to others, so that it might be published if he died, all reflect his troubled and fearful state of mind.[12]

There seem to be several elements involved in Lenin's fears. Since he was a basically mistrustful person, he might in any situation be expected to react with more suspicion and reservations than an optimist like Trotsky. Moreover, unlike Trotsky, Lenin had a real sense that he was a dangerous person. He was very serious in his aggressiveness and his willingness to use violence and he undoubtedly believed that others perceived him in the same terms. How, then, could even a relatively weak authority like the Provisional Government fail to act against him? Had he not just tried to overthrow them? Would not they now return the compliment in kind? True, the liberals collectively constituted a weak father, but even a weakened father possessed the strength to wreak revenge on a rebellious son.

Additionally, Lenin had a sense of the unique moment in history, the one time when a certain action might succeed. This attitude probably stemmed in part from the fact that his brother's attempted terroristic act had a very sharp and sudden outcome—one must strike at the right moment or death will result. In July the Bolsheviks had clumsily started an insurrection. They had failed and now it was the government's turn. If, however, the authorities failed to control the situation now, the Bolsheviks would have another chance. But they would have to be prepared to strike swiftly, to attack the liberals before they were attacked in turn. Lenin viewed his world in kill-or-be-killed terms— he who struck first and best would rule; the laggard would die.[13]

[12] Possony, pp. 235-39.

[13] As Trotsky emphasizes and as Lenin's writing during this period shows, Lenin lived in real dread that the Bolsheviks would not act soon or vigorously enough. Time and time again in the latter part of 1917 Lenin argued for imminent and violent overthrow of the government. See, for example, Trotsky, *Lenin*, pp. 91-96, and Lenin's

Because he foresaw the possibility of another chance at insurrection, Lenin did not despair while he was in hiding, although he apparently went through a brief period of depression during the first few days.[14] He managed to maintain some contact with his forces in St. Petersburg and completed, to the extent that it was ever completed, *State and Revolution*. Faced with the possibility of winning power, in this work Lenin turned his attention to the kind of society he hoped to build and the way in which it would be reached. In dealing with the latter, Lenin enunciated his version of the doctrine of the withering away of the state. According to Lenin the withering away of the state was to take place only after the socialists had gained control of state power via violent overthrow of the existing regime. There would then exist the dictatorship of the proletariat, which would utilize state power for the suppression of capitalist elements in the society. Eventually the lower, then higher, stages of communism would be reached, and with their realization the state would gradually disappear, for the state was merely an instrument of class domination and hence would be unnecessary once class distinctions disappeared.[15] In other words, Lenin put forward a picture of successive approximations of a utopia of a particular kind. In the present one starts in the least utopian of conditions: someone else is in control of massive means of suppression, has authority and threatens one. Violence must be used against this threat of violence. Thus in the first case Lenin merely summarizes, utilizing judicious selection of quotations from Marx and Engels, his view of the world as it is.

---

sharp note to the Bolshevik Central Committee in September entitled "The Bolsheviks Must Assume Power," in his *Collected Works* (New York, 1932), XXI, Book 1, 221-23. This theme, it might be mentioned, that there is only one right time for an action, is related to another major current in Lenin's psychology, that there is only one right line, one correct interpretation of events, at any juncture. On these points see Part II of Leites' *The Study of Bolshevism*.

[14] Possony, p. 237.

[15] Lenin, *State and Revolution* (New York, 1932), *passim*.

All the themes we have previously discerned in Lenin are succinctly recapitulated here.

Lenin, in order to give direction to his life, in order to see some way out of the tense emotional environment in which he lived, then had to posit the route of escape. Thus the first step was to change roles with the authorities. Although there would still be a world of conflict, now the proletariat (acting through the party which is its vanguard) would control the power of the state and rule over those who were formerly in power. In short, Lenin would be the father and his father would be a persecuted son who would have to suffer all the penalties Lenin felt his father wanted to inflict on him. But the dictatorship of the proletariat was not to be the final answer. Lenin needed to believe in the possibility of a world in which men could trust each other and conflict would end:

> But, striving for Socialism, we are convinced that it will develop into Communism; that, side by side with this, there will vanish all need for force, for the subjection of one man to another, and of one part of the population to another, since people will *grow accustomed* to observing elementary conditions of social existence *without force and without subjection.*[16] (Emphasis added.)

Thus the higher phase of communism was to involve the end of domination of any kind. This equality was to be made possible by the breaking down of the fundamental distinctions of precommunistic life: the end of classes, the end of the antagonism between mental and physical labor, and so on.[17] Lenin's present-day world, which was based on the existence of authority, distinctions, and antagonisms was to give way to one characterized by the absence of these qualities. From a world in which a dreaded father had to be fought, one would travel to a world in which the distinction between father and son had been obliterated. For

[16] *Ibid.*, p. 68.
[17] *Ibid.*, p. 79.

Lenin it was better to be father than son, to wield power rather than to suffer at the hands of the authorities. But it was better yet to escape from the situation altogether, to exist in a world free from the guilt and strain which would accompany the exercise of power. Clearly such a world exists only in phantasy—there are differences between fathers and sons, men and women, adults and children, which cannot be eliminated with changes of social structure (along with many other things which are, practically speaking, immutable in this regard). Lenin's life was predicted on a dream which could only remain a dream, but in terms of which he could justify his efforts and communicate with others. He did not expect his utopia, which he claimed was not unrealistic, to come overnight; the whole bent of his personality led him to anticipate a long struggle, a long wait. Moreover, there were gratifications to be had as long as the root aspect of the dictatorship of the proletariat, namely Lenin's ascent to the top position of authority, was obtained. Thus Lenin was unusually well suited to rule patiently should he get into power. Yet to some extent he would have to ward off the feelings of despair that come with incomplete realization of one's goals, as well as the guilt which results from the ultimate usurpation of paternal prerogatives. As we shall see in the case of Trotsky, it is sometimes impossible to make the jump from rebellious son to ruling father.

The actual transition to power was accomplished without great difficulty. Although Lenin was apprehensive right up to the moment the takeover began that the party was held back by inertia and timidity, with his prompting and Trotsky's leadership it easily eliminated the Provisional Government. When Lenin joined Trotsky at the Smolny Institute during the evening of November 6 he quickly turned his attention to two tasks: the details of control[18] and the drafting of decrees and proclamations.[19] Despite the fact he was still uncertain about the ultimate success of the ef-

[18] Trotsky, *Lenin*, p. 100.
[19] Possony, p. 250.

fort, he appeared to Trotsky to be delighted with the careful measures that had been taken, the efficiency of the operations and the seriousness of the attempt.[20] Trotsky also reports the following incident, noting that it was the only really personal remark Lenin made during the first few days of Bolshevik control. On the morning of November 7 Lenin "smiled and said: 'The transition from the state of illegality, being driven in every direction, to power—is too rough.' 'It makes one dizzy,' he at once added in German, and made the sign of the cross before his face.' "[21] Lenin, predictably enough, was somewhat overcome by the shift in roles. About to undertake to father a nation he appealed to the Father of his childhood for guidance.

From the moment he joined Trotsky in the Smolny until the spring of 1922, when he had the first of the cerebral attacks which eventually led to his death, with the exception of infrequent holidays and a period of recuperation after he was shot and wounded by Dora Kaplan in the summer of 1918, Lenin worked perseveringly at the tasks of organization of the many functions of the state, administration, ideological justification, and policy declaration. He continued to write at a prodigious rate and few government actions escaped his attention. It is not possible, in the space available, to give any substantial picture of the range of Lenin's activity, but one theme in particular runs through most of his behavior during this period: he was terrifically afraid of failure on the one hand (through inadequate performance of duty on his and the party's part), and of being overwhelmed by enemies on the other. To ward off failure, to avoid being an inadequate father to his revolutionary children, Lenin devoted endless hours to the most minute details of administration, firmly and patiently chaired meeting after meeting—and made decisions. His concern is shown in his reproaches to others. "Where have we a dictatorship? Show it to me. It is confusion we have, but not dictatorship."[22] Confusion and lack of orderliness were al-

[20] Trotsky, *Lenin*, p. 100.   [21] *Ibid.*, p. 102.
[22] Cited in Trotsky, *Lenin*, p. 138.

ways there to plague him, a man with an extraordinary need to have things neatly catalogued and distinctions clearly made. Lenin, who had to compartmentalize his thinking and categorize the people around him in order to control the original ambivalence of his emotions, found himself in a world where reality, in all its confusion and untidiness, had to be faced. The strain of living in such a world was very great.

Lenin's sense of responsibility is reflected in some words of admonition he gave to restive workers in the days just before Brest-Litovsk. This body of men was determined to go to the front and fight; Lenin, seeking to preserve manpower and prepared to retreat far eastward into Russia if necessary, ended his (successful) plea not to go with these words:

> "I will give you now a special train to the Front. I will not stop you. You may go. But you will take my resignation with you. *I have led the Revolution. I will not share in the murder of my own child. . . .*"[23]
> (Emphasis added.)

Lenin felt a father's responsibility for the movement he had led. He challenged his errant "children" to kill, symbolically, their father if they must have their way. Needless to say, Lenin would have chosen other measures if persuasion had failed. But judging by his own experience he surmised that he had chosen an effective tack: he knew only too well himself how hard it was to bear the burdens of overthrowing a father.

Additionally, Lenin lived in daily expectation of being overthrown. For example, Trotsky records a conversation with Lenin that took place sometime during the first weeks of power:

> "And what," Vladimir Ilyich once asked me quite unexpectedly, during those first days—"what if the

[23] In the impressions of Raymond Robins, cited in Albert R. Williams, *Lenin: The Man and His Work* (New York, 1919), p. 138.

White Guards killed you and me? Will Svyerdlov and Bukharin be able to manage?"

"Perhaps they won't kill us," I rejoined, laughing.

"The devil knows what they might do," said Lenin, laughing in turn.[24]

Lenin thought of his possible demise, of how his successors might manage. Trotsky could not treat the matter seriously. Lenin, in fear of his life, wanted to know what would happen to his "family" when he was gone. Trotsky did not feel the paternal obligation.[25]

Lenin's great emphasis on decrees during the early phases of the stay in power is another indication of the expectation of being overcome. He had constantly in mind the history of the Paris Commune, an ill-fated revolutionary effort that had come before the time was ripe for socialist rule. So, like the leaders of the Commune, he was concerned to leave behind a declaration of principles, an affirmation of his revolutionary dedication and his Marxist class-consciousness. As Trotsky put it in retrospect:

> It was impossible to tell in advance whether we were to stay in power or be overthrown. And so it was necessary, whatever happened, to make our revolutionary experience as clear as possible for all men. Others would come, and with the help of what we had outlined and begun, would take another step forward. That was the meaning of the legislative work during the first period.[26]

He had worked for and applauded the killing of the father and, symbolically, now possessed the mother, mother Russia. Surely this offense would not go unpunished, surely he

[24] Trotsky, *My Life*, p. 338.

[25] The men's reactions in this case parallel their reactions to earlier political experience. During his first political activity in St. Petersburg, Lenin had been very conscious of the need for a "successor" if he were arrested. Trotsky, during his period of revolutionary activity in the Ukraine, did not look ahead to the fate of the movement if he should be removed from the scene.

[26] *Ibid.*, p. 342.

would not be allowed to enjoy such forbidden fruit. Fear impelled Lenin to strenuous efforts of defense. Out of fear he reacted swiftly to new situations—anything to preserve the hold on power. But always, when time permitted, past actions were justified in Marxist terms, contact with the ideology in terms of which he conceived himself was maintained.

The responsibility for the direction of policy, guilt at the consequences of his action, his fear of punishment and the frustrations of his position, both in terms of the things that others failed to do and the inability of the country to reach the utopia of which he dreamed, took its toll of Lenin. Sukhanov reports, for example, that within a year and a half of Lenin's taking power his speeches became "flat, faded, and trivial, losing both . . . power and originality."[27] This was in great contrast to Sukhanov's characterization of Lenin's speaking before he attained power, at which time he found it to be of "enormous impact and power."[28] There were other, and more serious signs of strain as well. Although cerebral arteriosclerosis seems to have been a family trait (presumably his father had died from a stroke), it is very likely that the number of attacks Lenin had and the prolonged nature of the decline was in part a result of the strain under which he operated.[29]

Lenin, then, did show pronounced signs of the tension under which he operated; but given the difficulty of the job itself, that of leader of a new government in an extremely hostile environment, and the added burdens of guilt and fear associated with being a governmental leader after having been a revolutionist, Lenin managed the role extremely well. His lifelong orientation to long-run goals, the extension of his view of the world-as-conflict to apply to all time before the realization of communism (rather than just socialist control of government) and his pre-existing pattern of leadership, his secure identification with the paternal forces in his environment (notably his father and Marx)

[27] Sukhanov, *Russian Revolution*, I, 280.
[28] *Ibid.*
[29] Possony, pp. 394-96.

seem to be the primary factors which made the adjustment possible.

Perhaps the text which most clearly exemplifies Lenin's conception of his role as leader of the Bolshevik Party and the Soviet State is *Left-Wing Communism: An Infantile Disorder*, written in the spring of 1920. In it Lenin seeks to interpret for the Communist parties of other European countries the lessons to be learned from the Russian experience. It is, like *What Is To Be Done?*, a handbook for revolutionists; now, however, an organizational basis is assumed and Lenin goes on to discuss the tactics the organizations should use, the alternatives their leaders should select.

Lenin begins by claiming that other Communist parties must base their actions on the Bolshevik experience: "the Russian model reveals to *all* countries something, and something very essential, of their near and inevitable future."[30] Although the Russian Revolution will not be recapitulated in all its details, there will be important similarities between it and all other socialist revolutions. Just as in *What Is To Be Done?* Lenin viewed the Russian revolutionists as the vanguard of the world proletariat, so now others must look to the Bolsheviks for instruction. By this contention Lenin places his experience at the center of the revolutionary universe. He is *the* leader, not only of the Russians, but of all Marxist revolutionists as well. This reflects, in fact, Lenin's basic orientation that there is only one revolution, one worldwide in scope, just as each man has only one nuclear family. The battle is between Lenin and evil paternal authority. Now that one representative of that authority, the Tsar, has been defeated, the other oppressors must be faced.

This continuation of the conflict, however, creates certain difficulties, for "it was easy for Russia . . . to *start* the socialist revolution, but it will be more difficult for Russia than for the European countries to continue the revolution and bring it to its consummation . . . [and] it will be more

[30] Lenin, *Left-Wing Communism: An Infantile Disorder*, in his *Selected Works* (Moscow, 1961), III, 375-76.

difficult for Western Europe to *start* a socialist revolution than it was for us."[31] It took an unusual combination of circumstances to make revolution possible in Russia, despite which Russia remains a backward country incapable of moving to socialism on her own. In short, Lenin believed the success of even the Russian revolution was contingent upon revolution in the West. But this "fact," as we have seen, put Lenin in the uncomfortable and dangerous position of having to rely on the spontaneous advent of revolution in areas which seemed to be out of his control. Lenin now sought a doctrine and, in the Russian dominated Third International, an organization which would minimize his reliance on spontaneity, augment the possibilities of consciousness and vanguard direction.

The form of this doctrine has been implied above; Lenin simply extended the concept of the vanguard developed in *What Is To Be Done?* to include the Third International as well as the Russian Communist Party. He claimed for himself the fathership of the world revolution, just as he had previously done for the Russian. That Lenin is playing a father's role is indicated by his castigation of those who do not understand his directives and the lessons of the Russian experience as "childish," and by his emphasis on the educative nature of proper revolutionary preparation. For example, in stressing the need for Communists to infiltrate the trade unions, he characterizes the unions as "an indispensable 'school of communism' and a preparatory school that trains proletarians to exercise their dictatorship."[32] Lenin has become a veritable school superintendent of revolution, just as many years before his father had been school superintendent of Simbirsk.

The lesson Lenin seeks to teach the Europeans is essentially threefold: to avoid dogmatism of either the left or the right; to utilize any means that advance the revolutionary cause; and to maintain a tightly disciplined organization. The first point, as indeed all three points, is a familiar Leninist position. In the 1890s Lenin rejected Mikhailovsky

[31] *Ibid.*, pp. 412-13.   [32] *Ibid.*, p. 401.

on the right and the earlier Narodniks on the left. In *What Is To Be Done?* he battled against the Economists and the Terrorists. Now once again he tries to guide Marxists away from rightist opportunism and leftist infantilism. The leftists argue for direct action and against joining the trade unions, participating in elections, forming temporary alliances with the "liberals," and any and all compromises. But this policy, Lenin argues, is childish, immature, and sure to lead to defeat—just as, we may add, Sasha's fierce revolutionary spirit, untempered by caution and the lessons of revolt, made his defeat child's play for the Tsar's police.

In the face of a dangerous foe, involved in a revolutionary "war which is a hundred times more difficult, protracted and complicated than the most stubborn of ordinary wars between states," any means may be used.[33] The underpinnings of this flexibility seem to be first, as we have seen throughout this study, that Lenin viewed the struggle in kill-or-be-killed terms, that therefore one armed oneself as well as possible against the foe and felt free to use any weapons available for the combat. Secondly, we know that Lenin managed to liberate himself to an unusual degree from psychological involvement with other people. As a result, he was able to guard himself extraordinarily well from the danger of trusting unreliable allies too much or believing too easily in others' promises.[34] Hence he advocated for others the same kind of dispassion, an "objective" and manipulative view of one's human environment.

Finally, Lenin held first and last to his belief in the need for an organizational weapon, a band of brothers having "perseverance, discipline, firmness, implacability and unity of will."[35] Only with such a party could Lenin feel that he and the revolutionary cause were safe in a malevolent

[33] *Ibid.*, p. 417.

[34] It is of course true that Lenin was subject to "spasms of enthusiasm" about other people, as Trotsky put it (*My Life*, p. 338); but usually this response was followed by hard second thoughts, especially if the individual involved was to be trusted with any matter of vital concern.

[35] *Ibid.*, p. 378.

world; only if one mastered "all the means of struggle" would victory be assured.

Lenin's incapacitation from his seizures became increasingly severe as time went by. After the first one, in the spring of 1922, he was away from his work for only a few months, but after the second, in December of the same year, he never really regained his grasp of affairs. Just before his second attack, he had tried to set up a system of deputation which would divide power sufficiently so that no one man could again control—either in his absence or in the event of his death. As time passed, however, it became increasingly clear that the party was splitting into two groups, with Stalin and the bureaucrats on one side and Trotsky, with scattered support, on the other. Thus, over a period of days early in 1923 Lenin worked on what has since been called his "testament," which contained an analysis of party problems and leaders.[36] Trotsky and Stalin were termed the two most able leaders; each was observed to have faults. As more information on Stalin's activities gradually found its way to him, however, and after Stalin had been strangely rude to Krupskaya, Lenin added a postscript to the memorandum, recommending that Stalin be relieved of his post of general secretary of the party. He did not, it would seem, anticipate pushing Stalin out of the party; he was merely going to demote him so that the latter would learn restraint and manners. In order to effect this move, he convinced Trotsky to join him in an anti-Stalin bloc over the question of Great Russian chauvinism in Georgia (Stalin, despite his Georgian background, being the chauvinist). But he was struck down by his third stroke before the plan could be put into operation and Trotsky, as we shall see in the next section, did not realize what kind of game was being played and threw away his advantages.

Lenin, then, did give some attention to the question of succession. As a person sensitive to organization he had been involved in training others for the better part of

[36] The following discussion of the "testament" is based on Fischer's *Life of Lenin,* pp. 634-49.

his life. But he had created an organization which could not generate a successor of whom he would approve. As Sukhanov put it, Lenin was the "Thunderer"; any other men of similar stature had been forced out of the party during one split or another. All that was left was, on the one hand, Trotsky, who had many of the right ideas but did not understand the rules of the kill-or-be-killed game, and, on the other, Stalin, who understood the game but lacked the intellectual refinement and the ideological skill that Lenin so valued. To be sure, it was, in any case, unlikely that another man of Lenin's combination of abilities would be available when needed, but Lenin's need to be the head of the party made it not only unlikely but impossible.

In some ways, then, Lenin failed to set a basis for the continuation of the practices in which he believed. Yet no matter how distorted, and how much more distorted it was to become over time, the Leninist tradition was embodied in the Communist Party of the Soviet Union for some years. The effects of this tradition on the party after Lenin's death on January 21, 1924, the ways in which Stalin was and was not a Leninist and the degree to which Leninism is still relevant to Soviet politics is, however, more than sufficient subject matter for another study.

Trotsky: The Loss of Power

The outbreak of the Revolution found Trotsky and his family in New York. They undertook to return to Russia immediately, but were detained for a month in Canada pursuant to the orders of the British government.[37] Thus Trotsky did not arrive in St. Petersburg until early May. Unlike

[37] The British and the western allies generally considered Trotsky, as an avowed revolutionist, a danger to them as well as to the Provisional Government in Russia. Hence they sought to delay his return by the Canadian internment. Trotsky could not understand why he should be thus delayed. After all, he and his companions were "irreproachable Russian revolutionaries returning to our country, liberated by the revolution." (*My Life*, p. 280) He did not grasp, what the British and Lenin so well did, that revolution was a serious and deadly business. For him it still seemed a game in which the winners won applause.

Lenin, whose followers had arranged a conspicuous welcome for him, Trotsky entered the city without fanfare;[38]
in fact, it was uncertain what role he would be able to play
in the current political situation. In 1905 he had been one
of the first to return from exile, now he was one of the last
and "no appropriate vacancy seemed to be open for a man
of his gifts and ambition."[39] The Mensheviks and Social
Revolutionaries were in control of the Petersburg Soviet
and, although they did appoint him as an associate member
of the executive committee of that body, he clearly did not
control it. Nor were the Bolsheviks ready to accept him;
after all, he had been at odds with them since 1903. For-
tunately for Trotsky, however, there was much that could
be done without organizational support. The Revolution
was in many ways a St. Petersburg affair and in that urban
context there was ample room for any man who was an
effective speaker. With his great oratorical talents Trotsky
quickly established a rapport with the city's masses and the
military detachments stationed at nearby Kronstadt. He,
more than any other one man, came to control the people
and the military of the city, and on that basis was able to
project himself into a leading, if not the leading, position in
the revolution. It was not until he merged these resources
with the organizational basis Lenin had developed, however, that all the necessary ingredients, from the insurrec-
tionist's point of view, came under his (and Lenin's)
control.

It should be noted that Trotsky was not quite isolated
organizationally before he joined the Bolsheviks in September. He was the acknowledged leader of a group of former
Mensheviks and Bolsheviks known as the Inter-Borough
organization, which had many brilliant leaders and lieuten-
ants but virtually no organized following except in a few of
the working class districts of St. Petersburg.[40] But because
it was composed of so many useful men, it would clearly be

[38] Sukhanov, I, 339.
[39] Deutscher, *The Prophet Armed*, p. 250.   [40] *Ibid.*, p. 255.

to Lenin's advantage to incorporate it, and therefore Trotsky, into the Bolshevik Party if he could. But the incursion of this element into the top ranks of the party, especially when it developed that Trotsky was, next to Lenin, the most widely acclaimed leader of the group, could not but leave injured pride and restiveness in its wake—especially when someone as abrasive verbally as Trotsky was involved.

As stated above, the primary basis of Trotsky's leadership in 1917 was the effectiveness of his verbal appeals to the working class. Trotsky later told Sukhanov that he saw his role as an agitational one: " 'Only one path is permissible for a revolutionary: to go to his *own* class and call on it to fight!' "[41] Although Trotsky did in fact address audiences from other classes, he really felt in his element only with the workers. In addressing others there were all too frequent interjections of ridicule, but in the Cirque Moderne, where he most often spoke, the audience was his own and the response gratifying. In that setting his verbal prowess yielded what he had always demanded of it—the admiration, love, and attention of others; there his love of and flair for the dramatic, combined with his well developed talent for striking and emphatic expression of even very complex ideas, made him the master of his audience and the object of acclaim. He could openly express his hatred for authority and win approval. Later, as we shall see, the peace negotiations at Brest-Litovsk and the task of organizing and directing the Red Army had similar elements of excitement, self-display, and the uninhibited expression of aggression. These situations were the ones in which Trotsky functioned efficiently and unhesitantly. Away from such sources of support and stimulation his powers faltered and his actions became inhibited and tentative.

In his autobiography Trotsky presents a striking picture of the atmosphere at the Cirque Moderne and of his reactions to it:

[41] Quoted in Sukhanov, II, 383.

Every square inch [of the Circus] was filled, every human body compressed to its limit. . . . I made my way to the platform through a narrow human trench, sometimes I was borne overhead. The air, intense with breathing and waiting, fairly exploded with shouts and with the passionate yells peculiar to the Modern Circus. . . . I spoke from out of a warm cavern of human bodies; whenever I stretched out my hands I would touch someone, and a grateful movement in response would give me to understand that I was not to worry about it, not to break off my speech, but keep on. No speaker, no matter how exhausted, could resist the electric tension of that impassioned human throng. . . . At times it seemed as if I felt, with my lips, the stern inquisitiveness of this crowd that had merged into a single whole. Then all the arguments and words thought out in advance would break and recede under the imperative pressure of sympathy, and other words, other arguments, utterly unexpected by the orator but needed by these people, would emerge in full array from my subconsciousness. On such occasions I felt as if I were listening to the speaker from the outside, trying to keep pace with his ideas, afraid that, like a somnambulist, he might fall off the edge of the roof at the sound of my conscious reasoning.

Such was the Modern Circus. It had its own contours, fiery, tender, and frenzied. The infants were peacefully sucking the breasts from which approving or threatening shouts were coming. The whole crowd was like that, like infants clinging with their dry lips to the nipples of the revolution. . . .

Leaving the Modern Circus was even more difficult than entering it. The crowd was unwilling to break up its new-found unity. . . . In a semiconsciousness of exhaustion, I would float on countless arms above the heads of the people, to reach the exit. . . . When I found myself outside the gate, the Circus followed me. The street became alive with shouts and the tramping of feet. Then some gate would open, suck me in, and close after me. . . .[42]

Trotsky was almost always an effective speaker; but here, at the high point of his effectiveness, he describes his actions in peculiarly passive tones. Ideas well up from his unconscious, he observes himself as speaker, is carried overhead and sucked into repose away from the crowds. In this crowd situation the tight controls of consciousness, the inhibiting forces of guilt, have been broken down. Trotsky is thus at his best when he urgently and imminently feels that he is being borne by something greater than himself. The crowd in terms of personal contact is analogous to the inevitable forces of history in terms of ideology and abstraction, in each case a benevolent force carrying him safely forward.[43]

At the same time Trotsky feels himself to be the mother of the revolution, nursing it as the mothers in his audience are nursing their children. He unconsciously views himself as a better mother to his revolutionary children than his mother was to him. Trotsky claimed that his mother had, as we saw in Chapter 2, ignored the children. He remembers seeing one of the younger children at his mother's breast, although he thinks at first that he is remembering his own experience.[44] And now he shows his mother that there is room for all at his breast—he can suckle and love the whole revolution.

Needless to say, this is a very different impression of Trotsky's oratory from the one that I developed of Lenin. Lenin conspicuously based his presentation on the controlled and professorial mannerisms of his father. He came by his style in the normal course of things. Trotsky, by contrast, developed his style out of the books and experiences

[42] Trotsky, *My Life*, pp. 295-96.
[43] Trotsky here provides us with material for an important supplement to Freud's *Group Psychology and the Analysis of the Ego*, which views the leader of just such crowds as these rather as an unmoved mover. Trotsky's description gives us an insight into how much the leader responds passively to and is controlled by the crowd's activity.
[44] *Ibid.*, p. 2.

of his late childhood and adolescence, and in it are combined diverse elements. There is, moreover, a lack of clarity
in the blend, a hint of incongruity. In most settings Trotsky
was the brilliant schoolboy, answering questions and bet-
tering his opponents. Yet sometimes he was able to speak
with the calm authority of a father and here a mixture of
fatherly and motherly emotions are involved. This emotional eclecticism worked predominantly in his favor until
1920 and the end of the Civil War, but it was a liability
after that, when mass appeals were no longer the order of
the day and the abrasiveness of the schoolboy's style was
absorbed almost entirely by colleagues instead of class enemies—and when the lack of inner sureness which this
stylistic flexibility revealed would manifest itself in compromise and retreat.

The build-up of support for the Bolsheviks and Trotsky's rise were temporarily interrupted after the rioting of
the July Days. As was mentioned earlier, in the face of possible reprisals Lenin went into hiding. Trotsky, on the other
hand, who was not at first on the list of those to be arrested,
courted imprisonment by proclaiming his unity with the
wanted Bolshevik leaders and by displaying himself at
meetings for several days—until, in fact, he was arrested.
Here the basic difference in the attitudes of the two men
toward authority is revealed. Lenin was willing to overthrow authority and viewed it as willing to eliminate him.
Accordingly he took as many measures as possible to save
himself from unexpected attack or danger. Trotsky, who
was both more optimistic and who took the game much less
seriously, whose attitudes toward authority were much
more mixed and whose sense of his own potential for in-
juring others was much less developed (his father was still
alive at this time), took virtually no preventive measures.
Again, during this period, his ambivalence worked in his
favor. He was able to carry on his activities from prison
and his prestige rose on the basis of the courage of his
actions.

Trotsky also differed from Lenin in his view of the conditions under which the takeover of power should take place. Lenin's only concern was that the effort be made at the most auspicious time; there would be only one chance and one could not afford to miss it. Trotsky felt there was more leeway, that one could afford to wait for a moment when the action could be justified as one necessary for the preservation of the rights of the working class. Throughout 1917 Trotsky insisted on this defensive posture and continued to answer arguments from opponents.[45] Because he was more concerned with preserving the favorable response of his audiences and because he had a greater need for justification of his actions, he advanced his claims cautiously, step by step, putting the Bolsheviks into a position where only a precipitating action on the part of the government, some significant act of enmity, would be needed to occasion an insurrectionary response. One aspect of this mode of operation was that it gave the anxious Lenin an impression of hesitancy; and undoubtedly, as Trotsky himself later affirmed, Lenin's incessant calls to action did much to activate the revolutionary forces—and probably to resolve whatever internal waverings Trotsky still had.

Two governmental actions served to initiate the takeover: the closing down of the Bolshevik press and the interruption of telephone communications.[46] To these Trotsky reacted with alacrity; as a publicist he must have viewed the inhibition on communication as the most serious governmental provocation. The press was quickly reopened, the telephones were put back in operation and Bolshevik units rapidly occupied all the strategic centers of the city. By the morning of November 7, 1917 the Bolsheviks held effective power.

In a short time the question arose of what function Trotsky was to perform in the new government:

> The conquest of power brought up the question of my government work. Strangely enough, I had never even given a thought to it; in spite of the experience of

[45] Deutscher, *The Prophet Armed*, pp. 295-306, *passim*.
[46] Trotsky, *My Life*, pp. 321-22.

1905, there was never an occasion when I connected the question of my future with that of power. From my youth on, or, to be more precise, from my childhood on, I had dreamed of being a writer. Later, I subordinated my literary work, as I did everything else, to the revolution. The question of the party's conquest of power was always before me. Times without number, I wrote and spoke about the programme of the revolutionary government, but the question of my personal work after the conquest never entered my mind. And so it caught me unawares.

After the seizure of power, I tried to stay out of the government, and offered to undertake the direction of the press.[47]

Up to this time, as he says, Trotsky had been devoted to only one goal, the overturn of tsarism. It had been the anchor of his life, something definite to hold onto amidst the uncertainties and viscissitudes of life in exile. He had been able to envision himself as the tribune of the people, but he had not conceived of himself as one of their leaders once tsarism had been conquered. In other words, he had mastered his guilt sufficiently to eliminate the father but he could not see himself stepping into the father's shoes. Thus it was only with great difficulty that he was persuaded to take a governmental post, that of minister of foreign affairs. Lenin had even suggested that Trotsky be elected chairman of the Soviet of People's Commissars, the post the former was to hold until his death, but Trotsky found the idea "inappropriate."[48] Gradually, however, he adjusted himself to working under Lenin.

Between November and the effective end of the Civil War in 1920, Trotsky was primarily involved in two major activities. First, he led the Russian delegation in the peace negotiations with the Germans at Brest-Litovsk and, once they were concluded, was put in charge of the organization of the Red Army and the defense of the revolutionary fa-

[47] *Ibid.*, pp. 339-40.
[48] *Ibid.*, p. 339.

therland. In each case he did a magnificent job and, especially in the latter instance, increased his prestige enormously with the mass of the population; at the same time, however, the existing antagonism between him and the old-line Bolsheviks was further accentuated.

The Bolsheviks had come to power in part as a result of their claim that they would bring peace to Russia. Hence they quickly initiated negotiations with the Germans to try to end the war. Their original goal was an end to the war as a whole; but when the Allies did not respond to their request that there be a general peace without annexations, they undertook to negotiate by themselves. Soon after the talks began Trotsky was sent to take charge. His fundamental task was to drag out the talks as long as possible, so that the truce that had been established when they began would be prolonged, giving the Bolsheviks time to solidify their hold on the government. Trotsky, additionally, saw this as an opportunity for the Bolsheviks to address the workingmen of the world.[49] He felt he could put the case for communism and revolution so well that the masses of Europe would rise up against their capitalist masters, establish socialist regimes—and end the war. He thus viewed Brest-Litovsk in terms which made it a continuation of the revolution itself. Trotsky would stand as the tribune of the Russian people, addressing his class in other lands and using as the mechanism for this the besting of his diplomatic foes in argument. Although he did not in fact succeed in inspiring revolution abroad, he did present the Bolshevik case effectively, attracting much favorable attention to himself and his cause.

As the weeks passed, however, it became clear that the Germans intended to occupy as much territory to their east as they could. The representatives of the German general staff at the negotiations were becoming increasingly impatient with the diplomats and an end to discussions was near. At this juncture Lenin, fearing a German attack, wanted to give in to the German conditions for ending the

[49] *Ibid.*, pp. 362-78.

war. Others in the party wanted to refuse the terms and fight, if necessary, a revolutionary war. Trotsky proposed the formula of neither war nor peace: Russia would withdraw from the war and refuse to fight but would not sign an unjust peace treaty unless the Germans actually attacked.[50] The party followed Trotsky's lead, the Germans did attack, and Russia was forced to accept terms even worse than the original ones. Trotsky seems to have believed that, rather than sign a humiliating treaty, a revolutionary war should have been attempted, and in fact he could easily have carried a majority of the Central Committee with him in support of such an effort. But Lenin was adamant for peace and Trotsky refused to risk splitting the party. He did not feel that he could undertake the leadership of the party and a vote for revolutionary war would have entailed that.[51] Hence he supported Lenin but resigned as Commissar for Foreign Affairs.

In the above events Trotsky had acted with his characteristic optimism and dedication to public pronouncement and oratorical appeal. He did not believe the Germans would attack, and when they did, he believed they could be effectively resisted. Lenin by contrast thought only of preserving the regime; he saw mortal danger in the force of German arms and moved to protect himself against it. Although Lenin was far from insensitive to the opinion of the European proletariat, when it came to a preservation of *his* government he would take no risks. Trotsky, who was not the leader, who could not envision himself as the leader, did not feel Lenin's paternal responsibility. The preservation of Bolshevik control was no more important to him than the opinion the proletariat—and history— would form of him. But after years of fighting against it he had accepted Lenin's leadership and he would not risk losing his position of favorite son to the father of the party.

Simultaneously with his resignation as Commissar of Foreign Affairs Trotsky accepted assignment as Commissar of War. For two years, from the spring of 1918 through

[50] Deutscher, *The Prophet Armed*, p. 375.   [51] *Ibid.*, p. 395.

〖　268　〗

the middle of 1920, he virtually lived in a railroad train which served him as his military command center. He moved from front to front in the war against the White armies, inspiriting the men, developing strategy, and using repressive measures whenever necessary to maintain discipline and effectiveness. In most respects this period, like his short period of guidance of foreign affairs, was a continuation of the revolution, a constant struggle against the class enemy whom one fought by the development of strategies of conflict, deployment of forces, and inspiration of troops. In one way, however, it differed: violence had to be used on one's own people to insure the successful outcome of the conflict.[52] Trotsky defended his use of harsh punishment vigorously, and received full support from Lenin for his actions, but his justifications for his actions always had a defensive tone. Apparently he was not quite easy in the role of disciplinarian; it was easier for him to fight against authority than to enforce the prerogatives of authority.

To some extent Trotsky's rapid assumption of a set of minority positions in the party once the war was under control indicates his feelings of guilt about his past actions, his eagerness to disassociate himself from the position of authority. At the same time, however, he continued to argue for the need for centralized control and loyalty to the party; as Deutscher says, Trotsky was wrestling with "the dilemma between authority and freedom."[53] Before he had attained power, the underlying ambivalence of Trotsky's attitude had not proved very incapacitating. It had made difficult any factional alignment during the years of exile, but under the stress of events in 1917 this handicap was readily overcome (although only because Lenin had built an organization and was willing to work with Trotsky). But now the underlying tension was starting to manifest itself in crucial ways. From the end of the war until well into his final exile Trotsky attempted to argue for both "authority and free-

[52] *Ibid.*, pp. 420-21.
[53] Deutscher, *The Prophet Unarmed*, p. 52.

dom." Having conceived of himself and his life in terms of the revolutionary conquest of power, and having performed the functions of authority under the aegis of Lenin, Trotsky could not deny the legitimacy of the state he had helped to found or its policies without denying the very basis of his personality and admitting to his guilt, as well as Lenin's, in betraying the cause of the son for the role of the father.

Trotsky had mastered the problems of his adolescence by constructing a system of justification of revolutionary action against authority and now he found himself in the position of authority fighting to repress, both with respect to rebellious or timorous troops and opposition currents within the country and the party, revolutionary tendencies. He did not have Lenin's firm identification with a paternal model to ease the difficulty of the transition. He was, in fact, in an extraordinarily tension-ridden psychological position, one which was made tenable only by his relationship to Lenin. Although he continued to differ with him with great frequency, Trotsky had adjusted to working under Lenin. As long as Lenin lived, Trotsky could hold the strains of his position in check; but when Lenin died the question of authority and freedom was reopened on a new scale: Trotsky would have to overcome his guilt and claim Lenin's mantle, step into a clear oppositionist position vis-à-vis Stalin and the party bureaucracy, or fall into a confused and confusing middle position, a hesitant uncertainty. He did the latter.

Needless to say, the whole bent of Trotsky's personality and past experience predetermined his ineffectiveness during the 1920s, but there had been specific intimations of the problems ahead after 1920, of which the following is the most indicative. As early as the spring of 1922, even before he had his first stroke, Lenin had wanted to make Trotsky a deputy chairman of the Soviet of People's Commissaries.[54] He had appointed Stalin as general secretary of the party and now sought to balance power within the movement by giving Trotsky a countervailing position with

[54] *Ibid.*, p. 35.

respect to the governmental apparatus. But Trotsky refused the post, ostensibly because he found in the offer a needless multiplication of administrative functionaries. More fundamentally, however, Lenin's offer, which was repeated many times subsequently and each time turned down, was refused because it made obvious the incongruity of Trotsky's position. Trotsky was enough of a leader in his own right, his need for self-assertion was great enough, so that he could not formally acknowledge that he was second to Lenin as long as the latter lived. He had a half-rebellious, half-submissive relationship to Lenin which could not survive in a position of open lieutenantship, especially when there were to be other deputies as well—it would have been hard to preserve a self-image of favorite son under such conditions, much less one of co-equal father. The fact that the others who were appointed as deputies were clearly to be inferior to him fell far short of making the situation bearable.

Viewed another way, the problem with Lenin's offer was that it created a pair of equally unpalatable alternatives. Either the position of deputy made Trotsky heir apparent, in which case it was unacceptable because Trotsky's feelings of guilt about becoming head of the state and replacing Lenin were so great; or it made him just one of Lenin's top subordinates, which was unacceptable for the reasons indicated above. Thus Trotsky could not but refuse, and refuse again, thereby straining his relations with Lenin, giving others the impression that he was too proud to accept and disadvantaging himself tremendously in the struggle for power which would follow the death of the leader. Additionally, Trotsky did not believe Lenin was going to die in the near future, either when the first offer was made or even just before Lenin's totally incapacitating stroke in the spring of 1923.[55] He counted on his "father" to remain alive, to recognize the brilliance of his ideas, to manage the personal relations of the party so that Trotsky could continue to pursue his own ideas. It is not surprising, then,

[55] Trotsky, *Lenin*, p. 215.

that Trotsky reacted to the news of Lenin's death with bewilderment and a sense of bereavement.[56]

Trotsky was on his way to the Caucasus for a rest when Lenin died. He had been chronically ill for several years, perhaps as a result of a persistent malarial infection picked up on a hunting trip, and the anti-Trotsky campaign in the party was already well advanced under the direction of Stalin, Zinoviev, and Kamenev. He thus felt the need to escape from the Moscow environment. When he received the news of Lenin's death he continued on his journey; he contacted Moscow to ask whether he should return but Stalin told him the funeral would take place before he could return. Hence he missed Lenin's funeral, which in fact did not take place for several days, and gave the public as well as other party members the impression of being disrespectful to the fallen leader.[57]

Lenin's death had the immediate and quite persistent effect of immobilizing Trotsky. From 1924 through 1926 Trotsky traveled, wrote, studied the Soviet economy, and did many other things. But he did virtually nothing about the question of succession. The father's chair was now empty—although Stalin was moving toward it with increasing rapidity, virtually unperceived by Trotsky and the other intellectuals of the party as well, who could not take this uncouth mole of the revolution seriously—but Trotsky could not move himself to sit in it. Lenin, shortly before his death, had formed an anti-Stalin bloc with Trotsky and had given the latter enough material to insure Stalin's ouster from the general secretaryship of the party. But Trotsky compromised with Stalin and his allies in exchange for party commitments to his economic program. Trotsky

[56] Deutscher, *The Prophet Unarmed*, pp. 133-34 and Trotsky, *My Life*, pp. 508-10.

[57] The very fact that he accepted Stalin's word about the funeral, of course, indicates the degree to which Trotsky underestimated his opposition and his reluctance to return to Moscow and face up to Lenin's death. Ostensibly his illness delayed his return, as it later prevented him from attending crucial meetings at which his fate was at stake. It is rather striking, however, that these illnesses did not inhibit Trotsky's activity before the end of the Civil War.

thus continued to ignore the question of leadership while Stalin was working for control. He still saw the situation in terms of a battle of ideas, but Lenin was no longer there to reward him for his brilliance. With Lenin's death the game had become cruder; until that time a combination of Marxist incisiveness and a commitment to organization was needed to achieve and maintain power. Now, at least in the short run, only a sense for organization and personal susceptibilities was requisite. The internal affairs of the party had become as kill-or-be-killed as the struggle between the party and the state had formerly been; but Trotsky, who had never fully come to grips with the seriousness of the struggle before 1917, could not understand the nature of the situation. He was too much of a Menshevik, too optimistic, too committed to the sophisticated complex of ideas that was Marxism to comprehend the significance of Stalin's actions. This, combined with his own inhibitions about exercising power and his inability to disavow his past actions, foredoomed the Trotskyist opposition from the start. He was a semi-Menshevik in the Bolshevik camp, a perpetual outsider, and thus bound to lose.[58]

It is not possible here to trace the course of Trotsky's loss of power, the tortured yielding of one position of strength after another and the final and unsuccessful effort to go to the people in 1926-27. As Eastman comments, throughout this time Trotsky did not grasp that the attack was really on Trotsky, not some ideological position called "Trotskyism," and that proof that his position on issues was historically correct and unheretical would not lead to his acclamation by his foes.[59] He continued to interpret the success of Stalin as the ascendancy of the bureaucracy and the coming of the thermidorian phase of the revolution, instead of in terms of a set of opportunities and options which Stalin maximized and he did not. It was, of course,

[58] The most comprehensive study of the opposition movements in Russia in the 1920s, which argues a similar position on Trotsky and Menshevism, is Robert V. Daniels, *The Conscience of the Revolution* (Cambridge, Mass., 1960).

[59] Eastman, *Since Lenin Died*, pp. 93-96.

psychologically impossible for him to do anything else. Except with respect to the moment of revolutionary action itself (which is the one way in which he differed from the Mensheviks), Trotsky saw the world in terms of an inevitable dialectic which man was powerless to change in any very substantial way. This passivity in his personality grew out of his need for assurance that the outcome of the struggle to achieve manhood did not depend solely on his actions, that other forces were at work aiding him; but it now became the rationalization for his inaction and lack of comprehension of the reasons for his failure. In effect, he claimed that he did not fail—failure for someone holding his views was inevitable at this time in history:

> In view of the prolonged decline of the international revolution the victory of the bureaucracy—and consequently of Stalin—was foreordained.[60]

When the game had already been lost and Trotsky forced into exile, he gradually started to sort out what had happened. Although he never viewed his loss of power differently from the way he discussed it above, he took cognizance, retrospectively, of the arguments of Kamenev and Zinoviev that Stalin viewed the conflict in different, less sophisticated (in terms of Marxism) and bloodier terms.[61] Belatedly he broke away from his loyalty to the regime under Stalin and founded the Fourth International (in early 1933). Now, when it was too late, he was willing to assume the father's position, to accept the responsibility to lead by himself the international socialist movement, and to try to insure that the movement would survive:

> Thus I cannot speak of the "indispensability" of my work while Lenin was alive. But now my work is "indispensable" in the full sense of the word. . . . There is no one except me to carry out the mission of arming a new generation with the revolutionary method

[60] Trotsky, *Diary in Exile, 1935* (New York, 1963), pp. 93-96.
[61] *Ibid.*, p. 23.

over the heads of the leaders of the Second and Third International. . . . I need at least about five more years of uninterrupted work to ensure the succession.[62]

Thus Trotsky took up the problems Lenin had dealt with all his revolutionary life, those of building an organization and trying to insure continuity. But the combination of the limitations on his freedom of action placed upon him by Stalin's unrelenting opposition and his own inability to play with assurance and grace the role of leader doomed the Fourth International as an effective organization just as surely as the same characteristics had destroyed the opposition in Russia in the 1920s.[63] When he died in 1940, at the hands of one of Stalin's agents,[64] he had not managed to "ensure the succession," and, even if he had, what would succession to the control of an organization without a chance of gaining power mean? Trotsky was admirably suited to attaining power, but not to holding it. And if one cannot maintain power the question of succession is never really raised.

Gandhi: The Avoidance of Power

The final phase of the Indian struggle for independence began with the advent of the Second World War. Gandhi and the other Indian leaders deplored the outbreak of violence in Europe and were, by and large, pro-British in the European context. Gandhi, in fact, was moved to tears at the thought of the possible destruction of such things as Westminster Abbey.[65] Although with the passage of time he had lost his infatuation with the British way of life and had come to regard British imperialism in India with increasing dislike, he still maintained a deep affection for many in-

[62] *Ibid.*, pp. 46-47.

[63] The last phase of Trotsky's life, from his expulsion from Russia in 1939 to his death, is brilliantly covered in Deutscher's *The Prophet Outcast* (London, 1963).

[64] Deutscher's discussion of Trotsky's assassin and death is in *ibid.*, pp. 483-509.

[65] Cited from Gandhi's statement of September 5, 1939, in Tendulkar, *Mahatma*, V, 197.

dividual Englishmen and for those aspects of British culture which he could reconcile with his commitment to non-violence. And as he put it, "it almost seems as if Herr Hitler knows no God but brute force."[66] He did not support violent reaction to aggression but gave his moral support to Britain because, whatever her offenses in the Indian context, she was clearly the less aggressive party in the current international situation.

Congress, under Jawaharlal Nehru's direction, viewed the nascent war in somewhat different terms. As Nehru put it, they resented the fact that "One man, and he a foreigner and a representative of a hated system, could plunge four hundred millions of human beings into war, without the slightest reference to them."[67] The Viceroy had brought India into the war against the express wishes of the Congress leadership and Nehru now wanted to agree to support the British war effort only in return for British recognition of Indian independence. Gandhi, who was later to take the lead in pressing for immediate recognition, now held back; but he soon agreed that some action was needed to disassociate India from the British position of having India fight now and discuss with Britain possible ways of achieving independence only after the war. At the same time he did not want to hinder the British war effort. He thus found himself in what was, for him a relatively unusual situation: his feelings about what course of action to take were decidedly mixed. On the one hand he had residual affection for the British and lingering admiration for the determined masculinity of their resistance to nazism, as well as a repugnance for nazism; on the other hand he had bonds of loyalty to the Congress leadership (especially Nehru whom he regarded with fatherly affection), was dismayed by the violence which characterized the time and was repelled by the imperialistic intransigence of the English position on India. The former factors inclined him toward support of

[66] *Ibid.*
[67] Nehru, *The Discovery of India* (New York, 1946), p. 432.

the British, the latter toward nonviolent resistance. The result was a compromise: individual *satyagraha*.

On October 13, 1940 Gandhi outlined this compromise policy:

> Let me repeat the issue. On the surface it is incredibly narrow, the right to preach against war as war, or participation in the present war. Both are matters of conscience for those who hold either view. Both are substantial rights. Their exercise can do no harm to the British, if their pretensions that to all intents and purposes India is an independent country is at all true. . . .
>
>   *   *   *
>
> This right of preaching against the participation in war is being denied to us, and we have to fight against the denial. Therefore, while that right will be exercised only by those whom I may select for the purpose, all other activities of the Congress will continue as before unless the Government interferes with them.[68]

In part as a result of his barrister's training, Gandhi's mind always had a legalistic bent. He thought in terms of formulas, vows, and symbolic acts. In order to control the underlying ambivalence of his emotions the world, especially in abstract, was viewed in terms of rigid and unbending categories. One break in this pattern, be it positive or negative, marked the end of that state of affairs. (Similarly Lenin always feared that if one gave in a little to one's affectionate emotions, one was quickly prone to being overcome by them.) Thus if the British allowed the individuals whom Gandhi selected to speak against war to have their say, they would have given de facto recognition to the rights of Indians to behave in the manner of free citizens. If, alternatively, they suppressed the acts of free speech, they would tacitly admit their guilt in holding the Indians in a subject position and provide the occasion for further non-

[68] Tendulkar, V, 430-31.

violent resistance until, as Gandhi viewed it, British hearts and heads would be won over to the Indian position as a result of the selfless action of these few *satyagrahis*.

The campaign began in October with the speech and arrest of Vinoba Bhave, one of Gandhi's followers, and was gradually broadened to include the representatives of Indian nationalist organizations, provincial leaders and finally rank and file Congressmen in April 1940. Gandhi himself responded to the pleas of his followers and did not offer civil disobedience himself, both because he was needed out of prison to keep the campaign from expanding so rapidly that it would impede the war effort and because he did not want Britain to have to undergo the embarrassment of imprisoning him.[69] Because he viewed himself as God's leader in *ahimsa*, nonviolence, for his nation, he felt that Britain would place itself under a great moral handicap if its officials arrested him. His significance and his strength appeared to him to be a consequence of this special relationship with a protective deity, so that an act against him was an act against Truth. Although action against his followers also imposed a moral handicap on the British, it was presumably not as severe.

From Gandhi's position the movement could not fail if the *satyagrahis* did not resort to violence; but politically the activity was inconsequential. As Louis Fischer puts it, "people were tired of going to jail."[70] And the only one whose imprisonment could attract widespread interest was Gandhi. Thus by the end of 1941 the movement petered out and the British felt secure enough in India to release those already arrested; Gandhi's first attempt at Satyagraha during this crucial period was a failure in terms of advancing India and the Congress Party toward power.

Gandhi's second effort during the war period was occasioned by the Japanese victories of 1942. Fears increased that a Japanese invasion of India was imminent

[69] Nanda, pp. 437-46, provides an analysis of Gandhi's conception of this movement.
[70] Fischer, *Life of Gandhi*, p. 358.

〚 278 〛

and that were it not for the British presence in India there would be an invasion. And as Allied troops were brought into India to prepare for her defense, fears rose that from Japanese victory if the Allies lost or from the existence of this new element of armed force if they won, the path was being prepared for an even stronger subjugation of India than had hitherto existed. Gandhi's reaction to the armaments and troops was that they were:

> a tremendous price to pay for the possible success of allied arms. I see no Indian freedom peeping through all this preparation for the so-called defense of India. It is a preparation pure and simple for the defense of the British Empire, whatever may be asserted to the contrary. If the British left India to her fate as they had to leave Singapore, non-violent India would not lose anything. Probably, the Japanese would leave India alone.[71]

England had brought India into the war against the latter's will and now India was being forced to bear the consequences of British actions. She had been forced into a partnership in violence and now would have to pay for her sins. But Gandhi saw an out: if Britain would leave, Japan would have substantially less reason for invading India. It was, after all, the masculine mode of defense which carried with it the threat of paternal vengeance and left its user guilt-ridden. Feminine resistance at worst brought a guiltless death and at best led to the institution of harmonious relations with the erstwhile foe. Thus from India's standpoint there was nothing to lose by the British departure, as Britain was sure to lose anyway as long as she carried the burden of her immoral behavior toward India. In his own experience Gandhi had found that success came to him only when he was pure; that is, he was able to speak, lead, and win over others to his position only when he had renounced masculinity and aggressiveness. The extension of this idea to the political arena had been his singular con-

[71] Quoted from *Harijan* of April 26, 1942, in Tendulkar, VI, 93.

tribution to Indian revolutionary politics and now he brought it to bear, in theory at least, on international relations. But before international Satyagraha could take place, the British had to leave India.

Gandhi did not regard a British evacuation of India as a weakening of the British position in the war. Just as he felt that he was adequately armed only when he had renounced all aggressive intensions, so Britain could be strong only if she rid herself of the guilt of holding India in bondage:

> One thing and only one thing for me is solid and certain. This unnatural prostration of a great nation India —it is neither 'nations' or 'peoples'—must cease, if the victory of the allies is to be ensured. They lack the moral basis. I see no difference between the fascist or Nazi powers and the allies. All are exploiters, and all resort to ruthlessness to the extent required to compass their end. . . . They have no right to talk of human liberty and all else, unless they have washed their hands clean of the pollution.[72]

From their position the British could not understand, much less act upon, Gandhi's suggestion; for Gandhi their hostility to these ideas meant that civil disobedience was necessary. He now viewed the situation in such a way that there was no alternative to "embarrassing" the British government by such activity. He was even willing to risk violence among Indians, which he had previously avoided. Until now he had refused to lead any *satyagraha* campaign if there seemed a chance of Hindu-Moslem rioting or other disorder, but now he accepted the risk. Clearly this was an action born of desperation, occasioned by the national unrest and fearfulness of the Indian people in the face of possible Japanese invasion. From 1906 on Gandhi had been preaching that *swaraj*, home rule, achieved through nonviolence would bring harmony to India and give her moral authority of uncalculable value. Now it seemed that noth-

[72] Quoted from Gandhi's June 6, 1942 interview with Louis Fischer in Tendulkar, VI, 127.

ing less than *swaraj* would suffice to ward off the current danger and accordingly Gandhi planned a massive but speedy nonviolent movement to catapult India into independence.

On July 14 the Working Committee of the Congress Party published a resolution which echoed Gandhi's call to have the British leave India and proposed that Congress authorize Gandhi to lead a Satyagraha movement. On August 8, 1942 the All-India Congress Committee passed the "Quit India" resolution and Gandhi, speaking first in Hindustani and then English, addressed the assemblage. He first emphasized that he was severely disturbed by the continued hostility between Moslems, as led by Mohammed Ali Jinnah and the Moslem League, and the Hindus over the question of independence. Jinnah did not want the English to leave until communal differences had been settled by partitioning India into two states, Hindu India and Moslem Pakistan.[73] For Gandhi, however, the idea of partition was anathema and, until after the war when it became clear that the British did not have an independent policy on partition, he persisted in blaming communal differences on the British colonial policy of "divide and rule." Now, feeling an overwhelming need for freedom, he came to believe that communal unity could grow out of the struggle:

> You may take it from me that [Independence] is with me a matter of life and death. If we Hindus and Musalmans mean to achieve a heart unity, without the slightest mental reservation on the part of either, we must first unite in the effort to be free from the shackles of this empire.[74]

As he wrote in a later note to Jinnah, "the only real though lawful test of our nationhood arises out of our common political subjection. If you and I throw off this subjection by our combined effort, we shall be born a politically free na-

[73] Cf. Fischer, *Life of Gandhi*, pp. 397-404.
[74] Quoted in Tendulkar, VI, 196.

tion out of our travail."[75] Nonviolent means were thus to lead automatically to a nonviolent and unified society. In order to ward off his own feelings of guilt, which were awakened by aggression of any kind, Gandhi needed to see at least India and perhaps the world moving towards a non-violent harmony. And because Gandhi "identified" himself with the Indian masses as much as it "was possible for a human being to do,"[76] he felt that he was responsible personally for any act of violence in India. If he was to be free from the torments of guilt, the Indian people would have to free themselves from the sin of violence. And in order to save himself from feelings of helplessness, now as earlier, Gandhi enunciated the doctrine that out of nonviolent struggle must inevitably come a harmonious world.

Communal disorder created a problem for Gandhi in another way as well. Although on concrete levels he viewed all men as brothers, in abstract terms he viewed the world as dichotomized between British governance and *Hind Swaraj* (which meant Indian home rule, not Hindu rule), materialism and spiritualism, truth (*ahimsa, brahma*) and *maya* (illusion). In order to maintain that system intact, and doing so was necessary in order to keep separate the originally mixed emotions of love and hate, the notion of *Hind Swaraj* had to be preserved; and this was only possible on the basis of communal harmony. Thus the breakdown in communal relations in 1942 and even more markedly on the eve of Indian independence after the war, created a "spiritual" crisis for Gandhi. Communal enmity was growing despite Gandhi's (and to some extent India's) dedication to *ahimsa* and despite the supposedly unifying effects of the struggle for independence. What was wrong? Was *satyagraha* after all merely an effective means of revolutionary action when the rebelling party was very much the weaker of the two combatants? Or could *ahimsa* be the

[75] Cited in *ibid.*, p. 345, from a letter from Gandhi to Jinnah of September 15, 1944.
[76] *Ibid.*, VI, 198.

way of life of a powerful majority in its relation with a weaker minority? This question was the pervasive theme of the last years of Gandhi's life; his response to it will be dealt with briefly below.[77]

Gandhi's division of the world into realms of *maya* and truth is reflected in his plea to his followers to think of themselves as free:

> [Although the struggle itself will not actually begin for two or so weeks] every one of you should, from this moment onwards, consider yourself a free man or woman, and act as if you are free and are no longer under the heel of this imperialism.
>
> It is not make believe that I am suggesting to you. It is the very essence of freedom. The bond of the slave is snapped the moment he considers himself to be a free being.[78]

It is man's spirit that determines the meaning of his material circumstances, not the other way around. Gandhi felt that just as he had avoided the subjugation of guilt by renouncing the pleasures of the body, so the Indians would break the British raj by thinking of themselves, and hence acting, as free men. Gandhi felt that his soul had won over his body, that through an act of faith his fellow Indians would conquer their material circumstances and that therein would lie the defeat of British materialism and the attainment of *Hind Swaraj*.

The struggle Gandhi asked the Indian people to wage he conceived not to be for them alone but for all mankind. The world was in need of truth and God therefore commanded Gandhi to lead a Satyagraha campaign:

> In satyagraha, there is no place for fraud or falsehood, or any kind of untruth. Fraud and untruth today are stalking the world. I cannot be a helpless witness to such a situation. . . . How can I remain silent at

[77] See pp. 289-91.   [78] Quoted in Tendulkar, VI, 199.

this supreme hour and hide my light under a bushel?
. . . If today I sit quiet and inactive, God will take me
to task for not using up the treasure He had given me,
in the midst of the conflagration that is enveloping the
whole world.[79]

Opposition to the English is thus not viewed as an act of
volition, but as a sacred duty resulting from Gandhi's special relationship to God, to Truth. From a boy whose desire for an independent manhood was in radical conflict
with his love for his parents and his desire to submit to
them, Gandhi had evolved into a man who felt that he was
God's chosen instrument, and the possessor of a great
power which God now dictates that he use.

This power, this "treasure" of Gandhi's, is his because
for "the last twenty-two years, I have controlled my speech
and pen and have stored up my energy. He is a true *brach-
machari* who does not fritter away his energy."[80] By re-
fraining from sexual intercourse and from other forms of
uncontrolled behavior, Gandhi felt he kept within himself
the vital fluid of life, that he prevented the ebbing of his
powers and the loss of his manhood. And Gandhi was able
to exert the necessary self-control because he had made a
compact with God. When he yielded to God the preroga-
tive of sexual and other forms of indulgence, he received in
its place union with God's power, assurance of God's guidance and grace. He had become one with both mother and
father.

Now God (that is, his conscience) spoke to Gandhi of
the ensuing conflict and of his duty:

That something in me that never deceives me tells me
now: 'You have to stand against the whole world,
although you may have to stand alone. You have to
stare the world in the face, although the world may
look at you with bloodshot eyes. Do not fear. Trust
that little thing which resides in the heart.' It says,

[79] *Ibid.*, p. 198.   [80] *Ibid.*, p. 203.

'Forsake friends, wife, and all; but testify to that for which you have lived, and for which you have to die.'[81]

The alternatives are starkly drawn. Gandhi must face a hostile world and gain victory—or die. Up to this time, the aim of *satyagraha* had been relief of grievances or imprisonment. Now, however, the time for halfway measures had passed. As Lenin in 1917 had put on the scales of fate death or the dictatorship of the proletariat, now Gandhi put forward death or *Hind Swaraj*. In a world which accused him by its very violence, with India, the repository of his dreams and hopes, endangered, with the British continuing the policies which had made them anathema to Gandhi and other Indians for decades—and with his own old age hard upon him, connoting the possibility of not reaching *swaraj* in his lifetime and the question of the time and manner of his demise—Gandhi reduced his world to simple alternatives. India and he, Gandhi, more than others, must face a hostile world unafraid, must destroy evil authority or be destroyed by it.

In his speech, Gandhi makes explicit the dreadful simplicity of the possible outcomes of the *satyagraha* campaign:

> Here is a mantra, a short one, that I give you. You may imprint it on your hearts and let every breath of yours give expression to it. The mantra is: 'Do or Die.' We shall either free India or die in the attempt; we shall not live to see the perpetuation of our slavery. . . . Let every man and woman live every moment of his or her life hereafter in the consciousness that he or she eats or lives for achieving freedom and will die, if need be, to attain that goal. Take a pledge, with God and your own conscience as witness, that you will no longer rest till freedom is achieved and will be prepared to lay down your lives in the attempt to achieve it. He who loses his life will gain it; he who

[81] *Ibid.*, p. 205.

will seek to save it shall lose it. Freedom is not for the coward or the fainthearted.[82]

The Indian people must thus "do or die." This formulation, however, is not the Leninist kill-or-be-killed. The British may use arms if they wish, they may kill; but the Satyagrahi must not allow himself to be provoked into violence. Even now, or rather especially now, at what Gandhi viewed to be the most critical hour in the history of the Indian people, Gandhi did not dare to incur the wrath of a vengeful God by an act of violence. Aggression, even in the face of death, had to be disguised and moderated in order to make the voice of conscience speak softly and reassuringly.

Having justified and explained his course of action, Gandhi moved ahead with plans for a largescale *satyagraha* campaign and announced that he would communicate his position to the Viceroy before commencing nonviolent resistance. He never had a chance: he was arrested the next day and imprisoned. The next two years were spent in prison, with little communication allowed with other *satyagrahis,* much less with the Indian public. Britain under fire and under Churchill did not react to Gandhi's activity like the Britain of 1930. Against a foe who viewed things in total victory or total defeat terms, *satyagraha* was, at least in short-run terms, impotent. For, despite Gandhi's hopes, *satyagraha* depended on leadership. Without at least a model the people did not know what to do or did not care to do it. The Indian reaction to Gandhi's arrest was terror and violence, which did not fully subside until 1944.[83] Thus in his expectation of both British and Indian reactions Gandhi was deceived. Instead of death there was imprisonment, instead of *swaraj* and *ahimsa* there was military domination and violence.

On August 15, 1942 Mahadev Desai, Gandhi's longtime companion and secretary, died in prison. Gandhi, immensely saddened by the sudden loss, stated that "Mahadev

[82] *Ibid.*, pp. 199-200.   [83] Fischer, *Life of Gandhi*, p. 386.

has lived up to the 'Do or Die' mantra. . . . This sacrifice cannot but hasten the day of India's deliverance."[84] In February 1943 he undertook a twenty-one day fast in an attempt to gain relief for India from the violence of the British reaction to the "Quit India" movement. He survived the fast but the British remained firm in their policy. For the next year Gandhi was virtually without contact with the outside world and on February 22, 1944 Kasturbai, Gandhi's wife, died. Again Gandhi was very much saddened but as in 1942 when Desai died he conquered his grief and proclaimed that Kasturbai had died "with 'Do or Die' engraved in her heart."[85] In May 1944 Gandhi was released from prison because his health was poor and the Government felt strong enough to allow him to leave and recuperate in a more congenial atmosphere.

In the summer of 1944 Jinnah agreed to discuss communal differences, although Gandhi was not the official head of Congress and thus could not enter into any binding agreement. Gandhi seemingly was impelled to this move by the failure of the "Quit India" movement. The British were still adamant that communal differences would have to be settled before they would leave and hence Gandhi, who had not been able to force them to leave through *satyagraha*, had to turn his attention directly to the problem of Hindu-Moslem enmity. The price he paid in order just to converse with Jinnah was high: he had to recognize at least the possibility of an independent Pakistan. The talks led to nothing, as Jinnah, who realized that he had the advantage as long as Gandhi was impatient for independence and he was not, made his demands more and more stringent in the face of those concessions which Gandhi was prepared to grant.[86] Gandhi tried to deal with Jinnah as he did with most others: he appealed to his reason and sentiment, he was prepared to compromise and was more than willing to grant Jinnah the prestige he desired. But these tactics failed with Jinnah, as they failed with Churchill. *Ahimsa* was an

[84] Quoted in Tendulkar, VI, 224.
[85] *Ibid.*, p. 297.   [86] Fischer, *Life of Gandhi*, p. 404.

effective policy only under three mutually compatible conditions: when one could work on one's foe's conscience, when one's opponent had little to lose by giving in or when giving in would be less costly for him than opposing. Against men like Jinnah and Churchill, who had power of one kind or another, who were willing to use it and had no inclination to be moved by appeal, *ahimsa* was without the desired effect.

With respect to British policy in India the situation changed radically in the summer of 1945: a Labour government had been elected in Britain, embodying those elements in British society which had always been more inclined to Indian independence and which were more susceptible to the moral appeals of Gandhiism. Gandhi was one of the first Indian leaders to sense that the governmental pronouncements indicating that India would soon be free were at last genuine and to turn his attention to reasonable negotiation with the British. This was, in fact, a situation in which he was more comfortable, working for a mutually acceptable basis of agreement with someone who would treat him and his ideals with respect. Were it not for the adamant Jinnah and the Moslem League, in fact, the transition to Indian independence might have taken place without further abrasion. Instead, the two years during which the model of an independent India was constructed were filled with bad feelings and intercommunal violence, and when independence came in the summer of 1947 it was to two nations, India and Pakistan.

Before turning to Gandhi's reaction to the communal unrest during the period just before and after India's independence, it should be noted that Gandhi never became a member of the government of free India. He had, in fact, given up his membership in the Congress Party in 1934 and temporarily retired from public life, which for Gandhi meant pursuing the goals of the so-called "constructive program," a set of activities like handweaving and village sanitation which he conceived to be a necessary corollary to *satyagraha.* Now that independence had come he avoided office and, when not involved with questions of interreligious relations, pressed for fulfillment of the constructive program, which at that point consisted of such things as the removal of untouchability, the production and wearing of *khadi* (homespun cloth), promotion of village industries and sanitation, of a national language, increased status for women, economic equality, and nature cure clinics. While some of these could be worked into a program of governmental administration, many of them, such as *khadi*, were incompatible with the needs of a new state in an increasingly industrialized world. Gandhi, in other words, made no effort to adjust his program or his way of life to the exigencies of the exercise of power. Unlike Lenin, who mastered the politics of power and the administration of the state, and unlike Trotsky, who avoided power but designed workable administrative programs, Gandhi avoided governmental authority altogether.

It was argued in Chapter 4 that the leader is one who can exercise the prerogatives of "fatherhood" with relatively few qualms and convince others of his right to those prerogatives. Gandhi, it was stated, attained a position of parental authority, not by emulating the father but by identifying with his mother to the greatest possible degree. The extent of this feminine identification is suggested by Gandhi's relationship with a grandniece named Manu, who became his ward after Kasturbai's death. He decided that he would be a mother to this nineteen year old girl and he took her with him on his walking tour of Noakhali (in Bengal) in 1946-47 when he went there to try to still communal unrest. He supervised her life in every detail and to test her innocence and his own achievement of *brahmacharya* had her sleep in the same bed with him. At one point during the trip he remarked to her:

> If out of India's millions of daughters, I can train even one into an ideal woman by becoming an ideal mother to you, I shall thereby have rendered a unique service

to womankind. Only by becoming a perfect Brahmachari can one truly serve the woman.[87]

Gandhi thought of himself at least as much in motherly as
in fatherly terms and predominantly acted in accordance
with feminine ideals. Hence he had no desire to exercise
power, which is the function of political fatherhood. His
image of *Hind Swaraj* was of a free India ultimately not
needing a government, not of a new government to replace
the old. Although he was willing to work with a free Indian
regime, he had no need to hold a position of governmental
authority. He had long ago given up, at least for himself,
the ideal of masculine assertiveness in the manner of his
father or the British. Thus he was not inclined toward or
suited for administration, just as his ideas were inadequate
for coping with the problems of a new state.

By 1947, in fact, Gandhi had taken to referring to himself as a "back number."[88] He was plagued by depression
and thought increasingly of death. He at times thought that
he would live 125 years, at others he thought death was
imminent. Increasingly his attention was turned to the violence and strife which characterized Hindu-Moslem relations and he found it unbearable.[89] When by his actions he
was able to reduce the turmoil, his spirits would temporarily
rise, only to sink at the news of fresh outbursts. In part, of
course, his depression is attributable to age—he was, after
all, seventy-eight—but there seems little doubt that intra-
Indian violence came close to overwhelming him. It was
the ultimate reproach, the ultimate failure, the final indication that *ahimsa* was for the weak, not a way of life that
could be shared by the strong. Gandhi's adult life had been
predicated on the assumption that India left to herself
would attain *swaraj*, peace and nonviolence, and that he,
Gandhi, would be the instrument of that achievement. If
India was torn by violence, it could only mean that he had

[87] Pyarelal Nair, *Mahatma Gandhi: The Last Phase* (Ahmedabad,
1956), I, 578. See also Rudolph's treatment of this episode in "Self-
Control and Political Potency," pp. 93-94.
[88] Tendulkar, VIII, 165.　　[89] *Ibid.*, p. 176.

failed, that either *ahimsa* was inadequate for this world or he an inadequate instrument of it. He finally came to admit that up until this time India had merely achieved passive resistance, not true nonviolence, no real love of her enemies or respect among her citizens.[90] As 1947 drew to a close, however, he was able to restore peace to Calcutta, which had been one of the bloodiest cities, by a short fast, and in January 1948 undertook a fast which finally brought peace to Delhi. Again, he was doing or dying for India: there would either be peace or he would starve himself to death.

As a result of his success in Calcutta and Delhi Gandhi's spirits again rose in January 1948. He again talked of living to be 125 years old, but it is impossible to tell whether his optimism would have remained in control, for he was assassinated by a Hindu extremist on January 30, 1948, and died with the name of *Rama*, God, on his lips.

Long before his death Gandhi had insured that his successor as the leader of Congress would be Nehru. In 1934 and again in 1946 he had backed Nehru for the Congress presidency and secured his election. He often referred to him as his successor and viewed him as a son.[91] Although he was not able to pass on to Nehru his highly personal hold on the loyalties of the Indian people, nor to insure that his policies would become part of the program of free India (rather the opposite), he succeeded better than either Lenin or Trotsky in controlling the succession. Several things seem to have facilitated this. First, because he did not relish office himself, Gandhi was able to place the man he favored in office before his death. He was able to oversee the establishment of Nehru in power without losing his own authority and without therefore feeling endangered. Second, Gandhi had always maintained much more intimate relations with other human beings than either Lenin or Trotsky. As a result there were people available who were personally loyal to him and whom he in turn respected and loved. Thus he was not, like Lenin, faced with choosing between two men, neither of whom he found truly compatible

[90] *Ibid.*, p. 224.   [91] Tendulkar, VI, 52.

with what he wanted in a successor. And finally there was a man available who realized Gandhi's ideal of a head of government: Nehru, the most English of Indians, a handsome man who had been able to incorporate much of the English into himself.[92] As long as there must be a government, he supported the man who most nearly approximated his own discarded ideal of authority. And because Nehru was loyal to him and willing to subordinate himself to Gandhi as long as the latter lived, Gandhi could share vicariously the achievement of power without acting in such a way as to build up new feelings of guilt. When Nehru announced to India and the world that Gandhi was dead, that "the light has gone out of our lives,"[93] the relationship was equalized as he partook thereby of at least part of Gandhi's vast moral authority. And with his death, at least for the time being, communal strife diminished from a roar to a whisper.

The Transition to Power

In this chapter we have addressed ourselves to three central questions. First, how does the revolutionist behave during the takeover of power, while exercising power and with respect to passing on power? A summation and generalization of the points that have been made in relation to these questions seem appropriate at this time.

During the phase of actual insurrectionary action the revolutionary leader is well suited to exploit the opportunities inherent in his environment. He has tended to view the world in terms of two camps, one of which contains his enemies. Under the conditions which prevail when governments fall, such a world-view channels activity in strategically efficacious directions: while the Mensheviks in 1917 were, along with several other groups, still searching for a middle ground and an accommodation for sharing power, Lenin and Trotsky were working for Bolshevik control of the state apparatus; under the dangerous conditions

[92] Michael Brecher, *Nehru: A Political Biography* (London, 1959), p. 315.
[93] Quoted in Tendulkar, VIII, 348.

of wartime India in 1942 Gandhi called for a do or die struggle against British imperialism—but not, it should be emphasized, a kill-or-be-killed struggle.

The revolutionary leader is also equipped to deal with the chaotic social and political conditions which are characteristic of the period. At least in our three cases, he is not a man who has been a member of a governmental hierarchy or bureaucracy or who has found it necessary or possible to live a life neatly bounded by established social ties and accepted ways of behaving. He has been from the beginning of his career a person who has had the strength to impose his own order and his own code of rectitude and rightness on his relations with other men. And because he substantially impersonalized these relations he is less likely than most men to be overwrought by the loss of comrades or the pain of bearing the accusations of enemies and former friends. Thus Gandhi, for example, despite his quite advanced age, managed to overcome his grief at the deaths of Kasturbai and Desai and carry on with his work.

At the same time, the leader's freedom from dependence on the directives and guidance of a living superior stands him in good stead in a situation in which many hierarchical relations are breaking down. He does not need the direction of others to enable him to perform his tasks (although Trotsky, who was less of a leader, probably was to a considerable degree reliant upon Lenin's prompting toward action in the summer and fall of 1917) and he is prepared to direct others. His longstanding association with some supernatural authority, his conviction that it has been given to him to know the one correct path, the divinely given moment of action, aid him in giving concrete and emphatic direction to people who are in need of such guidance.

Needless to say, leaders are not uniformly well prepared for the insurrectionary situation; moreover, there is variability with respect to what specific assets and debits they bring to bear on the problem of the seizure of power. Lenin and, to some extent, Gandhi were able to provide an organizational basis for whatever activity they found necessary during the period of struggle and Trotsky did not; each of the former two had been able to envision himself in the role of parental authority and had tried to build up a loyal family of followers. Trotsky, who always wanted to be the favorite son of a father toward whom he had very mixed feelings, and who was not able to convey to other revolutionists the impression of impersonal truth combined with a lack of personal ambition, did not have an organized following until he was brought into the Bolshevik Party.

On the other hand Trotsky had an agitational talent which neither of the other two men had to the same degree. In the tumultuous months of revolutionary conflict his highly developed sense of the dramatic, coming from long years of being "on stage," on display in whatever he did and growing out of his need for attention and respect, served to create a basis of power for him in public opinion and support which not even Gandhi was always able to equal.[94] Each of the other two had organizational talents which were critical during this phase; each might succeed without the support of a Trotsky. But the existence of an orator of Trotsky's caliber augments the resources of any revolutionary movement and produces for the party and the individual a lever to use against opposition as long as the intensity of mass support can be maintained. But as we saw in the case of Trotsky, popular approval is a commodity of limited duration: as time passes the public's role in the governmental process declines[95] and the agitator is left to face his revolutionary peers without his army at his back.

Finally, the revolutionist may be variously disposed toward violent or nonviolent action. In most insurrectionary situations the individual who, like Lenin, is uninhibited about using force will be at an advantage. India in 1942 and Russia in 1917 both provided environments in which superior force and the willingness to use it were the crucial

[94] For Lasswell's analysis of the attributes of the agitator or dramatizer see *Psychopathology and Politics*, pp. 262-63.
[95] Brinton, p. 219.

elements. Hence Gandhi, who was psychologically unable to resort to violent means, was ill-equipped to deal with the English at that time. On the other hand, the individual who is willing to use force may resemble Lenin in another respect as well: he may see so much danger to himself in his immediate environment that he finds it necessary to find some retreat where he will be safe from molestation. This severely limits the kind of contact he can maintain with the public and, as in Lenin's case, even with his own followers. But too trusting a response to the environment can lead to imprisonment, as it did for a while in Trotsky's case and for a more extended period of time in Gandhi's. On balance, an individual who, like Trotsky, feels relatively free to use any means that further his cause, uses secrecy when necessary in response to his situation at any given time and starts from the position that one should operate openly until such time as there is sufficient evidence to indicate that this is too risky, is probably the individual most likely to maximize the possibilities of the revolutionary period. He is the individual who is neither so involved in working out the consequences of Oedipal guilt that he is unable to act aggressively against authority nor so mistrustful of his environment that he constantly feels in danger of being overwhelmed.

If the movement of which the individual is a part, or the leader, succeeds, the individual must in some way adjust to his change in status. He is no longer merely an opponent of an ongoing regime but a member of one; he must, if his regime is to last, come to grips with the problems of administering state power instead of simply opposing the administrative actions of others. He must, in other words, accept the burdens of political fatherhood, especially if he is the leader of the movement but also, to some extent, if he is a follower who is to be given a high governmental post.

As Edward Shils points out in regard to the intellectuals in the new nations, once the goal of the movement is achieved many individuals who have worked for the attainment of power find it difficult to shake the oppositional tenor of their lives.[96] They have built up their personalities in terms of rebellion against the father; once they take up the father's role, they suddenly find themselves guilty of the same acts which for so long provided the aim of their opposition. Trotsky, in particular, suffered in this way; ultimately he found it impossible to accept the father's role and opted for an oppositional position.

The revolutionist may also, again like Trotsky, bring another disability with him into the newly formed arena of politics which is the revolutionary state: he may be unable to deal with peers, convinced that individuals do not count, that battles within the regime will be won on the basis of superiority in argument and the proven worth of one's ideas. Agitators generally will tend to have this configuration of attributes, for they have won approval from their environments and mastered their own internal conflicts in terms of the above kinds of behavior patterns.

All the above problems are minimized (but not eliminated) if the individual has been able to assume and manage the position of ultimate authority to his followers before the takeover of power. His adjustment is simpler than is that of the nonleader, for he essentially has only to extend his paternity to a broader range of people. He may or may not succeed in so doing, depending on the needs of the population which he strives to control, but no basic psychological reorientation is needed to accomplish this. To the extent that the achievement of power fulfills his dream of taking the father's place, however, some added burden of guilt arises. How great this burden is, of course, depends on how much residual guilt was left unmanaged in the original assumption of revolutionary leadership. In Lenin's case, for example, the assumption of the broader paternity

<hr />

[96] Edward A. Shils, "The Intellectuals in the Political Development of the New States" in John H. Kautsky, ed., *Political Change in Underdeveloped Countries* (New York, 1962), p. 219.

seems to have had only marginal effects. His loss of some of his former vibrancy, continually endangered feeling, and relatively frequent threats to resign the leadership if his policy recommendations were not acted upon indicate that there was some strain involved in continuing to play the father's role. But these are relatively minor problems in comparison with those with which a person like Trotsky, who had not made the earlier adjustment to leadership, was confronted.

Gandhi, as was mentioned earlier, had a peculiar disability with respect to exercising governmental leadership: his concept of authority was based on a feminine identification and accordingly he was not impelled to seek an office. Had he done so the inadequacies of his "constructive program" for the direction of Indian affairs would have been even more obvious than they were. Both Lenin and Trotsky, by contrast, were able to think of policy goals compatible with the demands of governing. Neither of the latter were dependent on the notion of the spontaneity of the masses to the degree that Gandhi was.

Even if the individual is a leader and has based his leadership on masculine models, problems of adjustment remain. All revolutionists see as the result of the revolutionary struggle the relatively rapid establishment of a new society devoid of conflict and inequality. The dictatorship of the proletariat as originally conceived was not to be of long duration (although Lenin by 1917, when he was writing *State and Revolution*, already foresaw the necessity of not specifying when this phase would end); *Hind Swaraj* would soon be attained. Thus the revolutionist is bound to be disappointed by the results of his actions, as old problems and conflicts live on and new ones grow up to take the place of those that have died. The revolutionist is thus forced to look for some new locus of conflict, compatible with his ideology, in order to keep intact his hardwon and in many ways delicately integrated personality. Hence the revolution is turned into a "permanent revolution," external enemies and recalcitrant elements in society become the new objects of struggle.[97] The revolutionist believes that when the new battles are won utopia will at last be reached.

The idea of a "permanent revolution" has another advantage as well; it enables the individual to continue thinking and acting in terms of patterns of means and ends which have become habitual and vital. The original impulsion to adopt the particular world-view has been augmented by long practice of its dictates. Should, in fact, the quite genuinely longed for utopia arrive, the revolutionist would be ill-adapted to its demands—just as many revolutionists are not attuned to the exercise of governmental power. They are men who have worked out their lives in terms of the externalization of conflict and, should the external world no longer provide an outlet for the expression of the aggressive drives which underlie their behavior, they would be forced to confront once again the original conflict or continue to rebel against a system which had long been their goal. In either case the strains would be enormous.

Neither the pre-existing ability to be a leader nor the transformation of the anticipated utopia into a permanent revolution suffice to make the adjustment to power easy. The strains of playing the father's role, as mentioned above, and those attendant upon having to postpone the realization of one's goals, are sure to exist. Just as Lenin continued to suffer from fears of defeat, so Trotsky suffered from depression and various nervous maladies and Gandhi was distressed by the violence which accompanied independence; to some extent a diminution of vigor takes place after the revolutionary act has been consummated.

If an individual succeeds in attaining a leadership role and has hopes that his organization, be it a national government or an ephemeral body like the Fourth International, will outlive him, he must at some time face the question of succession—and his own death. Each of the three

[97] Sigmund Neumann was one of the first to indicate the implications of Trotsky's phrase when applied to an ongoing regime in his *Permanent Revolution* (New York, 1942).

men did in fact confront this problem, but only Gandhi was able to handle it successfully. Erik Erikson's analysis of the crisis of maturity or old age indicates some of the relevant variables here. He characterizes the successful management of the problems of old age and the facing of death as "ego integrity," some of the constituents of which are:

> It is the ego's accrued assurance of its proclivity for order and meaning. It is a post-narcissistic love of the human ego—not of the self—as an experience which conveys some world order and spiritual sense, no matter how dearly paid for. It is the acceptance of one's one and only life cycle as something that had to be and that, by necessity, permitted of no substitutions. . . .
>
> The lack or loss of this accrued ego integration is signified by the fear of death: the one and only life cycle is not accepted as the ultimate of life. Despair expresses the feeling that the time is now short, too short for the attempt to start another life and to try out alternative roads to integrity.[98]

Lenin, in a sense, did not live long enough to have to confront the problem as Erikson sets it up. If he did question the worth of his life, it most probably was after the third stroke (assuming that his mental powers were not completely impaired); he certainly felt that time was too short and that much remained undone, but there is no evidence that he questioned the worth of his life or despaired because there was not time to start anew.

Trotsky and Gandhi, on the other hand, did reach more advanced ages, both were exposed to the infirmities and dilemmas of that period. And although both shared with Lenin the concern that there was not enough time left to insure the victory of their cause, neither were overwhelmed by the depression that occasionally marred the final phase of their lives. Rather all three men were convinced that their lives were something "that had to be and . . . per-

[98] Erikson, *Childhood and Society*, pp. 268-69.

mitted no substitutions"; for each the problem was to enable others to follow them after their withdrawal or death.

With respect to succession it seems that in no case is it fully accomplished, but that considerable variability is possible. The pervasive problem is what Max Weber termed the routinization of charisma.[99] Lenin and Gandhi, the two men who evolved to full leadership status, come close to meeting the Weberian criteria for charismatic authority. They were men who claimed, and got accepted by others, a special relationship with a supernatural entity and who did not depend on office for their authority.[100] As such, in order to pass on to their followers the authority which accrued to them on a personal basis they had to try to establish offices which would legitimate those who held them in terms of their own moral code. In the process, of course, the authority becomes no longer charismatic but bureaucratic; unless, however, the charismatic leader lends the weight of his authority to the establishment of such offices a stable bureaucratic structure may not, in fact, develop.

Lenin, who devoted most of his adult life to the development of the party and Gandhi, in his selection of Nehru and his support of the Congress Party, both did much to legitimate the regimes of which they were the effective founders. Lenin, however, was not able to go beyond this and select the one man he would have wanted to follow him. He had, over time, driven many talented men out of the party, so that in 1922 he was left with the unpalatable choice of Trotsky or Stalin. One embodied his policies, the other his political methods. Confronted with the possibility of his own withdrawal from the scene he opted to support Trotsky, who was close to him in Marxist perspective, but he was struck down before he could consummate his ac-

[99] Weber, *The Theory of Social and Economic Organization*, pp. 363-69.

[100] *Ibid.*, pp. 358-62. Weber lists several other attributes of charisma without ever adequately defining it. It is a vague term, which really covers an undeveloped area of Weber's theory, but it does lead one to consider the question of how personal authority is transformed into institutional authority.

tion. Thereafter Lenin's follower in political manipulation easily bested his near-equal in Marxist theorization.

Gandhi, by contrast, was able to select the man whom he felt was exactly right to lead the new government. Although Nehru did not agree with many of his policies, and did not even emulate many of his methods, he had those qualities which Gandhi felt were needed to lead India governmentally toward *swaraj* in the ultimate sense. Because he did not seek an exact replica of himself, fewer strains were involved in this act. Where Lenin had to give up some of his authority, which had already become "routinized," in order even to narrow the field of successors to two major figures, Gandhi could insure Nehru's ascendance without losing any essential part of his own authority.

Trotsky, as was mentioned earlier in this chapter, was never in a position to come to grips with succession as did the other two. He was very concerned in the years before his death to insure that there would be others who would believe as he did. As a result the Fourth International, to the extent that it existed, was exclusively a propagandizing organization. And at no time, moreover, at least not after the death of his son Leon Sedov in 1938, did Trotsky attempt to establish a line of inheritance to the leadership of the organization.

In brief summary, then, the revolutionist tends to be well adapted to the period of revolutionary conflict. There are a variety of strains attendant upon the adjustment to power, but these can be handled relatively well by the individual who was the leader of a movement before attaining power and who has based that leadership on the assumption of a paternal role. Succession is in all cases difficult to arrange, especially with respect to the charismatic aspects of a leader's authority, but is facilitated when the leader can place someone in office without thereby jeopardizing his personal authority.

summary

The basic concern of this study has been to arrange a confrontation between psychoanalytic theory and the lives of three men, hoping thereby both to gain some insight into the personalities of the men themselves and to generate a set of useful psycho-political propositions about revolutionary involvement and leadership. My interest has been quite exclusively in the motivations of the subjects and certain emotional capabilities related to these. As a result I have been forced to forego any systematic analysis of the men's cognitive characteristics and of the more broadscale social psychological and sociological aspects of revolutionary behavior. It has not been my purpose, however, to deny the importance of these other kinds of considerations. As Freud put it, "in general it doesn't often happen that psycho-analysis contests anything which is maintained in other quarters; as a rule, psycho-analysis only adds something new to what has been said. . . ."[1] In other words, my goal has been to broaden, not narrow, revolution as a field of social science inquiry. Hopefully, I have not created a procrustean bed of psychological reductionism, in which there is no room for analysis of other aspects of the revolutionary process. At the same time it seems desirable that others, in theorizing about the problems of revolutionary participation and leadership, should leave room for the kinds of issues which have been raised here.

In conclusion, then, let us briefly review the major analytic points of the study. We began by asking the question

[1] Freud, *A General Introduction to Psycho-analysis*, p. 42.

of why a man becomes a revolutionist. In attempting to answer it, we examined the existing materials on our three men covering the period from earliest childhood through young manhood, by which time all three had embarked upon revolutionary activity as a vocation. Using Erikson's formulation of the stages of psycho-sexual development as a guide, the following picture emerged. For the oral phase, when trust and mistrust are at issue, there is no consistent pattern for revolutionists. Lenin apparently was very mistrustful from an early age, Trotsky and Gandhi seemed to have had considerable faith in the underlying benevolence of their environments. Thus in later life Lenin was difficult to betray, but also pessimistic—so that, for example, in the summer of 1917 he beat a rather too hasty retreat in the face of relatively negligible force. Trotsky, on the other hand, was constantly surprised by antagonistic responses from others—he did not expect to be punished for school pranks or struck down by his "enemies" for his revolutionary activity. Nor was he able to see the world in the kill-or-be-killed terms which was a necessary component of one's political orientation in post-Lenin Russia. During those times when boldness and daring yielded returns, however, such as during the Revolution itself and the Civil War, his optimism allowed him to act in ways that added greatly to his prestige and power. The contrast between Lenin and Trotsky is clearly seen in their attitudes toward the Germans at Brest-Litovsk; Trotsky felt the Germans would not attack even if a peace treaty were not signed and that if they did the results would not be disastrous. Lenin was convinced that the Germans *would* attack and that the very life of the Revolution was being endangered.

Gandhi, with a personality combining basic trust with great needs to suffer punishment, resembled Trotsky in his response to his circumstances. He expected others to react to his nonviolent provocations with restraint, although toward the end of his life expectations about the imminence of death developed. Thus in 1930 he was able to lead the Salt March, fully expecting that the British would allow him to carry on as if he were their friend; and in 1930 he was largely right. In 1942, however, when he adopted the same approach, based on the same confidence in his foes, the result was immediate arrest and failure.

For the anal phase, as for the oral, considerable variability exists for revolutionists. Lenin developed a firm sense of autonomy and of his own worth, so that in adult life he seldom found it necessary to react, to insult or to insist on personal prerogatives. Trotsky and Gandhi, by contrast, both had severe problems with shame, which they mastered in contrasting ways. During his school days Trotsky was able to develop a talent, namely an ability to manipulate the tools of intellect, which he used as a lever against those who had formerly humiliated him (such as his father and the peasants on the estate at Yanovka). It was a lever he continued to use throughout his life. With it he demonstrated to others their manifest inferiority and with it he was able to assert his right to center stage during the climax of the revolutionary drama. But it also contributed to the creation of the antipathies and jealousies which help to account for his isolation from 1905 through 1917 and his downfall after Lenin's death.

Gandhi also was plagued by great feelings of shame, but he did not find in his school work or anywhere else in his early life sufficient support for his shaky feelings of self-respect. It was not until his arrival in South Africa that he found that, in this new context, his gifts and training provided him with the kind of esteem Trotsky had been able to win as a schoolboy. By that time Gandhi had already developed too strong a feeling of lowliness to transform himself into a man of selfless confidence like Lenin or powerful arrogance like Trotsky. Instead he viewed himself as the most humble of the humble and took upon his shoulders the abuse directed against all Indians in South Africa. He escaped from his personal shame by asserting the autonomy and dignity of the lowly.

The genital phase we treated together with adolescence, for in all men, but in the present cases especially, the prob-

lems of the latter phase are the problems of the former—
with complications. The intervening period is latency, in
which feelings of inferiority must be warded off so that industriousness can emerge. All three men had substantial
success during this period, and hence we suppose that the
capacity for sublimation which is the hallmark of competent management of the Oedipal conflict is also a pre-
requisite of the successful revolutionist.[2] The sustained capacity for work which all three developed was to be of
great value to them later on. Lenin's ability to give almost
pedantic attention to the most minute details of organization, communication, and policy helped him to maintain
his control of the Bolshevik Party both before and after the
seizure of power; and Trotsky's sustained intellectual cre-
ativity in adulthood, which won him Lenin's respect and
thus in part accounts for his position as co-leader of the
party before Lenin's death, was largely a continuation of
the behavior patterns of the brilliant schoolboy. Gandhi,
who performed dutifully but not excitingly during latency,
never relished intellectual achievement as the other two
did. Where Lenin and Trotsky found a basis for superiority
in this kind of activity, Gandhi found his in other areas. In
the Indian context, however, intellectual prominence was
not as essential an attribute of leadership as it was in the
Russian, especially, in the latter case, as it was during the
period of the exile to western Europe before 1917. Among
the Russians one had to be an accomplished Marxist to gain
the respect of others, in the Indian case there was no such
universally agreed upon canon of intellectual legitimacy.

Turning then to adolescence, we found the following situation to be common to all three men. Each had an un-

[2] As has been stressed earlier, and as is emphasized below, the
ability to manage the problems of guilt which result from the Oedipal
phase does not connote that the problems were minimal. Far from it.
For all three men the conflict was unusually intense and was much
aggravated by the events of adolescence; but all three found the resources, both within themselves and in their environments, to master
it. And in that mastery lay the origins both of their commitment
to revolutionary activity and, especially in the cases of Lenin and
Gandhi, of their ability to assume leadership roles.

usually ambivalent relationship with his father. In Lenin's case there was a sturdy identification with his father, combined with a residue of strained feelings resulting from his father's frequent and prolonged absences combined with his loving attention when he was with the family. Trotsky admired his father greatly and considered him to be a superior to his mother in many ways, but resented his monopolization of his mother's time and affection and was irked by his inability to emulate his father successfully in the performance of those tasks which gained respect from others at Yanovka. Moreover he had been separated from the family during latency, when he went to Odessa to school, and thus the talents which he did develop were not immediately relevant to his familial competition: his ability to write a brilliant theme did not help him to cut wheat. At the same time this separation meant that he carried with him a more infantile view of his father than did Lenin or Gandhi—and hence one more awe-inspiring and difficult to combat.

Gandhi, whose masculine self-assurance was tenuous in any case, found his emotional life enormously complicated by his early marriage. He was forced to act like a man in the most basic way when he was still unsure of what it meant—or required—to be a man. He was haunted by fears and struggling to solidify his masculinity through, for example, the eating of meat as well as through the assertion of his prerogatives vis-à-vis his wife. All three men were thus forced to come to grips with the problem of forming a masculine identity under tense and difficult circumstances.

Although perhaps without quite the same intensity, this kind of ambivalence is far from uncommon during adolescence. For it to be transformed into revolutionary energy it must be accentuated rather than diminished as adolescence progresses. In Lenin's case the successive deaths of his father and his brother, the latter indirectly at the hands of the Tsar, created a great burden of guilt—and at the same time a way out from under that load. The death of Gandhi's father at the very moment when Gandhi was in bed with his wife also radically intensified feelings of guilt and precipitated a flight from India and his family. In Trotsky the trauma was neither as great nor as clear-cut. Rather there was an increasing alienation from his father and his father's way of life which resulted in a rather sharp break with the family when he had finished high school. But in all three cases contact with the father was cut off when the emotional involvement with him was still extremely high, so that the feelings of guilt that accompany the adolescent break with paternal authority, and which in the present cases were already so strong, were kept alive and problematical.

Because late adolescence and young manhood is not only the period of separation from the family but also the time when the individual must turn his attention to creating an occupation for himself, the psycho-sexual conflicts of adolescence are an important part of the context of vocational choice.[3] Thus when the nature of the youth's relation to paternal authority is very much at issue, it is extremely likely that the individual will be responsive to occupations, of which revolutionary activity is one, which allow him to work through his conflicts and hopefully resolve them. This was in fact what happened here, and thus we hypothesized that the revolutionist is one who escapes from the burdens of Oedipal guilt and ambivalence by carrying his conflict with authority into the political realm. For this to happen two conditions must exist: the conflict with paternal authority must be alive and unresolvable in the family context as adolescence draws to a close, and there must exist a political context in terms of which the conflict can be expressed. The former condition was met in the cases of Lenin and Gandhi by the death of the father, which made it impossible to outgrow him and difficult to learn to live with the memories of him. Surrogate fathers had to be found in terms of which the issue could be resolved if neurotic involvements were to be avoided. For Trotsky the break was not as sharp—hence he had a lingering desire to

[3] Erikson, *Young Man Luther*, pp. 17-18.

be the favorite son until after the deaths of his father and Lenin in the 1920s.

The second condition, the existence of an appropriate precipitant, was also met in all three cases. The death of his brother as the result of a revolutionary action provided both a partial model for political action and the enemy against whom Lenin was to fight. In Gandhi's case the insult from the British political agent in Kathiawad and the subsequent experiences during his confrontation with himself at the Maritzburg station were the occasions for what was to become his revolutionary response (although it was to take many more years before he was ready to call for a change in the nature of government and social structure). For Trotsky his arrest and the strains of imprisonment as the result of his relatively playful "revolutionary" activity with the Southern Russian Workers' Union changed him from a rather aimless adolescent to a confirmed enemy of tsarism.

In this way, then, a man becomes a revolutionist; but until he has defined his relations with other men much more specifically he is not ready to be an effective advocate of his cause—in fact, at this juncture, he is still uncertain of the nature of his cause. But the event which activates the revolutionary potential of the individual, along with his previous experiences which resulted in that potential, provide the material out of which the revolutionary personality is built. The basic attribute of this personality is that it is based on opposition to governmental authority; this is the result of the individual's continuing need to express his aggressive impulses vis-à-vis his father and the repressive action of governmental officials. The latter permits the individual to externalize his feelings of hatred—previously he had been tormenting himself because his feelings of antipathy toward his father were balanced by feelings of love, respect, and the desire to emulate him. Now the situation is much less ambivalent; governmental authority is clearly malevolent, unlike one's father who served as the basis for one's standards of morality, and hence can be fought with a clear conscience. And because, at least in the three cases studied, the aggressive governmental action came as a consequence of individual actions which were representative, rather than personal, the individual finds a cause to defend. Sasha, with whom Lenin identified, had been fighting for the Russian people, Trotsky had been defending the rights and dignity of the working class, and Gandhi was insisting that Indians be treated as men. Thus far the cause is crudely conceived and unelaborated; with time an ideological superstructure is based upon it so that the individual can fulfill his needs for self-justification.

In this manner the revolutionist dichotomizes his world, and with it the emotional complex of his ambivalent feelings toward his father. As a consequence his feelings of guilt are substantially reduced, so that in all three cases we saw the men turning from introspection and inaction to vigorous pursuance of their revolutionary vocations. Lenin read his brother's books and sought out exiled populist terrorists in order to learn from them of his brother's cause and the techniques of revolutionary struggle; Trotsky composed revolutionary songs in prison and undertook a Marxist study of freemasonry; and Gandhi set about organizing the Indian community in South Africa. In addition each man turned his attention to creating or subscribing to some system of justification which would complement the aggressive aspect of his personality, each sought a benevolent father, concretely and abstractly, to set up in opposition to the evil father that was tsarism or the British raj. This is necessary for the revolutionist for two reasons. First, it satisfies his need to feel that he is not betraying his father's moral standards, which formed the basis of his superego and which therefore can be flaunted only with great strain. Second, in this manner he can assure himself that he is fighting under the aegis of a strong, protective, and righteous paternal authority who guarantees victory over his powerful foes. Thus Lenin could not simply subscribe to his brother's Narodism, for that was only the creed of a rebellious son and had not safeguarded Sasha, and

therefore could not safeguard him, from the blows of aveng-
ing tsarism. Hence he evolved into a Marxist, finding in its
doctrine of the inevitable victory of the working class and
in the confident and assertive personality of Plekhanov both
justification and protection. The identification with his
brother was very strong, however, and hence Lenin's Marxism was really a blend of Russian voluntaristic populism
and scientific socialism.

Trotsky, of course, was also a Marxist, although he
fought against it for several months before he discovered
that it satisfied his need for a total explanatory and justificatory system better than his amorphous and not very
deeply held populism. Later in London he was to find in
the editorial board of *Iskra* that concrete embodiment of
Marxism that Lenin at first found in Plekhanov. In contrast to the two Russians, Gandhi had no intellectual re-
source like Marxism available to him, but he gradually
evolved the idea of *Hind Swaraj*, which contained or implied some of the core attributes of revolutionary Marxism.
Although it differed from Marxism in many ways, it shared
with it a dichotomized view of the world (between spir-
ituality and materialism, truth and *maya*), a justification
of the rebellion of the lowly and an image of a utopian
society which was to result from the revolutionary struggle.
In sum, all three men met their personal crises by adopt-
ing a revolutionary political stance and an ideological justification for their actions.

The next question the inquiry was directed to was why a
revolutionist does or does not become a leader. The answer
was formulated in terms of the individual's attitudes toward
his fellow revolutionists (superiors, peers, and inferiors)
and toward governmental authority. For each of these I
attempted to analyze both the individual's relations with
these other actors and his rationalized view of these relationships.

We found that Lenin and Gandhi, who maintained
greater control over their followers—and who had more
followers—found it possible to do away with a leader medi-

ating between them and their gods, while Trotsky, who was not as successful as a leader, did not. Lenin broke with Plekhanov as soon as he had any extensive contact with him and Gandhi, while acknowledging Gokhale as his political guru, never accepted the authority of another man as binding. Both men claimed to be in direct contact with their respective truths and each claimed that at any given juncture the alternative that he chose was the only correct one. Each found subservience to others unbearable. As long as there was a living man to whom they owed the respect and obedience they formerly owed their fathers, the strains of the earlier relationships would be perpetuated; because the constant tendency of these men was to act in such a way as to reduce psychic strain, followership was exceedingly difficult for them. Trotsky, whose father's death had not been involved in his choice of revolution as a career, and who consequently was not bearing as large a burden of guilt as were the other two, found it less difficult, although not easy, to work under others. He eventually came to accept Lenin's authority and to see in him the father to whom he could be the favorite son.

The inability to be a follower, of course, does not account for the ability to be a leader. For this something more is needed, namely a firm identification with parental authority, an underlying feeling of connection with the moral standards and behavior of one parent or the other. Thus Lenin, who identified with his father as he did with Sasha (that is, as a result of childhood emulation of him and in order to ward off the feelings of loss and guilt at his death), was able to play the political father's role naturally and effectively. Gandhi, through his incorporation of many of his mother's characteristics, was also able to make decisions without recourse to any higher earthly authority. But Trotsky found much less that was useful in the model his father provided. Moreover, he was separated from his father, except for summer vacations, from the age of eight on and thus had less of an opportunity to emulate him. Hence

Trotsky was not able to envisage himself in the role of *the* leader until very late in his life.

Just as the leader casts off all superiors, so he eliminates all peers. Lenin began as one of three "brothers," Potresov and Martov being the other two, but soon found that his brothers were ineffective or "soft." Gandhi worked with others without insisting on that clear demarcation of relations which was a hallmark of Leninism, but his self-proclaimed status of the most humble of men—but one to whom God spoke—insured him against serious rivalry. Trotsky found it difficult to work with peers (his conflicts with party members during the Civil War is just one example), but he was never able to achieve a position of uniqueness which would save him from having to deal with men who considered themselves his equal and whom he viewed as brothers. Thus while Lenin and Gandhi lived in an emotional world populated only by followers and enemies, Trotsky had to live with superiors and peers as well. The lower intensity of his original familial conflicts enabled him to live a more normal life, to allow his relations with others to be somewhat more jumbled—and hence it prevented him from ascending to the top rung of leadership. For, as Erikson says, the psychological requisites of leadership include the mastery of great personal conflict:

> Still others, although suffering and deviating danger-ously through what appears to be a prolonged adoles-cence, eventually come to contribute an original bit to an emerging style of life; the very danger which they have sensed has forced them to mobilize capacities to see and say, to dream and plan, to design and con-struct, in new ways.[4]

Although the leader eliminates superiors and peers in terms of personal relations, he maintains both in abstract form. Lenin does not follow Plekhanov, therefore he follows Marx all the more fervently; Gandhi has no guru but follows absolutely the dictates of his inner voice. At the

[4] *Ibid.*, pp. 14-15.

same time, the idea of a political brotherhood and of the brotherhood of man (or the working class) is exalted while, for example, Lenin willingly split the party and Gandhi withdrew from political life to the confines of his *ashram*.

The leader needs and is able to bear the responsibility of having followers. At a minimum he will accept those who acknowledge his leadership, who come to him as children needing protection and guidance. In his followers the leader sees the child he once was; and he can therefore relieve somewhat his residual burden of guilt about his feelings toward his father by showing the latter (that is, the remnants of his father preserved in his superego) that, not only has he become like him, but he has become an even better father in the process. He tries to take care of his children, his followers, better than he feels his father took care of him.[5] As a result, he expects them to be grateful and, what is more, because he sees himself in them he expects betrayal from them—just as he feels he has betrayed his father. Thus Lenin was always suspicious of the intentions of his followers and Gandhi took any failure of his followers to be his own. The fasts by which he punished himself for the weaknesses of his fellow Indians reflect both this projection and identification and the degree to which he took any falling away from the truth as an act against him.

Normally the effective leader will have to organize his following. Lenin, who lived in a world which he perceived in kill-or-be-killed terms, constructed an organization that would protect him from his enemies and enable him to strike at them with impunity. But he did not trust even those who were the members of his vanguard, hence he tried to build an organization of rules rather than men. The rules would control the behavior of others and he would control the rules. Gandhi revitalized the Congress Party in India and gave it new direction and form, but he was less apprehensive of his environment than Lenin and therefore

[5] There is also, it might be mentioned, an important maternal theme here, but one which I have not had opportunity to explore systematically in this study. Gandhi, of course, reflects this theme most clearly.

did not go to the lengths the latter did in building up a tightly centralized organization. Trotsky never assumed the leadership of a substantial bloc of followers, but he was similar to Gandhi in placing rather great faith in his environment and thus in 1903 he opted for spontaneity and loyalty to his friends when Lenin tried to make centralized and efficient command a governing principle of the Russian Social Democratic Party. All three of the men, it might be noted, had extraordinary organizational abilities, but only Lenin elevated organization to a central position in his doctrine and practice.

The revolutionist's relationship with governmental authority has already been specified. The leader, who feels the challenge of that authority more powerfully than others,[6] goes beyond simple opposition to the creation of doctrine and practice of opposition, a conception of revolutionary means. This doctrine is certain to involve the leader's followers, who are its instruments. Thus the root conception of Leninism is *kto-kovo*—who will kill whom. The organization has been built up to fight tsarism in a life-or-death struggle in which he who is more powerful and better armed will win. The lesson Lenin learned from Sasha's death was transformed into the main operative principle of bolshevism.

Trotsky, who in 1905 and again in 1917 temporarily emerged as the leader of the masses, also evolved a doctrine of means. His concept of permanent revolution served to focus all attention on the current struggle as the final engagement out of which the Socialist utopia would emerge. For Trotsky its underlying meaning was twofold. On the one hand it focused attention on the insurrectionary period itself, the period when Trotsky could dramatically display himself to the world. On the other, it promised a cessation of struggle and release from the psychic strains under which

---

[6] The leader feels the might of authority more than his followers because he has set himself up in opposition to it and has no superior to rely on—for the follower the conflict is between the brotherhood and the evil father; for the leader it is a war of father against father.

he was laboring. It was hence exceedingly useful during the period of struggle, but left him unprepared for the far from utopian world which followed the defeat of the White armies.

Both Trotsky and Lenin were thus men of violent means. Gandhi, by contrast, was a nonviolent revolutionist. His doctrine of *satyagraha*, of truth-force, or passive resistance, was based on the principle of conversion, not domination. Because of the manner of his father's death, Gandhi felt that any aggressive impulse was enormously dangerous, both to himself and to others. As a result he was constrained to act without violence, but action was necessary if he were not to be defeated by the challenge of achieving independent maturity. (The long period during which Gandhi only very gradually came to find a suitable role for himself indicates the intensity of the struggle and the proximity of failure.) Gandhi's solution to his difficulty was to identify himself increasingly with his mother and her ways of "resisting." Fasting, suffering, dietary regulation, spinning, and the lack of manifest sexual desire were all components of *satyagraha*, and all attributes of his mother's behavior in particular or Gandhi's idealized view of women in general. Thus in 1906 Gandhi vowed to refrain from sexual intercourse—and shortly thereafter evolved the idea of *satyagraha*, his unique contribution to the waging of revolutionary war. *Satyagraha* was simply womanly resistance applied to politics on a mass scale, but, as Susanne Rudolph puts it, it provided not only Gandhi but also India with a "new courage."

As was the case with the genesis and characteristics of the revolutionary personality, the psychological attributes of the leader have been examined in more detail earlier.[7] We can therefore turn to the questions related to the transition to power, treating these rather briefly as they were the last topic discussed in the main body of the study.

We analyzed the transition to power in terms of three questions. The first had to do with the adequacy of the

[7] Cf. Chapter 4.

revolutionist's preparation for the period of insurrectionary activity itself. Here, as one would expect, we concluded that the revolutionist is in fact well prepared for this occasion. His simplified model of the world as two warring armies allows him to strike against his foes without the hesitation that beset nonrevolutionists. There is, however, considerable variability in terms of efficacy among revolutionists. We saw that Trotsky was maximally prepared for this period. His agitational skills brought him to the fore in the revolutionary hotbed that was St. Petersburg and his cautious daring was perfectly suited to dealing with the weak but not quite impotent Provisional Government. Lenin, on the other hand, provided the organization vital to his and Trotsky's success, but his fears of annihilation after the July Days forced him into hiding and minimized his effectiveness until after the takeover of power. Gandhi, whose revolutionary tactics were based on keeping faith with the opposition, and vice versa, was, as mentioned earlier, effective as leader of the Salt March in 1930 but impotent when he tried to organize the "Quit India" movement in 1942. Led by Churchill and laboring under the exigencies of war, Britain was actually more repressive than the Provisional Government in Russia.

As to the adjustment to power itself, we found that Lenin, who was the only one of the three to base his leadership upon full assumption of the father's role, adjusted best; Trotsky, who was not able to face up to assuming that position, never achieved full control of the state and was unable to take advantage of several chances to do so; and Gandhi, whose authority was based on his identification with his mother, wisely refrained from attempting to exercise power. The latter found, however, that he and his ideals seemed somehow out of tune with free India. Thus we concluded that the person who achieves leadership on a masculine basis before taking power is most likely to be able to wield it effectively after power has been attained.

We also found that all three men had the adjustment

made easier for them in some ways and harder in others by the fact that revolution did not bring either socialism or the *Hind Swaraj* of Gandhi's conception. It made things easier for them because it enabled them to continue to act, to continue to work through the conflicts which precipitated them into revolutionary activity. Although the utopian goal is fervently wished for, these are men who are too acclimated to struggle to live in such a world, even if it were to arrive. Hence "permanent revolution," the means of struggle, come to substitute for the ends. On the other hand, each man felt that to some extent the revolution was a mockery of itself: men had struggled and died and there was still no peace. As a result each of the men showed signs of stress and hints of despair as they contemplated their life's work.

Finally we touched on the question of succession. Here we found that Lenin was able to create, to a degree, a party in his own image but was unable to control the choice of a successor. Lenin had constructed an organization which made it virtually impossible that a man with his combination of theoretical and practical aptitudes would be available when he weakened. Thus he had to choose between the ideologically correct Trotsky and the politically clever Stalin, and when he finally faced the issue and opted for Trotsky it was already too late. Trotsky, of course, never really had to face the issue; he had no power to pass on, except in the nascent (and stillborn) Fourth International; and while he was very concerned with who would keep his ideas alive after his death, he was not able to think of ways to create an organizational succession. Finally Gandhi, who unlike Lenin did not savor power and who unlike Trotsky was seldom in a quandary about it, did in fact manage to control succession—in a restricted sense. He was partially responsible for Nehru's ascendancy in the Congress Party and insured his election to the presidency of the party in 1946. But Gandhi was able to do this only because he gave away no essential part of his own authority in yielding governmental control to his beloved Nehru.

Political men and political processes, like revolution, are complicated things; and it is not presumed that the ideas developed in this study provide definitive solutions to any of the problems we have raised. Indeed, until these ideas about the revolutionary personality and revolutionary leadership are subjected to rigorous testing, I am not entitled to treat them as anything more than tentative hypotheses, rough approximations growing out of the application of psychoanalytic theory to a restricted number of cases. Even if, in fact, the ideas stand up under the burdens of future testing and refinement, we will still have achieved but a partial understanding of the men who make revolutions and the revolutions they make. For there is more to understanding men than can currently be gleaned from psychological knowledge; and there are other useful perspectives on revolution than the psychological. Yet it is psychological analysis, in any deep and systematic way, which is most often lacking in the study of politics. Here I have sought to restore somewhat the balance, to reaffirm the need to understand human nature in its most concrete and individual manifestations.

BIBLIOGRAPHY

PRIMARY SOURCES

Chekhov, Anton. *The Horse Stealers and Other Stories*, trans. Constance Garnett. New York, 1921.

Chernyshevskii, N. G. *What Is To Be Done?* trans. Benjamin R. Tucker. New York, 1909.

Gandhi, Mohandas K. *An Autobiography: The Story of My Experiments with Truth*, trans. Mahadev Desai. Boston, 1957.

——. *The Collected Works of Mahatma Gandhi*. Vols. I-IX. The Publications Division, Ministry of Information and Broadcasting, Government of India, 1958-63.

——. *Communal Unity*. Ahmedabad, 1949.

——. *Delhi Diary*. Ahmedabad, 1948.

——. *Gandhiji's Correspondence with the Government, 1942-44*. Ahmedabad, 1945.

——. *Gandhiji's Correspondence with the Government, 1944-47*. Ahmedabad, 1959.

——. *Hind Swaraj*. Ahmedabad, 1938.

——. *The India of My Dreams*, ed. R. K. Prabhu. Bombay, 1947.

——. *My Appeal to the British*, ed. A. T. Hingorani. New York, 1942.

——. *"My Dear Child,"* ed. Alice M. Barnes. Ahmedabad, 1959.

——. *Non-Violence in Peace and War*, ed. Mahadev Desai. Ahmedabad, 1942.

——. *Satyagraha in South Africa*. Madras, 1928.

——. *Truth is God*, ed. R. K. Prabhu. Ahmedabad, 1955.

——. *The Way to Communal Harmony*, ed. U. R. Rao. Ahmedabad, 1963.

——. *Young India, 1924-26*. New York, 1927.

Gandhi, Prabhudas. *My Childhood with Gandhi*. Ahmedabad, 1949.

Krupskaya, Nadezhda K. *Memories of Lenin*. 2 vols. New York, 1930.

Lenin, V. I. *Collected Works*. Vols. 20 and 21. New York, 1929-32.

——. *Collected Works*. Moscow, 1960——.

——. *The Essentials of Lenin*. 2 vols. London, 1947.

——. *Imperialism: The Highest Stage of Capitalism*. New York, 1939.

——. *The Letters of Lenin*, ed. Elizabeth Hill and Doris Mudie. London, 1937.

——. *Selected Works*. Moscow, 1960.

————. *State and Revolution*. New York, 1943.

————. *What Is To Be Done?* New York, 1943.

————. *What the "Friends of the People" are and How They Fight The Social Democrats*, in his *Collected Works* (1960), Vol. I.

Nehru, Jawaharlal. *The Discovery of India*. New York, 1946.

————. *Nehru on Gandhi*. New York, 1948.

————. *Toward Freedom*. Boston, 1958.

Recollections of Lenin. Moscow, 1956.

Reminiscences of Lenin by His Relatives. Moscow, 1956.

Sukhanov, N. N. *The Russian Revolution 1917*, ed. and trans. Joel Carmichael. 2 vols. New York, 1962.

Trotsky, Leon. *Diary in Exile 1935*, trans. Elena Zarudnaya. New York, 1963.

————. *The History of the Russian Revolution*, trans. Max Eastman. 3 vols. New York, 1932.

————. *Lenin. New York*, 1962.

————. *Literature and Revolution*. Ann Arbor, Mich., 1960.

————. *My Life*. New York, 1930.

————. *The New Course*. New York, 1943.

————. *Our Revolution*, trans. and ed. Moissaye J. Olgin. New York, 1918.

————. *Permanent Revolution*. Calcutta, 1947.

————. *Problems of the Chinese Revolution*. New York, 1932.

————. *Problems of Life*. London, 1924.

————. *The Real Situation in Russia*. New York, 1928.

————. *The Revolution Betrayed*. Garden City, N.Y., 1937.

————. *Stalin*, ed. and trans. Charles Malamuth. New York, 1941.

————. *Stalin's Frame-up System and the Moscow Trials*. New York, 1950.

————. *The Stalin School of Falsification*. New York, 1937.

————. *Terrorism and Communism*. Ann Arbor, Mich., 1961.

————. *Their Morals and Ours*. New York, 1942.

————. *Whither Russia?* New York, 1926.

SECONDARY SOURCES—BOOKS

Abraham, Karl. *Selected Papers*, ed. Ernest Jones. London, 1942.

Adorno, T. W. *et al. The Authoritarian Personality*. New York, 1950.

Almond, Gabriel A. and Sidney Verba. *The Civic Culture*. Princeton, 1963.

Arendt, Hannah. *On Revolution*. New York, 1963.

————. *The Origins of Totalitarianism*. New York, 1958.

Bass, Bernard M. *Leadership, Psychology and Organizational Behavior*. New York, 1963.

Bondurant, Joan V. *Conquest of Violence.* Princeton, 1958.

Brecher, Michael. *Nehru: A Political Biography.* London, 1959.

Brinton, Crane. *The Anatomy of Revolution.* New York, 1952.

Brodie, Fawn M. *Thaddeus Stevens.* New York, 1959.

Brown, Norman O. *Life Against Death.* New York, 1959.

Bychowski, Gustav. *Dictators and Disciples.* New York, 1948.

Cantril, Hadley. *The Psychology of Social Movements.* New York, 1941.

Carr, Edward Hallett. *The Bolshevik Revolution, 1917-23.* 3 vols. New York, 1951-53.

――――. *Studies in Revolution.* London, 1950.

Chamberlin, William H. *The Russian Revolution, 1917-21.* 2 vols. New York, 1960.

Christie, Richard and Marie Jahoda, eds. *Studies in the Scope and Method of "The Authoritarian Personality."* Glencoe, 1954.

Dan, Theodore. *The Origins of Bolshevism,* ed. and trans. Joel Carmichael. New York, 1964.

Daniels, Robert V. *The Conscience of the Revolution.* Cambridge, 1960.

Deutscher, Isaac. *The Prophet Armed.* London, 1954.

――――. *The Prophet Unarmed.* London, 1959.

――――. *The Prophet Outcast.* London, 1963.

Dhawan, Gopinath. *The Political Philosophy of Mahatma Gandhi.* Ahmedabad, 1957.

Eastman, Max. *Leon Trotsky: The Portrait of a Youth.* New York, 1925.

――――. *Since Lenin Died.* London, 1925.

Eckstein, Harry, ed. *Internal War: Problems and Approaches.* New York, 1964.

Edwards, Lyford P. *The Natural History of Revolution.* Chicago, 1927.

Eissler, K. R. *Goethe: A Psychoanalytic Study.* 2 vols. Detroit, 1963.

Erikson, Erik H. *Childhood and Society.* New York, 1963.

――――. *Identity and the Life Cycle.* New York, 1959.

――――. *Insight and Responsibility.* New York, 1964.

――――. *Young Man Luther.* New York, 1958.

Fenichel, Otto. *The Psychoanalytic Theory of Neurosis.* New York, 1945.

Fischer, Louis. *The Life of Lenin.* New York, 1964.

――――. *The Life of Mahatma Gandhi.* New York, 1962.

Freud, Anna. *The Ego and the Mechanisms of Defense.* New York, 1946.

――――. *Normality and Pathology in Childhood.* New York, 1965.

Freud, Sigmund. *The Basic Writings of Sigmund Freud*, ed. and trans. A. A. Brill. New York, 1938.

———. *Civilization and its Discontents*, edited and trans. James Strachey. New York, 1961.

———. *The Ego and the Id*. New York, 1960.

———. *A General Introduction to Psychoanalysis*. New York, 1938.

———. *Group Psychology and the Analysis of the Ego*, trans. James Strachey. London, 1948.

———. *The Interpretation of Dreams*, in *The Basic Writings of Sigmund Freud*, ed. A. A. Brill.

———. *Leonardo da Vinci*, trans. A. A. Brill. New York, 1947.

———. *Moses and Monotheism*. New York, 1939.

———. *New Introductory Lectures on Psychoanalysis*. New York, 1965.

———. *The Problem of Anxiety*, trans. Henry A. Bunker. New York, 1963.

———. *Three Contributions to the Theory of Sex*, in *The Basic Writings of Sigmund Freud*, ed. A. A. Brill.

———. *Totem and Taboo*, trans. A. A. Brill. New York, 1946.

Fromm, Erich. *Escape From Freedom*. New York, 1941.

George, Alexander L. and Juliette L. George. *Woodrow Wilson and Colonel House*. New York, 1956.

Gilbert, Gustav Mark. *The Psychology of Dictatorship*. New York, 1950.

Gottfried, Alex. *Boss Cermak of Chicago*. Seattle, 1962.

Haimson, Leopold. *The Russian Marxists and the Origins of Bolshevism*. Cambridge, Mass., 1955.

Hartmann, Heinz. *Ego Psychology and the Problem of Adaptation*. New York, 1958.

Hilgard, Ernest R. *et al. Psychoanalysis as Science*. Stanford, 1952.

Hitschmann, Edward. *Great Men*. New York, 1956.

Hoffer, Eric. *The True Believer*. New York, 1958.

Hook, Sidney. *The Hero in History*. New York, 1943.

Hook, Sidney, ed. *Psychoanalysis, Scientific Method and Philosophy*. New York, New York University Press, 1959.

Hyman, Herbert. *Political Socialization*. Glencoe, Ill., 1959.

Kautsky, John H., ed. *Political Change in Underdeveloped Countries*. New York, 1962.

Kornhauser, William. *The Politics of Mass Society*. New York, 1959.

Lane, Robert E. *Political Life*. Glencoe, Ill., 1959.

Lasswell, Harold D. *Politics: Who Gets What, When, How*. New York, 1958.

———. *Power and Personality*. New York, 1962.

————. *Psychopathology and Politics*. New York, 1960.

Leites, Nathan. *A Study of Bolshevism*. Glencoe, Ill., 1953.

Lipset, Seymour Martin. *Political Man*. Garden City, N.Y., 1963.

Machiavelli, Niccolo. *The Prince and the Discourses*. New York, 1940.

Mannheim, Karl. *Ideology and Utopia*. New York, 1936.

Marcu, Valeriu. *Lenin*, trans. E. W. Dickes. London, 1928.

Marcuse, Herbert. *Eros and Civilization*. New York, 1962.

Marvick, Dwaine, ed. *Political Decision-Makers*. New York, 1961.

Meehl, Paul E. *Clinical vs. Statistical Prediction*. Minneapolis, 1954.

Money-Kyrle, R. E. *Psychoanalysis and Politics*. London, 1951.

Nair, Pyarelal. *Mahatma Gandhi: The Last Phase*. 2 vols. Ahmedabad, 1956-58.

Nanda, B. R. *Mahatma Gandhi*. Boston, 1958.

Nayyar, Sushila. *Kasturba: Wife of Gandhi*. Wallingford, Pa., 1948.

Neumann, Sigmund. *Permanent Revolution*. New York, 1942.

Parsons, Talcott and Edward A. Shils, eds. *Toward a General Theory of Action*. Boston, 1951.

Pettee, George Sawyer. *The Process of Revolution*. New York, 1938.

Plato. *The Republic of Plato*, ed. and trans. Francis Cornford. New York, 1945.

Possony, Stefan T. *Lenin: The Compulsive Revolutionary*. Chicago, 1964.

Rieff, Philip. *Freud: The Mind of the Moralist*. Garden City, N.Y., 1961.

Rogow, Arnold. *James Forrestal*. New York, 1963.

Schapiro, Leonard. *The Communist Party of the Soviet Union*. New York, 1964.

Scheidlinger, Saul. *Psychoanalysis and Group Behavior*. New York, 1952.

Selznick, Philip. *The Organizational Weapon*. Glencoe, Ill., 1960.

Shub, David. *Lenin*. Garden City, N.Y., 1948.

Tendulkar, D. G. *Mahatma*. 8 vols. Bombay, 1951-54.

Treadgold, Donald W. *Lenin and his Rivals*. New York, 1955.

Ulam, Adam B. *The Bolsheviks*. New York, 1965.

Weber, Max. *From Max Weber*, ed. Hans Gerth and C. Wright Mills. New York, 1958.

————. *The Theory of Social and Economic Organization*, ed. Talcott Parsons. New York, 1964.

Williams, Albert R. *Lenin: The Man and His Work*. New York, 1919.

Wilson, Edmund. *To the Finland Station*. Garden City, N.Y., 1953.

Wolfe, Bertram D. *Three Who Made a Revolution*. New York, 1964.

Wolfenstein, Martha and Gilbert Kliman. *Children and the Death of a President*. Garden City, N.Y., 1965.

Zimmer, Heinrich. *Philosophies of India*, ed. Joseph Campbell. New York, 1956.

SECONDARY SOURCES — ARTICLES

DeGrazia, Sebastian. "Mahatma Gandhi: The Son of His Mother," in *The Political Quarterly*, Vol. XIX, No. 4 (Oct.-Dec. 1948).

Edinger, Lewis J. "Political Science and Political Biography," in *The Journal of Politics*, Vol. 26, Nos. 2 and 3 (May and Aug. 1964).

Eckstein, Harry. "On the Etiology of Internal War," in *History and Theory*, Vol. IV, No. 2 (1965).

Freud, Sigmund. "Dostoevsky and Parricide," in his *Collected Papers*, Vol. V, ed. James Strachey. New York, 1959.

Freud, Sigmund. "Mourning and Melancholia," in his *Collected Papers*, Vol. IV, trans. Joan Riviere. New York, 1959.

Hartman, Heinz, Ernest Kris, and Rudolph Loewenstein. "Notes on the Theory of Aggression," in *The Psycho-Analytic Study of the Child*. Vol. III/IV, 1949.

Jones, Ernest. "The Symbolic Significance of Salt," in his *Essays in Applied Psychoanalysis*. Vol. II. New York, 1964.

Leites, Nathan. "Psycho-Cultural Hypotheses about Political Acts," in *World Politics*, Vol. 1, No. 1 (Oct. 1948).

Pye, Lucian W. "Personal Identity and Political Ideology," in Marvick, ed., *Political Decision-Makers*.

Rudolph, Susanne Hoeber. "The New Courage: An Essay on Gandhi's Psychology," in *World Politics*, Vol. XVI, No. 1 (Oct. 1963).

————. "Self-Control and Political Potency," in *The American Scholar*, Vol. XXXV (Winter 1965-66).

Shils, Edward A. "The Intellectuals in the Political Development of the New States," in Kautsky, ed., *Political Change in Underdeveloped Countries*.

Wolfenstein, E. Victor. "Violence or Non-Violence: A Psychoanalytic Exploration of the Choice of Political Means in Social Change," Princeton University Center of International Studies Research Monograph No. 20 (Oct. 1965).

Wolfenstein, Martha. "Death of a Parent and Death of a President: Children's Reactions to Two Kinds of Loss," in Wolfenstein and Kliman, *Children and the Death of a President*. Garden City, N.Y., 1965.

SECONDARY SOURCES — UNPUBLISHED MATERIALS

Eckstein, Harry. "Internal Wars: A Taxonomy." Memorandum No. 2, Princeton University Internal War Project (Center of International Studies), March 1960.

————. "The Concept Political System." A paper presented to the 1963 meeting of The American Political Science Association.

Johnson, Chalmers A. "Revolution and the Social System." A paper presented to the 1963 meeting of The American Political Science Association.

INDEX

adolescence, *see* Erikson; Gandhi; Lenin; Trotsky
Adorno, T. W. *et al.: Authoritarian Personality*, 165-66
ahimsa, 143, 278, 290
Ahmedabad, University of, 87-88
All-India Congress Committee: Quit India Resolution, 281, 316
ambivalence, 7, 233-34. *See also* Gandhi; Lenin; Trotsky
anal phase, *see* Erikson; Gandhi; Lenin; Trotsky
Antid Oto, *see* Trotsky
Arefeev, 107
ashram, 216
Asiatic Bill of 1906, 156

Babushkin: memory of Lenin, 118-19
Ballhorn, Johann, 179
Bhagavad Gita, 142
Bhave, Vinoba, 278
Bloody Sunday, 199-200
Bolsheviks, 247. *See also* Lenin and Trotsky
Bramacharya, 154, 156-57, 289
Brest–Litovsk, 252, 261, 266-67, 303
Bronstein, David Leontievich, 50, 57, 58
Bronstein, Lev Davidovich, *see* Trotsky
Bronstein, Mrs., 51-52, 57

Chekov, Anton: *Ward No. 6*, 111-13
Chernyshevsky: *What Is To Be Done?*, 105-106, 115
Churchill, Winston, 287, 288, 316
Cirque Moderne, 261-62
civil disobedience, *see* Gandhi
Committee for Illiteracy, 118

Dandi, 219. *See also* Salt March
Desai, Mahadev, 286-87, 293
Deutscher, Isaac, 49, 129-30, 196-98, 269

Eastman, Max, 49, 50, 57
Economists, 178, 179, 257
Engels, F., 120
Englistan, 268
Erikson, Erik, 17ff., 37, 158, 163, 263, 299, 303, 312; anal phase, 92; ego development, 13; latency, 96; identity crisis, 89-90; Oedipal phase, 94; oral phase, 90; origins of trust and mistrust, 41. *See also* Gandhi; identity crisis; Lenin; psychoanalytic theory; Trotsky

Fischer, Louis, 48-49
Fourth International, 301
Frazer, James: *The Golden Bough*, 6
Freud, Sigmund: dreams and ideology, 4; on the ruler, 6-7, 144, 302
  works: *Civilization and Its Discontents*, 6; *Future of an Illusion*, 6; *Group Psychology and the Analysis of the Ego*, 6, 8-9; *The Interpretation of Dreams*, 4; *Totem and Taboo*, 5-6

Gandhi, Mohandas Karamchand: adolescence, 78; affection for Britain, 275-76; anal phase, 93-94, 304; *An Autobiography: The Story of My Experiments With Truth*, 73; arrest in 1942, 286; as an attorney, 145-46; birth, 74; birth order, 77; caste, 74; civil disobedience, 217; death of father, 85-88; death of mother, 144-45; described, 30-31; desire for punishment, 149-50; dietetic experimentation, 141; efforts at becoming English, 139-40; father image, 143; fear of father, 77, 80-81; force, use of, 212, 237-38; friendships, 158; identity crisis, 100;

incident with British Political Agent, 145-46; incident at brothel, 182-84; incident at Maritzburg, 147-48; Indian elitism, 211; leadership ability, 224-25; Letter to Viceroy, 1930, 218; latency, 96; Oedipal conflict, 149; Oedipal phase, 95-96, 305-308; pride, degree of, 162; relation with Indian National Congress, 216-17; Salt March, 219-21, 316; search for masculinity, 81-82; status in South Africa, 148-49; study at University of Ahmedabad, 87-88; studies in England, 140; succession, 291-92; trust, degree of, 160; view of world, 282-83. *See also* Hind Swaraj; *satyagraha*
Gapon, Father, 200
Gokhale, K. G., 152, 215
Greyben, Ivan, 5, 6

Harijans, 222
Hind Swaraj, 207-15, 283, 290, 317; explained, 207-15
Hoffer, Eric, 23
Horkheimer, Max, 165

identification: with leader, 9; formation of, 18. *See also* Freud, *Group Psychology and the Analysis of the Ego*
identity crisis, 89-90, 96-101. *See also* Erikson; Gandhi; Lenin; Trotsky
Inter-Borough organization, 260
Iskra, 137, 184, 192, 193, 310; foundation and purpose, 175, 176

Jinnah, Mohammed Ali: dispute with Gandhi, 281-82; 287, 288

Kaba, 74-75, 77, 80-81
Kaplan, Dora, 251
Karamchand, *see* Kaba
Kasturbai, 85, 213, 297; death of,

287; relations with Gandhi in later life, 153-54
Khardin, A. N., 107
Kherson Prison, 135, 136
Kronstadt Military Detachment, 260
Krupskaya, 106, 118, 123, 158; memories of Lenin, 240, 246
Kzhizhanovsky-Claire, 137

Lasswell, Harold, 23; definition of political activity, 165; *Psychopathology and Politics*, 17, 164; *Power and Personality*, 164
Le Bon: *Psychologie des Foules*, 8-9
Lenin, 254; activities in exile, 104-106; adolescence, early, 97-98, 305-308; anal phase, 92, 304; as attorney, 107; authority, attitude toward, 264; birth, 33; cerebral seizures, 258-59; death, 259; death of father, effect of, 45-46; death of Sasha, effect of, 48-49, 100; democratic centralism, 232; described, 25-27; exiles: Kukushkino, 104, Shushenskoye, 123, Siberia, 175; father, relation to, 38-39, 45; force, use of, 237-38, 264-65; friendships, 158; identification with father, 119-20; identification with Sasha, 105; latency, 96; leadership ability, 224-25; marriage, 123; Marxism, early, 107-109, 116-17; Oedipal phase, 94-95; old age, 299-300; on Brest-Litovsk, 267-68; on populism, 115-16; oral phase, 91, 303; pride, degree of, 162; strategy of revolution, 180-82; succession, 252-53, 258, 300-301; superego, formation of, 39; trust, degree of, 160; at University of Kazan, 103-104

works: *Development of Capitalism in Russia*, 121, 123; *Discussion Between a Social Dem-*

ocrat and a Populist, 114; How The Spark Was Nearly Extinguished, 184; Imperialism, 191; Left Wing Communism: An Infantile Disorder, 255; New Economic Developments in Peasant Life, 114; State and Revolution, 247-48, 297; What Is To Be Done?, 118, 137, 176-77, 255, 256, 257; What the "Friends of the People" Are and How They Fight the Social Democrats, 114

Manu, 289-90
Martov, 63, 123, 124, 158, 176, 183, 188-90, 230, 312
Marxism, 110-11, 116-17
Marx, Karl, 106, 120, 187, 312
maya, 209
Mehtab, Sheik, 81, 82, 85, 91, 153
Mensheviks, 30, 192, 198
Mikhailovsky, N. K., 256; Russkoye Bogatsvo, 114
Mohd Banias, 74. See also Gandhi
Moslem League, see Jinnah
Mukhin, 127-28

Narodism, 71, 107, 182
National Legislative Assembly, 151
Nehru, J., 216, 276, 291-92, 317

Oedipal phase, see Erikson; Gandhi; Lenin; Trotsky
Oblomovism, 180

Paris Commune, 253
Parvus, 63, 199
Patel, 216
permanent revolution, 200
Pero, 137. See also Trotsky
personality, definition of, 12-13
personality, revolutionary, 9-10, 12, 16, 18-19, 21; model of, 225-38; "psychological role propensity," 23
Petersburg Soviet, 200, 260
Plato, 3-4

Plekhanov, G. V., 114, 123, 158, 183-86, 194, 312
Pokrovsky: memory of Lenin, 183
politics, definition of, 20
populism, see Lenin
Potresov, 123, 158, 176, 183, 188, 312
primal horde, 10
projection: of love and hate, related to revolution, 170-71
Provisional Government, 240, 245-46; 250, 316
psychoanalytic theory: application to politics, 3, 13. See also Erikson; Gandhi; Lenin; Trotsky
Putlibai: relation to Gandhi, 75, 76-77; use of fast, 141; death, 144-45. See also Gandhi

Rama, 77-78
Rank, Otto, 10
repression: relation to authority figures in later life, 8; of impulses, 14. See also Erikson; Gandhi; Lenin; psychoanalytic theory; Trotsky
revolution: definition of, 20-21
revolutionary leader: ability to fill role of father, 229, 308-10; described, 24; formation of ideology, 172-73; leadership, acquiring, 225-27, 310-14; relation to own children, 223-24; relation to followers, 223, 230, 233-34
Rudolph, Susan, 214
Russian Social Democratic Party, 30, 314
Russo–Japanese War, 199

Salt March, 219, 303, 316; results of, 221. See also Dandi
salt tax, 220
Sasha, 36, 37, 38, 103, 104, 115, 116, 178, 309, 314; compared with Lenin, 37-38; death of, 48-49; revolutionary activity, 42-44, See also Alexander Ulyanov; Lenin

satyagraha, 278, 315; individual, 276-77; origin of, 157; way to achieve, 214-15

Sedov, Leon: relation to Trotsky, 301

Shils, Edward, 295-96

Shivigovsky, 125-26, 193

Smolny Institute, 250

Sokolovskaya, Alexandra L.: relation to Trotsky, 125-26. *See also* Trotsky

Sokolovsky brothers, 127

Southern Russian Workers Union, 128-29, 200, 308; structure and function of, 132-34

Spentzer: relation to Trotsky, 63

Stalin, 270, 272

succession: issue of, *see* Gandhi; Lenin; revolutionary leader; Trotsky

Sukhanov: memories of Lenin, 245-46, 54; of Trotsky, 261

Trotsky, Leon: adolescence, 98-99; aggressive force, identifying with, 126; anal phase, 92-93, 304; authority, attitudes toward, 264-65; death, 275; described, 28-30; father, break with, 58, 65, 71-72, 124; force, use of, 237-38; on Freemasonry, 136; friendships, 158; imprisonment of 1899, 134; incident in second grade, 67-69; marriage, 136-37; Marxism, delay in conversion to, 126; Marxism, rejection of, 70-71; memories: of childhood, 53-54, of Martov–Lenin split, 188-89, of parents, 54-55, 58-59; mother images, 262-63; name, choice of, 137-38; Oedipal phase, 95, 305-308; old age, 299-300; oral phase, 91, 303; perspectives, ideological, 203-204; pride, degree of, 162; relations: with *Iskra*, 193-94, with Lenin, 192, 195-96, 246, with Mensheviks, 192, to Narodism, 71; revolutionary government, role in, 265-69; schooling, early, 62-63; school in Nikolayev, 69-72; speech, early failure in, 130-31; trust, degree of, 160; writing, first efforts at, 60-61

works: *Balance and the Prospects—Moving Forces of the Revolution*, 202; *Literature and Revolution*, 205; *My Life*, 73

Tsar: as Oedipal father, 117

Ulyanov, Alexander, *see* Sasha

Ulyanov, Anna, 34; memories: of father, 34, of Lenin, 104, 111, of mother, 35

Ulyanov, Dmitri, 36, 38

Ulyanov, Olga, 36; relation to Lenin's late walking, 40-41

untouchables, *see* Harijans

Uspensky, Gleb, 137

Webb: *Theory and Practice of English Trade Unions*, 123

Weber, Max: vocational and avocational politics, 21-22

Wolfe, Bertram, 37, 187

Wolfenstein, Martha: on mourning, 46-47

Zasulich, V. P., 120, 123, 176

Ziv, Dr., 128

BOOKS WRITTEN
UNDER THE AUSPICES OF THE
CENTER OF INTERNATIONAL STUDIES
PRINCETON UNIVERSITY

Gabriel A. Almond, *The Appeals of Communism* (Princeton University Press 1954)

William W. Kaufmann, ed., *Military Policy and National Security* (Princeton University Press 1956)

Klaus Knorr, *The War Potential of Nations* (Princeton University Press 1956)

Lucian W. Pye, *Guerrilla Communism in Malaya* (Princeton University Press 1956)

Charles De Visscher, *Theory and Reality in Public International Law,* trans. by P. E. Corbett (Princeton University Press 1957; rev. ed. 1968)

Bernard C. Cohen, *The Political Process and Foreign Policy: The Making of the Japanese Peace Settlement* (Princeton University Press 1959)

Myron Weiner, *Party Politics in India: The Development of a Multi-Party System* (Princeton University Press 1957)

Percy E. Corbett, *Law in Diplomacy* (Princeton University Press 1959)

Rolf Sannwald and Jacques Stohler, *Economic Integration: Theoretical Assumptions and Consequences of European Unification,* trans. by Herman Karreman (Princeton University Press 1959)

Klaus Knorr, ed., *NATO and American Security* (Princeton University Press 1959)

Gabriel A. Almond and James S. Coleman, eds., *The Politics of the Developing Areas* (Princeton University Press 1960)

Herman Kahn, *On Thermonuclear War* (Princeton University Press 1960)

Sidney Verba, *Small Groups and Political Behavior: A Study of Leadership* (Princeton University Press 1961)

Robert J. C. Butow, *Tojo and the Coming of the War* (Princeton University Press 1961)

Glenn H. Snyder, *Deterrence and Defense: Toward a Theory of National Security* (Princeton University Press 1961)

Klaus Knorr and Sidney Verba, eds., *The International System: Theoretical Essays* (Princeton University Press 1961)

Peter Paret and John W. Shy, *Guerrillas in the 1960's* (Praeger 1962)

George Modelski, *A Theory of Foreign Policy* (Praeger 1962)

Klaus Knorr and Thornton Read, eds., *Limited Strategic War* (Praeger 1963)

Frederick S. Dunn, *Peace-Making and the Settlement with Japan* (Princeton University Press 1963)

Arthur L. Burns and Nina Heathcote, *Peace-Keeping by United Nations Forces* (Praeger 1963)

Richard A. Falk, *Law, Morality, and War in the Contemporary World* (Praeger, 1963)

James N. Rosenau, *National Leadership and Foreign Policy: A Case Study in the Mobilization of Public Support* (Princeton University Press 1963)

Gabriel A. Almond and Sidney Verba, *The Civic Culture: Political Attitudes and Democracy in Five Nations* (Princeton University Press 1963)

Bernard C. Cohen, *The Press and Foreign Policy* (Princeton University Press 1963)

Richard L. Sklar, *Nigerian Political Parties: Power in an Emergent African Nation* (Princeton University Press 1963)

Peter Paret, *French Revolutionary Warfare from Indochina to Algeria: The Analysis of a Political and Military Doctrine* (Praeger 1964)

Harry Eckstein, ed., *Internal War: Problems and Approaches* (Free Press 1964)

Cyril E. Black and Thomas P. Thornton, eds., *Communism and Revolution: The Strategic Uses of Political Violence* (Princeton University Press 1964)

Miriam Camps, *Britain and the European Community 1955-1963* (Princeton University Press 1964)

Thomas P. Thornton, ed., *The Third World in Soviet Perspective: Studies by Soviet Writers on the Developing Areas* (Princeton University Press 1964)

James N. Rosenau, ed., *International Aspects of Civil Strife* (Princeton University Press 1964)

Sidney I. Ploss, *Conflict and Decision-Making in Soviet Russia: A Case Study of Agricultural Policy, 1953-1963* (Princeton University Press 1965)

Richard A. Falk and Richard J. Barnet, eds., *Security in Disarmament* (Princeton University Press 1965)

Karl von Vorys, *Political Development in Pakistan* (Princeton University Press 1965)

Harold and Margaret Sprout, *The Ecological Perspective on Human Affairs, With Special Reference to International Politics* (Princeton University Press 1965)

Klaus Knorr, *On the Uses of Military Power in the Nuclear Age* (Princeton University Press 1966)

Harry Eckstein, *Division and Cohesion in Democracy: A Study of Norway* (Princeton University Press 1966)

Cyril E. Black, *The Dynamics of Modernization: A Study in Comparative History* (Harper and Row 1966)

Peter Kunstadter, ed., *Southeast Asian Tribes, Minorities, and Nations* (Princeton University Press 1967)

E. Victor Wolfenstein, *The Revolutionary Personality: Lenin, Trotsky, Gandhi* (Princeton University Press 1967)

Leon Gordenker, *The UN Secretary-General and the Maintenance of Peace* (Columbia University Press 1967)

Oran R. Young, *The Intermediaries: Third Parties in International Crises* (Princeton University Press 1967)

James N. Rosenau, ed., *Domestic Sources of Foreign Policy* (Free Press 1967)

Richard F. Hamilton, *Affluence and the French Worker in the Fourth Republic* (Princeton University Press 1967)

Linda B. Miller, *World Order and Local Disorder: The United Nations and Internal Conflicts* (Princeton University Press 1967)

Wolfram F. Hanrieder, *West German Foreign Policy, 1949-1963: International Pressures and Domestic Response* (Stanford University Press 1967)

Richard H. Ullman, *Britain and the Russian Civil War: November 1918-February 1920* (Princeton University Press 1968)

Robert Gilpin, *France in the Age of the Scientific State* (Princeton University Press 1968)

William B. Bader, *The United States and the Spread of Nuclear Weapons* (Pegasus 1968)

Richard A. Falk, *Legal Order in a Violent World* (Princeton University Press 1968)

Cyril E. Black, Richard A. Falk, Klaus Knorr, and Oran R. Young, *Neutralization and World Politics* (Princeton University Press 1968)

Oran R. Young, *The Politics of Force: Bargaining During International Crises* (Princeton University Press 1969)

Klaus Knorr and James N. Rosenau, eds., *Contending Approaches to International Politics* (Princeton University Press 1969)

James N. Rosenau, ed., *Linkage Politics: Essays on the Convergence of National and International Systems* (Free Press 1969)

John T. McAlister, Jr., *Viet Nam: The Origins of Revolution* (Knopf 1969)

Jean Edward Smith, *Germany Beyond the Wall: People, Politics and Prosperity* (Little, Brown 1969)

James Barros, *Betrayal from Within: Joseph Avenol Secretary-General of the League of Nations, 1933-1940* (Yale University Press 1969)

Charles Hermann, *Crises in Foreign Policy: A Simulation Analysis* (Bobbs-Merrill 1969)

Robert C. Tucker, *The Marxian Revolutionary Idea: Essays on Marxist Thought and Its Impact on Radical Movements* (W. W. Norton 1969)

Harvey Waterman, *Political Change in Contemporary France: The Politics of an Industrial Democracy* (Charles E. Merrill 1969)

Cyril E. Black and Richard A. Falk, eds., *Future of the International Legal Order*, Vol. I, *Trends and Patterns* (Princeton University Press 1969)

Ted R. Gurr, *Why Men Rebel* (Princeton University Press 1969)

C. S. Whitaker, Jr., *The Politics of Tradition: Continuity and Change in Northern Nigeria, 1946-1966* (Princeton University Press 1970)

Richard A. Falk, *The Status of Law in International Society* (Princeton University Press 1970)

Henry Bienen, *Tanzania: Party Transformation and Economic Development* (Princeton University Press 1967, rev. edn., 1970)

Klaus Knorr, *Military Power and Potential* (D. C. Heath 1970)

Other Titles of Related Interest
Available in Princeton and
Princeton/Bollingen Paperbacks

AMOR AND PSYCHE: *The Psychic Development of the Feminine,* by Erich Neumann (P/B #239), $2.95

ART AND THE CREATIVE UNCONSCIOUS, by Erich Neumann (P/B #240), $3.45

COMPLEX, ARCHETYPE, SYMBOL IN THE PSYCHOLOGY OF C. G. JUNG, by Jolande Jacobi (P/B #241), $3.45

ESSAYS ON A SCIENCE OF MYTHOLOGY: *The Myth of the Divine Child and the Mysteries of Eleusis,* by C. G. Jung and C. Kerényi (P/B #180), $2.95

FOUR ARCHETYPES: MOTHER/REBIRTH/SPIRIT/TRICK-STER, by C. G. Jung, translated by R.F.C. Hull, Extracted from *The Archetypes and the Collective Unconscious,* Vol. 9, part I, Collected Works (P/B #215), $1.95

FROM CALIGARI TO HITLER: *A Psychological History of the German Film,* by Siegfried Kracauer (#45), $2.95

JOSEPH CONRAD: *A Psychoanalytic Biography,* by Bernard C. Meyer, M.D. (#188), $2.95

ON THE NATURE OF THE PSYCHE, by C. G. Jung, translated by R.F.C. Hull, Extracted from *The Structure and Dynamics of the Psyche,* Vol. 8, Collected Works (P/B #157), $2.95

THE ORIGINS AND HISTORY OF CONSCIOUSNESS, by Erich Neumann (P/B #204), $3.95

PSYCHOLOGY AND EDUCATION, by C. G. Jung, translated by R.F.C. Hull, Extracted from *The Development of Personality,* Vol. 17, Collected Works (P/B #159), $2.95

THE PSYCHOLOGY OF THE TRANSFERENCE, by C. G. Jung, translated by R.F.C. Hull, Extracted from *The Practice of Psychotherapy,* Vol. 16, Collected Works, (P/B #158), $2.95

THE SOCIAL MEANINGS OF SUICIDE, by Jack D. Douglas (#186), $2.95

SOCIETY AND THE ADOLESCENT SELF-IMAGE, by Morris Rosenberg (#111), $2.95

THE SOCIETY OF CAPTIVES: *A Study of a Maximum Security Prison,* by Gresham M. Sykes (#227), $1.95

THE SPIRIT IN MAN, ART, AND LITERATURE, by C. G. Jung, translated by R.F.C. Hull, Vol. 15, Collected Works (P/B #252), $1.95

WHY MEN REBEL, by Ted Robert Gurr (#233), $2.95

Order from your bookstore, or from

Princeton University Press, Princeton, N.J. 08540